TRUSTED GUARDIAN

To Jonan and Grayce

Trusted Guardian

Information Sharing and the Future of the Atlantic Alliance

DAMON COLETTA
United States Air Force Academy, USA

ASHGATE

Published by
Ashgate Publishing Limited
Gower House
Croft Road
Aldershot
Hampshire GU11 3HR
England

Ashgate Publishing Company
Suite 420
101 Cherry Street
Burlington, VT 05401-4405
USA

www.ashgate.com

British Library Cataloguing in Publication Data
Coletta, Damon V.
Trusted guardian : information sharing and the future of the Atlantic alliance
1. North Atlantic Treaty Organization 2. Crisis management 3. Security, International 4. United States - Foreign relations - 2001- 5. United States - Foreign relations - Europe 6. Europe - Foreign relations - United States
I. Title
327.7'3'04

Library of Congress Cataloging-in-Publication Data
Coletta, Damon V.
Trusted guardian : information sharing and the future of the Atlantic Alliance / by Damon Coletta.
p. cm.
Includes bibliographical references and index.
ISBN 978-0-7546-7481-8
1. United States--Foreign relations--2001- 2. North Atlantic Treaty Organization. 3. Security, International. 4. Pacific settlement of international disputes. 5. International cooperation. I. Title.

E895.C65 2008
973.93--dc22

2008019104

ISBN 978 0 7546 7481 8

Mixed Sources
Product group from well-managed forests and other controlled sources
www.fsc.org Cert no. SGS-COC-2482
© 1996 Forest Stewardship Council
FSC

Printed and bound in Great Britain by
TJ International Ltd, Padstow, Cornwall

Contents

List of Figures

Acknowledgements

This book would not have been possible without the encouragement and moral support of colleagues at the US Air Force Academy. Among the many people who have my gratitude are Tom Mowle, Douglas Murray, Cheryl Kearney, Brenda Vallance, Paul Bolt, Fran Pilch, Joe Derdzinski, Dave Sacko, Paul Carrese, Skip Shackelford, members of the International Institute for National Security Studies, Erik Gartzke at the University of California, San Diego, Jim Wirtz and David Yost at the Naval Postgraduate School, and Pascal Vennesson at the European University Institute. This book is academic work. Any errors are my responsibility, and it does not reflect official opinion of the United States Air Force or the United States Government.

Chapter 1

The Atlantic Alliance and Global Crisis Management

This study began with two premises about the course of world politics in the years to come. First, after September 11, the United States has decided to engage its dominant military and economic power in ambitious international projects. These include counter-terror combat missions in Afghanistan and Iraq, training missions in the Philippines, Colombia and several countries in North Africa, and forward deployments to Central Asia. They also include leadership in the maritime Proliferation Security Initiative and substantial budget increases apart from war expenses in order to maintain a large lead in defense capabilities with emphasis on force projection.

Second, despite spending more than $400 billion on defense in 2005—more than three times the estimated expenditures for China and Russia combined—the United States is not able to succeed in its proactive grand strategy without the cooperation of other nations and particularly the support of close allies in Europe.[1] Claims of unipolarity in the distribution of power not withstanding, indications that the United States cannot run roughshod over the opinions of others in pursuit of its national purposes repeatedly confront Americans who would prefer greater freedom of action. As operations progressed in Afghanistan and Iraq, the United States asked for more help and pleaded its case before a wider circle of friends.[2]

The paradoxical combination of awe-inspiring material capabilities on the one hand and clear limitations in attempts to dictate, or even articulate, a new world order on the other set the context for an extended reflection on the nuances of US leadership. In certain manifestations of power where the United States presently dominates, it can serve the national interest if relevant technologies are shared rather than hoarded. This counterintuitive approach to international leadership holds promise in the high profile area of information systems, even though similar technologies also underpin superior American force projection capability.

The current American strategy, not surprisingly, calls for closely guarding information technology, but this standard approach produces difficulties. The same advances that enabled lopsided US victories on the conventional battlefield

---

1 For a review of defense budget figures, see Table 1: US and Foreign Defense Spending (by Rank): Data from the International Institute for Strategic Studies (London) and US Department of State in Chamberlin (2004: 5). See also 2005 data from the Center for Arms Control and Non-Proliferation at www.globalissues.org/Geopolitics/ArmsTrade/Spending.asp.

2 Sciolino (2004); Hoge (2004); Armitage (2004).

also generated suspicions and jealousies among potential US partners.[3] NATO members often do not share in the data from America's most sophisticated national assets and have trouble operating within secure communication networks run by US forces. While information systems grant the United States a swift and terrible sword to protect the community of liberal democracies, exploitation of these systems erodes trust among America's closest allies, dramatically inflating the cost of sustaining US leadership.

As mentioned, one possible response to reassure other states would be to share access to the special devices and software used for collection, analysis and distribution of information. To some extent, organizations such as the Linked Operational Intelligence Centers Europe (LOCE) already facilitate the transfer and interpretation of data within the transatlantic alliance. Yet, after several crises involving multilateral uses of force, the effectiveness of LOCE has been limited by fear of information leaks that could expose the secrets of superior US information systems and, in worst case scenarios, increase the danger to American troops or airmen in the field.[4] These fears dominated US decision making during Operations Allied Force in Kosovo and Enduring Freedom in Afghanistan, both of which ended in allied victories but also in greater willingness of international partners to challenge, if only diplomatically, what they saw as growing American arrogance and reliance on unilateral action rather than cooperative deliberation.[5]

This book argues that the painful tradeoff between US legitimacy and US superiority can best be resolved by unpacking complex concepts—such as information superiority, national security and legitimacy—then searching for policy opportunities. Information superiority, for example, covers a vast range of activities for the Department of Defense and beyond.[6] The focus, here, remains on those information systems used for evaluating foreign threats and developing policy responses to improve US national security.

US security and defense can also be broken down in different ways, by strategy and tactics or by the different instruments for wielding power. Here, the analysis emphasizes gradations of risk, from ordinary diplomacy to general war, and it pays special attention to the mixed motives during international crises, which roughly speaking, take place in the stage before war.

Finally, legitimacy is a kind of political capital that offsets some of the material costs incurred from proactive foreign policy. International legitimacy comprises several elements, including economic strength, military capability, and ideological appeal. Here, the argument highlights the value of trust, especially among partners but at some minimal level even among adversaries, as an enabler for sustainable US leadership. Bringing together the three considerations—crisis information

3 Lloyd (2002: 8–9). For the official perspective of the French Ministry of Defense on the lessons of Kosovo, see Ministry of Defense, France (1999) and Whitney (1999).

4 Reuters (2000); Shenon (1999).

5 Kitfield (2002).

6 Department of Defense (2006). Joseph Nye and Admiral William Owens (1996) concisely described various facets of America's information advantage in the journal *Foreign Affairs*.

operations, crisis dilemmas, and trust—it appears there is, indeed, room to negotiate the tradeoff between maintaining technological advantage and winning international acceptance.

The exploitation of US systems in the context of international crises, when the goal is to reach a favorable settlement in multilateral bargaining, need not be exclusive as is required for securing decisive victory in war. Sharing a common crisis information system with close allies would help the United States earn the benefit of the doubt from partners. The added legitimacy would make it difficult for states arrayed against the United States to resist US demands, and this in turn, would have salutary consequences for US grand strategy.

The Role of Trusted Guardian

Allowing for comparable material capabilities, a "trusted guardian" deters more challenges from the rest of the world than a self-appointed sheriff.[7] For adversaries determined enough to challenge but not to make war, the trusted guardian can credibly back ambitious bargaining demands against an isolated opponent. Should negotiations fail against the most determined challengers, the trusted guardian, even if it must fight largely on its own, will find operations easier to accomplish with greater access for expeditionary troops. Eventually, in the war's aftermath, there will be fewer costs, overall, if the trusted guardian can inspire greater diplomatic support.

By contrast, America's performance in the world has occasionally inspired characterizations of a short tempered and simpleminded cowboy, donning a white hat on the urge to free a town from the clutches of one thug or another. Critics see America saddled by its own traditions: in the Old West, the bravest lawmen chose tactics and allies with pragmatic considerations in mind. If deadly shootouts were the only way to crush marauding criminals, in such circumstances, a solitary figure could count on neither the Federal army nor the letter of the law for protection.[8] Marshals sometimes adopted extralegal measures to raise their chances of survival, and they sought allies whose steadfastness in danger came by virtue of personal, not just legal, bonds. While life after the OK Corral might have been easier for the Earp brothers and the citizens they defended had they not compromised the role of trusted guardian, Americans instinctively comprehend that Wyatt and Virgil would not have survived their encounter with the Clanton gang if they had strictly adhered to what we today might call a multilateral institutionalist approach.

Nevertheless, in the contemporary struggle for a more benign world order after September 11, the mantle of trusted guardianship—by American reckoning—need not be unduly burdensome. The United States can gain legitimacy in the international community without leaving itself fatally exposed to criminal or terrorist threats

7 Colin Gray (2004) uses the metaphor of a sheriff to describe the role the US ought to play in supporting world order.

8 Gray (2004) selects the sheriff analogy to elaborate America's more aggressive leadership role in the world after September 11 in part because it resonates with American culture better than comparisons to previous colonial empires. For more on the tactics and allies of Wyatt Earp, see Lake (1931) and Boyer (1976).

because in a manner not available to the lone gunmen of old, the United States can offer the community of states a shield without depleting its own arsenal or compromising tactical independence.

For the international community, forewarned is forearmed, and today's technologies, available in the commercial world, could provide American allies a more comprehensive picture of crisis situations—a more robust foundation for refining, admittedly, but ultimately supporting US leadership in world affairs. Constructing a crisis information system with commercial-proprietary rather than defense contracts would still cost the United States in financial terms, and, technically, it would still mean an effort to buy legitimacy at the cost of diluting relative advantage. Now, though, the material capability traded away would be one that operated during crisis bargaining, when a putative information advantage can do more harm than good. In contrast, those defense systems that allow the United States to rapidly find, fix, target and destroy an enemy in combat would remain classified and under national custody.

Essentially, the American sheriff could keep his guns and his freedom of action, but on those occasions when he used them, a larger swath of the international community would know why. Perhaps more important, allies could trust that raw American power was harnessed in the service of larger political purposes, purposes that in the end were compatible with their own goals. Over the long haul, winning that modicum of trust from at least America's closest partners in the transatlantic alliance is the best protection against exhaustion as the United States works to parley its material advantage into a second, more peaceful and more prosperous, American Century.

Trust and American Grand Strategy

The basics of a grand strategy for bringing this century about have already been proposed.[9] Not since the peak years of the Cold War has the United States so aggressively committed its resources to defend freedom abroad.[10] For both major political parties, a secure, more prosperous world requires proactive US leadership, which means engagement of American power in just about every populated region of the world. In choosing among those instruments, the domestic debate has intensified over the appropriate mix of positive and negative options.[11] More positive appeals include economic carrots such as lowering trade barriers to the US market or dedicating

---

9 Bush (2002). The *National Security Strategy* generated interest in studying its implications for future international cooperation and conflict involving the United States. For sample articles, see Gaddis (2002; 2005), Hendrickson (2002), Albright (2003), and Powell (2004). The 2006 version of the strategy largely followed the outlines of its predecessor, though the update did include a chapter on nontraditional security objectives.

10 Cold War historian John Lewis Gaddis (2004) identified September 11 as one of the rare shocks in US history that have prompted a more coherent, and as it turns out, more expansive American Grand Strategy.

11 For a similar classification of foreign policy means available to great powers, see the section on "Benign vs. Coercive Engagement" in Miller (2001: 16–8).

billions of dollars to fight AIDS in Africa.[12] Other types of carrots comprise arms sales and military training missions. Economic and military incentives often make it easier to wield what former assistant secretary of defense Joseph Nye termed soft power: the moral appeals, public diplomacy and cultural interaction that can persuade other actors to support US goals.[13] Soft power is positive in the sense of providing people what they want by adjusting their desires to better match what the United States can give. Not surprisingly, it is less effective when accompanied by negative measures that deny other actors what they want through economic sanctions or war.

Most Americans agree the United States should support a more orderly world in which members of the international community pay special heed to liberal, democratic and free market principles. After the terrorist attacks of September 11, many also conceded the need for the United States to take a more internationalist approach as opposed to fortress America. The central partisan divide in Washington was instead over the importance of sticks, specifically offensive military force, for achieving US goals.[14]

During the run-up to the 2004 presidential election, Democrats, often echoing scholars in the liberal-institutionalist tradition, argued that in implementing his National Security Strategy, President Bush overemphasized unilateral preemptive force projection. He wasted tens of billions of dollars that might have been dedicated instead toward homeland security, if only his administration had exercised patience and first built legitimacy to support its initiatives, working through international institutions and compromising with allies.[15]

Meanwhile, Republicans, in defense of the president and often reinforced by scholars more closely identified with realism in international affairs, argued that the most important legitimizing factor for US leadership after September 11 was US power. Too much concern for the fears of minor powers on the United Nations Security Council was really an overly sophisticated prescription for paralysis, a thin rationalization for abandoning America's obligation to take sword in hand and battle the twin dragons of global terrorism and weapons proliferation, which ultimately threatened the entire interstate system.[16]

---

12 While much of the media attention on foreign affairs swung toward the US-led battle against insurgents in Iraq, major initiatives in trade and aid continued (Borden 2004; Sontag 2004).

13 Nye (2004).

14 *Agence France-Press* (2004); Lowry (2004); Guggenheim (2004); Harwood and Schlesinger (2004).

15 Examples of scholars in this line of thinking included Ikenberry (2001), Nye (2003a), Nye (2003b), and Etzioni (2004). In a rising chorus after the election, writers like Robert Kagan (2004) and Stephen Walt (2005) coming out of the realist tradition urged prudent policies that would court legitimacy and not provoke as much resistance from other states, especially allies. For a practitioner-scholar critique in a similar mode, see Daadler and Lindsay (2003).

16 Scholars drawing from the realist tradition and generally supporting the Bush administration's more aggressive approach to grand strategy included the aforementioned Kagan (2002), Gray (2004), and Gaddis (2004). Also, see Art (2003), Mead (2004), and Lieber (2005). Two very important realist *opponents* of the war were John Mearsheimer of

Casting the debate over grand strategy into two main camps helps to understand the major issues at stake, but actual positions admit more complex variation.[17] In particular, the Republican flank in Washington and the realist flank in academia soften at the prospect of imperial overstretch. Hans Morgenthau, the influential realist scholar from the University of Chicago, urged America after World War II to keep sword firmly in hand as a precaution against expanding Soviet power, but in later decades, he also famously counseled the United States to avoid over commitment in Vietnam.[18] The dual message of realism, indeed, runs very deep. In Thucydides' *History of the Peloponnesian War*, a multilateral regime that established order for independent cities within Hellenic civilization crumbled in the face of rising Athenian power, but Thucydides also made clear that Athens eventually overreached in Sicily and hastened the collapse of its own influence.[19]

Indeed, it is fair to say that the Bush administration itself took the possibility of overstretch seriously after the occupation in Iraq turned increasingly bloody. As costs soared beyond $100 billion and American deaths neared one thousand, several commentators noted that, after one clear application, the Bush Doctrine seemed to lose much of its force as a governing principle. Overtones of unilateral action and preemptive force faded in extended, multilateral negotiations with North Korea and Iran over their nuclear programs.[20] The administration's caution was striking because North Korea and Iran had been mentioned alongside Iraq by President Bush in his 2002 State of the Union address as part of an "axis of evil" and because the reluctance to threaten force in the latter cases emerged against a backdrop of tour extensions and reserve call-ups to cover the first application in Iraq.[21]

If the Bush Doctrine appeared to be running out of steam, it was not because senior foreign policy voices in the administration lacked an appreciation for the role of power, material capabilities in particular, for shaping international outcomes. From the first term, Paul Wolfowitz and Donald Rumsfeld heading the Defense Department, Colin Powell as Secretary of State, and Condoleezza Rice as National Security Adviser all had experience with the types of policy dilemmas attending military operations. All had publicly expressed philosophies closer to realism than liberal idealism.[22] In fact, during the 2000 presidential campaign, then candidate

---

the University of Chicago and Stephen Walt of Harvard University (Mearsheimer and Walt 2003; Mearsheimer 2005; Walt 2005; Mearsheimer and Walt 2007).

17 For an insightful review of the debate in academia, albeit sympathetic toward the realist perspective, see Lieber (2004). A high profile group during the 2004 campaign calling themselves Diplomats and Military Commanders for Change included officials from both Democratic and Republican administrations (Selvin, 2004).

18 Morgenthau (c1950). For his commentary on Vietnam, see Morgenthau (c1966; c1968). A more recent appreciation for how realist principles could be interpreted in different ways to fashion contrasting approaches to Vietnam is found in Hilsman (1987).

19 Provocative arguments on imperial overstretch from the post-Vietnam era but before September 11 include Kennedy (1987), Snyder (1991), and Kupchan (1994).

20 Sanger (2004).

21 Freedberg (2004); Mazzetti (2004).

22 Wolfowitz was identified with the Pentagon draft document, *Defense Planning Guidance for Fiscal Years 1994–1999*, which was leaked to the *New York Times* and published

Bush called for a more "humble" foreign policy that involved less extravagant rhetoric and greater prudence with respect to the deployment of forces for missions other than the defense of vital American interests.[23]

The problem after September 11, though, was the ubiquitous nature of the terrorist cells. Within such loose networks, commanders accustomed to Clausewitzian, state-on-state conflict had difficulty finding a center of gravity. They could, however, see that al Qaeda benefited from sanctuaries, financial support and widespread, if often quiet, sympathy in the Middle East. Toppling the Taliban in Afghanistan brought a temporary respite, but al Qaeda or splinter groups could still reorganize in a region critical to future energy supplies. Osama bin Laden was not simply attacking symbols of American global reach in New York and Washington. He also threatened Western supported, state-based regimes in the Middle East.

In order to deal with the strategic aspect of the threat from Islamic fundamentalism, realists in the Bush administration thought they saw an opportunity, a lynchpin that could be attacked in the name of preserving power rather than wasting it in an endless series of thrusts against shadowy networks. In terms of the usual elements of national power, Iraq was well endowed for the region, with several urban centers, an educated populace, and the second largest oil reserves after Saudi Arabia.[24] Compared to neighbors Iran and Saudi Arabia, religious fundamentalism had been brutally quashed by Saddam Hussein and his secular Baath party. The bet was that Saddam could be replaced by a more democratic, more cooperative government that would resist fundamentalist encroachments and translate increased foreign investment from the West into general prosperity.[25] A successful Iraq in the heart of the Middle East would shake the geopolitical foundations of anti-Americanism and religious fundamentalism based in the Levant, Egypt and North Africa, as well as to the east in Iran, Pakistan and Central Asia.[26]

To date, despite the enormous investment and sacrifice of Iraqi, allied, and American lives, the US engineered regime change has brought mixed results at

---

on March 8,1992 under the headline, "Excerpt from Pentagon's Plan" (section 1, 14). During the Clinton administration, Rumsfeld chaired two federal commissions chartered to find ways of countering potential rivals to the United States: the US Ballistic Missile Threat Commission and the US Commission to Assess National Security Space Management and Organization. Also, see Powell (1992–1993) and Rice (2000).

23 Text from the second presidential debate of the 2000 election campaign is available at www.c-span.org/campaign2000/transcript. See also Rice (2000).

24 Byman and Pollack (2003).

25 Kaplan (2002); Fallows (2004).

26 Mearshiemer (2005), as a realist, disputed the assessment of threat and American foreign policy goals by so-called neoconservatives in the Bush administration in degree more than kind. The threat from Saddam Hussein was not as radical or imminent as Paul Wolfowitz or Richard Cheney asserted, and the plan to democratize Iraq was far more risky and costly than the administration advertised. Here, I classify the Bush team's calculus as more or less realist, but the costs and benefits being input to the analysis seemed, in Mearsheimer's estimation, oddly distorted. Mearsheimer and Walt (2007) later fingered a decidedly non-realist and politically controversial cause, the strong pro-Israel lobby in the United States, for the government's skewed perceptions.

enormous cost.[27] At least until Iraq stabilizes politically and grows economically, the United States will not escape the basic strategic predicament realized after September 11: interests vulnerable to attack seemingly everywhere but material capability sufficient for military victory in only a few places at once. Just as during the Cold War, the United States has large incentives to extend the effects of its military resources by resorting to coercive diplomacy—the threat of force rather than combat operations—in order to influence states in the War on Terror.[28]

This is not to say that the United States will adopt a policy of fomenting crises around the world. As mentioned, the Bush administration has so far practiced something closer to crisis avoidance with North Korea and Iran. Terrorist cells, though, remain active in Asia, Africa, Europe and the Americas, and two large countries hang in the balance after American invasion. The United States is unlikely to admit defeat by pulling back from its internationalist posture. A forward leaning stance along with recognition that other states play important roles in determining the success of terror attacks make it almost inevitable that US statesmen over coming years will find themselves embroiled in crisis negotiations and saddled by divergent threat assessments that grate within the government and among close allies.

Crisis Management after September 11

The United States and its European allies had already begun to resurrect the art and science of crisis management before September 11. The rising demand for United Nations peacekeeping during the 1990s, accompanied by the failure to quickly contain civil violence in Somalia, Rwanda, the Democratic Republic of the Congo, and on NATO's borders in the former Yugoslavia, alerted European and American leaders to the need for doctrinal adjustments.[29] These were reflected in new publications on "military operations other than war," the so-called headline goals for a new European Union rapid reaction force and the shift in NATO doctrine from collective defense to a dual focus that included out-of-area crisis management.[30]

Before September 11, the challenge was to secure peace using the minimum possible force because leaders in the Western democracies could not mobilize their

27 Baker and Weisman (2007).

28 One of the foremost scholars on crisis management and deterrence produced two editions on the limits of coercive diplomacy, roughly corresponding to the middle and later years of the Cold War (George, Hall, and Simons 1971; George, Simons, and Hall 1994). More recent works on coercive diplomacy include Byman and Waxman (2001) and Art and Cronin (2003).

29 Kissinger (2001: 251–73).

30 Department of Defense (1995); Matsamura, et al. (1999). For more on the Helsinki Headline Goals and the objective of a 60,000 strong force to establish a European Security and Defense Identity, see Rutten (2001). The shift in NATO emphasis from collective defense to crisis management is covered in Yost (1998). NATO's movement toward better crisis management capability accelerated after Operation Allied Force (1999) and September 11 to include the development of a rapidly deployable NATO Response Force (NRF) (De Wijk 2004; Sciolino 2004; Appathurai 2007).

societies to send forces for all the world's trouble spots when humanitarian rather than vital national interests were at stake. Now, the threat of an attack on home soil using weapons of mass destruction has increased, but the cost of invasion and counterinsurgency operations to destroy terrorist cells has also skyrocketed well beyond the budget for humanitarian operations. While the supply of studies on crisis diplomacy dwindled after the dissolution of the Soviet Union, the return of a direct threat of global proportions along with soaring defense costs signaled the need for a second look at those lessons from the Cold War.[31]

Granted, the context of future crises will not be bipolar. Multiple, loosely affiliated states merely make the purposes of violent non-state actors or the odd rogue state harder to fulfill. The lack of a state-based center of gravity, however, does not vitiate traditional crisis management skills. It does make it more complicated to establish norms for crisis bargaining since there are likely to be fewer repeated interactions with any single group of opposing leaders. Still, the basic ingredients for future crises are latent in the present international environment.

Intense conflicts of interest will result when states, through policies on terrorism or weapons proliferation, come too close to the American jugular. The common desire to avoid war will also grow stronger as the United States presses the limits on its conventional force structure in additional deployments and as each individual challenger hesitates to become the primary target, drawing the ire of a US defense establishment backed by one half trillion dollars.

The enormous annual expenditure means that despite extended commitments in Afghanistan and Iraq, the US military still has the capacity to mount decisive attacks in a new theater. The money also drives a qualitative transformation based on the application of new information technology to simultaneous operations from land, sea, air and space, which means the Americans can do more damage to an opposing state with fewer troops and less equipment.[32]

This technological condition hearkens back, again, to the strategic environment of the Cold War.[33] In those days, quantum increases in the speed and scope of destruction enabled by nuclear technology altered the dynamics of great power competition.[34] Both the United States and the Soviet Union had good reason to fear gains by the

31 Classic works on crisis management from the Cold War era include Allison (1971), Holsti (1972), Snyder and Diesing (1977), George, Hall, and Simons (1971), George and Smoke (1974), George (1991), and George, Simons, and Hall (1994). Brecher and Wilkenfeld (2000) was published afterward, but its widely used dataset, which covered events from 1918 to 1994, and its research hypotheses relied heavily on the Cold War experience.

32 Small states may find asymmetric means for countering the US conventional advantage, but the Iraq conflicts with US-led coalitions in 1991 and 2003 provide striking evidence. In both cases, the speed, accuracy and lethality of fire from American units overwhelmed Iraqi defenders. The capture of Baghdad in March-April 2003 was accomplished with fewer troops in less time and with fewer casualties than the Defense Department's own analysts thought possible just months earlier (Boyer 2003; Freedberg 2004; White and Deutch 2004).

33 Others noticed these parallels. See the aforementioned *Surprise, Security, and the American Experience* by Gaddis (2004) and Hutchings (2004).

34 For a discussion of the "crystal ball effect," see Carnesale, et al. (1983) and the argument of Jervis (1989: esp. 5–8).

other side, but they also had better reason, as they pursued their conflicting goals, to avoid general war. These strong, yet contradictory, motivations led both sides toward a mode of dueling that came to be known as the superpower crisis.[35]

Although the information revolution has different implications for national capability than the nuclear revolution, it similarly encourages leading states, in this case the United States, to practice crisis diplomacy. The new technologies for collection, analysis and distribution of information, rather than accelerate massive destruction already made possible by nuclear warheads, facilitate the precise destruction of forces organized to defend a state. After mixed but still impressive results in Kosovo, the transforming American military, in stunning fashion, abruptly dismantled the state and whisked it away from seething populations in Afghanistan and Iraq.

The full consequences of information dominance as an offensive weapon, though, show that its greater precision does not free it from some of the same paradoxical concerns that attended nuclear weapons. After the Korean War, President Eisenhower took the controversial decision to embrace nuclear weapons in the so-called New Look strategy, which shifted resources from the Army to the strategic bombers of the Air Force. He also supported Secretary of State John Foster Dulles in aggressive rhetoric that linked nuclear superiority to diplomatic leverage for rolling back Soviet influence. On the other hand, when it came to the actual use of nuclear bombs in a general conflagration, Eisenhower was more circumspect because he realized that if the United States could somehow win a nuclear exchange, the aftermath of such a victory across the vast stretches of Soviet territory would pose grievous moral, economic and political problems for America.[36]

While the magnitude of destruction in a regime takedown by the information age US military is less than Eisenhower contemplated for preventive nuclear war, the disruption to millions of innocent lives still weighs on the geopolitical scale. Civil order and public services still transfer to the legal and moral responsibility of the occupying power. Bystander states—and there are many after a precise information age attack—perceive additional incentive to isolate and weaken the United States after it unilaterally employs any of its superweapons. Whatever the risks in frustrating the will of the leading state, these are balanced by fear of a world in which such a country assumes the role of judge, jury and executioner. Under such conditions, from the point of view of other states in the system struggling to distinguish between offensive and defensive intentions, the threat from American arms—be they nuclear or conventional—becomes more arbitrary and more worrisome.[37]

After the information revolution, as after the nuclear revolution, the leading state, if it is wise, comprehends the benefit of conserving its technological advantage

---

35 Hyland (1987); Brecher and Wilkenfeld (2000).

36 Eisenhower's skepticism toward the concept of nuclear victory is captured in notes from a conversation with military officers. "Gain such a victory and what do you do with it? Here would be a great area from the Elbe to Vladivostok and down through South East Asia torn up and destroyed and without government..." Eisenhower's 1954 conversation is quoted in Nathan (1995: 3); also, see Jervis (1989: 4). For a favorable review of Eisenhower's stewardship of national security policy from a former National Security Council staffer, see Bowie and Immerman (1998).

37 Jervis (1978).

in order to intimidate uncooperative adversaries at the same time that it appreciates the total cost of putting new technology to widespread use.[38] Again, the mixed motivations to escalate contests and yet pull back from all-out war also enter the calculations of savvy challengers. They sense the leader's reluctance to employ its superior military even as they dread the consequences of pushing the leader too far. In this manner, information-based military transformation, like nuclear transformation, sets the stage for interstate crisis dynamics.

Once crisis performance takes center stage, a set of special considerations involving deployment and custody of the weapon technology also come to the fore. If the main strategy of the United States is to threaten use of its information age military but bring it into action only on rare occasions, officials in the Executive and Congress must decide which units can best handle enhanced capabilities. In the current context, this means selecting which American and allied elements will be fully plugged in for "network centric" conventional warfare. Involvement of allied units helps with sharing the burden of defense modernization, but it also creates additional command and control protocols and information security issues.[39]

A regime killing force like that assembled under CENTCOM General Tommy Franks before Iraq in 2003, operating in a world that can still drain the capabilities of the leading state, may acquire more credibility under a form of joint custody. Although this flies in the face of Machiavelli's dictum to depend first on one's own arms, to control the costs of global leadership over the long run, the United States cannot launch sharp attacks in all directions. Especially after the experience in Iraq, it may be more willing to use force against the next recalcitrant adversary if important allies authorize the blow.

Some proposals have called for allies to participate in the decision making on future strikes by contributing fully interoperable forces. Members of the North Atlantic Treaty Organization are probably best positioned to accept this role. The alliance for several years highlighted interoperability as a top priority, and the less prepared, newer members spent significant portions of their defense budgets to upgrade weapons, doctrine and training to NATO standards.[40]

Unfortunately, the Herculean task of military transformation at the US pace is complicated by domestic politics on both sides of the Atlantic. In Europe, defense ministers by and large have planned their acquisitions within stagnant or decreasing defense budgets as a percentage of gross domestic product. Domestic opinion, moreover, tends to favor status symbols such as fighter aircraft over less glamorous but equally sophisticated gear to share secure information with US forces on the move.[41]

---

38 Haley (2004).

39 Mitchell (2006).

40 See, for example, the NATO communiqué (especially items 18–21 and 29) from the June 2004 Istanbul summit, available at www.nato.int/docu/pr/2004/p04-096e.htm. The US Department of State published a fact sheet, "NATO: Building New Capabilities for New Challenges," that listed some of the important national capabilities commitments; see, from the 2002 collection, www.state.gov/p/eur/rls/fs/15384.htm. Eventually these efforts to build new capabilities were rolled into the initiative "Transforming NATO for New Challenges;" see the US Department of State fact sheet from 2006 at http://www.state.gov/p/eur/rls/fs/76982.htm.

41 Butterworth-Hayes (2004); De Wijk (2004).

Meanwhile, Pentagon officials labor under competing goals. On the one hand, they want to increase burdensharing by promoting interoperability. Yet, they also desire to keep the US lead in information technology, which in turn drives US conventional superiority over potential great power rivals. Lowering the technology barriers to Europe inevitably raises the likelihood of leaks to hostile parties in the wider world.[42] Even if the technological cooperation with NATO allies were made airtight, American planners would still keep one eye peeled for emerging threats to US defense contractors whose capacity for new sales and future innovation sustains the superior quality of US equipment.[43] In the realm of military combat operations, then, there are stubborn obstacles to process sharing among allies and integrated execution.

The following chapters of this book explore a possible way out from the strategic and technological dilemma confronting US global leadership. The next two chapters extend propositions coming out of this introduction. First, strategic ambitions of the United States after September 11 combined with American ascendance in relative power, and continuing limitations on absolute power, will move the United States into more frequent crisis situations. Chapter 2 of the book, "Crisis, Information, War," discusses ways in which crisis management differs from combat in all-out war, and it reviews lessons learned on crisis diplomacy, largely from the Cold War experience.

A second claim motivates Chapter 3, "Testing Information Effects on Crisis Performance." The systems used for collection, analysis and distribution of information act as force multipliers for extending US military dominance, but they, like nuclear weapons, require special care in their application to crises. Relevant lessons have already cropped up in other endeavors such as emergency management, humanitarian relief, business and finance. The counterintuitive ways in which modern information systems sometimes interact with human organizations are reviewed with attention to how these patterns might be observed in the context of interstate crisis bargaining.

Case studies in Chapters 4 and 5 form the empirical heart of the analysis, providing a record of how principles of information management played out under

---

42 International cooperation was more difficult after a French officer admitted to passing general targeting information to the Serbs during the October 1998 precursor to Operation Allied Force. With regard to the main air campaign, security tightened sharply on the distribution of air-tasking orders, and flight plans for sensitive American platforms such as the F-117A Stealth Fighter were never shared (Graff, 2000). The French, for their part, complained that their efforts to help the Americans during Operation Enduring Freedom in Afghanistan were hampered when the Americans upgraded communications without properly coordinating with NATO (Brosky 2002).

43 Spiegel (2004); Scully (2005). American and European officials from government and the private sector entangle themselves in complex negotiations over missile defense. European cooperation could reduce the price and increase the technical effectiveness of missile defense subsystems, but it could also reduce America's relative standing in important defense technologies and nurture eventual competitors for large US suppliers such as Boeing and Lockheed (Pasztor and Karp 2004). See also the March 28, 2007 Foreign Press Center Briefing, US Department of State, "Missile Defense and Europe," on technology sharing with Italy, available at http://fpc.state.gov/82329.htm.

tense conditions between ordinary diplomacy and war. Each case study actually comprises a series of events that vigorously tested US leadership in transatlantic relations. Chapter 4 recounts the "low technology" case of the Berlin Crises between 1948 and 1962 and compares it against crises in the former Yugoslavia, 1998–1999 after the information revolution. The structured comparison marshals evidence to show that vast improvements in information technology over five decades did not relieve US decision makers from having to confront certain recurring dilemmas of crisis management. The cases reinforce the idea that crisis dilemmas are more resistant than opposing armies to solutions involving exclusive control of superior information technology.

Chapter 5 features a counterfactual analysis, taking the crisis leading up to the 2003 Iraq War as a basis for asking whether US crisis performance would have improved if a common infrastructure of collection, analysis, and dissemination systems for crisis decision making had existed for the NATO allies. The counterfactual explores how sharing the process rather than just the products of information technology could improve allied deliberation and overall outcomes of crisis bargaining.

Finally, Chapter 6, "Kantian Union in the Information Age," discusses the policy implications of common information infrastructure and the plausibility of trusted guardianship in the future of the Atlantic Alliance. The level of institutionalization at NATO, as opposed to loosely connected bilateral relationships in, say, East Asia, facilitates technology sharing among transatlantic allies. One policy implication from this study would be to invest in this favorable environment by launching a new crisis information system under the auspices of the NATO Common Infrastructure Program. The requirements for such a system could be met by proprietary technology. Unlike systems for US national security, these designs could be built and operated without military classification barriers that discriminate among NATO allies.

As the United States searches for ways to leverage its power and shape a more benign world order, strategic gains are possible through a synthesis of crisis management and information management. The astronomical costs of projecting conventional military force everywhere and limits on the utility of the most advanced information technology under crisis conditions turn crisis information systems into a double-edged sword, more safely employed with many hands rather than America's alone.

In the short run it may be easier for US presidents to reject the meddling of friends during crisis diplomacy, and for reasons of military effectiveness, it may make sense on occasion for America to fight as a lone sheriff. Most Americans, however, would prefer that US preeminence remain not just for years but decades. Before America notches too many combat victories and takes on too many commitments for postwar reconstruction, it will want to weigh the advantages of becoming a trusted guardian. Successful cooperation against rogue forces that could fracture the system of states may hinge on the willingness of the leading state to share—if only in the context of crisis decision making—a key source of strength with a community long accustomed to internecine competition.

Chapter 2

Crisis, Information, War

In order to understand why there might be a fundamental shift between information system design for the contingency of crisis versus combat, it makes sense to explore whether the incentive structure for crises is distinguishable from the type of challenge faced by commanders in conventional war. That, in turn, requires a definition of crisis apart from war. Any such definition is open to criticism because the term "crisis" appears in so many different contexts, including within a war.

Nevertheless, definitions offered during the Cold War era of superpower showdowns provide a useful guide to what makes crises different. After settling on a definition, it is reasonable to separate international conflicts conforming to the crisis definition from war events that do not. In reviewing the essential differences, it becomes clearer how the art of crisis management differs from the art of wartime command. Moreover, it is easier to see how the introduction of new technology with greater capacity for the collection, analysis, and distribution of information could affect the course of events in either case. Setting aside the argument over whether the next generation network of computers and sensors will work as advertised—still an important concern for the future of military transformation—if new technology functioned perfectly, it might very well reduce the logistical and human costs of fighting for the superior force but at the same time make the art of crisis management more demanding and the crisis game more dangerous.

That is, unless the information superior party found a way to reassure allies and adversaries against its early exit from crisis bargaining in favor of a high-technology offensive strike. Shifting objectives from combat attrition to crisis reassurance imply a corresponding change in information system design from exclusive access toward common network infrastructure. The last section in this chapter discusses how sharing information technology for crisis management among sovereign states should be easier and more effective if they are also democracies.

Defining Crisis

For the purpose of distinguishing modes of behavior and understanding the implications of improved information technology, an international crisis is defined here in terms of a particular strategic dilemma confronted by policy makers. While many different situations are called crises in common parlance, reliable distinctions can be made using three criteria: 1) the competition against another state places serious national interests at stake, 2) decision makers on all sides have limited time to find a settlement before events slip from their control and a devastating mutual loss takes place, and 3) decision makers labor under surprise conditions that are not accounted for in standard operating procedures.

This definition appears narrow given the number of crises popping up in newspaper headlines. The classical definition, by contrast, refers broadly to circumstances harboring the potential for dramatic change, a turning point, from the regular stream of events.[1] Contemporary American scholars with an eye turned toward political competitors in Asia note that the Chinese character for crisis denotes the concept of "opportunity" as well as danger.[2] For those promoting change within the bureaucracy, identifying a situation as a crisis can serve as a bid for resources. If only extra money or manpower or authority can be spared during the crisis period, long-term benefits—whether the context is advancing disease, spiraling debt, or a foreign arms build-up—might be secured against an urgent threat.

Accordingly, the language of crisis makes frequent appearances in government circles. Americans muddle through health care crises, a social security crisis, and sundry environmental crises without a rigorous understanding of what distinguishes the urgency of crisis from everyday politics. A line of constructivist thinking explains why this odd predicament might develop. In this theoretical approach, normal policy is seen as evolutionary, with the everyday stream of political conflicts generally perceived and resolved on the basis of language games. These games, almost like international trade agreements, are built over time to facilitate communication between bureaucratic actors in complex environments. Even states with the most powerful material capabilities have trouble unilaterally erasing precedents for negotiation or coercion that precluded all-out war in the past.[3]

Crisis may be thought of as a dreadful situation in which parties to a conflict perceive that the old language game has suddenly collapsed. Unless a replacement is socially constructed in short order, parties cannot avoid their *ultima ratio* for addressing conflict. In most policy contexts, the final arbiter usually imposes extraordinary costs for all stakeholders. An interesting implication of the constructivist approach is that policy entrepreneurs might invoke the language of crisis early, not in a transparent attempt to redirect political capital but to defend an existing language game from collapse. That is, they could use the descriptive language of a crisis already in process as a warning to head off a real crisis. This explains the common proliferation of crisis rhetoric and, for example, why the Bush administration during the winter of 2003 could brush aside a so-called nuclear crisis with North Korea.[4] It implies that true crises are likely to occur in only a small subset of cases identified as such in the news. The policy arena for national security hardly differs from other political contexts in the sense that contemporary crisis rhetoric often elicits wary discounting and prudent defenses from the bureaucracy against raids on its resource allocation.

In a previous era, though, the term "crisis management" drew serious attention from both scholars and practitioners. After the Cuban Missile Crisis, Secretary of Defense Robert McNamara testified in a congressional hearing that "there is no

1 Robinson (1972: 22).

2 Lord (2003: 204). Using crisis to seek advantage is not unique to China, but China often bears the brunt of this kind of charge in American analyses (Gudgel 2004). Alastair Iain Johnston (2003) recognized and challenged this habit.

3 Howard (2004).

4 Perry (2003); Kessler (2003).

longer any such thing as strategy; there is only crisis management."[5] Strategy, of course, could not be lightly discarded. In the heat of Great Power conflict, it provided the foundation for leaders struggling to organize enormous industrial age forces. Strategy connoted calm detachment from the immediate temptations of frightening circumstances. Strategy enabled expert analysis that would cull critical information from otherwise overwhelming detail. Correct strategy protected against reckless crisis reactions by capturing the larger pattern embedded in current difficulties. It prioritized various state activities from the theater level down to sectors within individual battlefields. Top-down coordination succeeded through long-range planning against a relatively accurate forecast of coming challenges extrapolated from the historical pattern, be they natural or man-made.[6]

True to form, McNamara's terse lesson-learned before Congress suggested to some a naked claim on resources, especially authority, on behalf of civilian officials and at the expense of military professionals.[7] Graham Allison's widely read study of the Cuban Missile Crisis included an episode in which McNamara railed against Admiral George Anderson, Chief of Naval Operations during the quarantine on Cuba against additional Soviet missiles. McNamara relentlessly probed the details of naval maneuvers until the admiral became uncomfortable. The complexities involved in blockading ports had been thought through; highly skilled sailors had been trained in order to successfully complete the mission; the strategy was already "in the book" that, for emphasis, he waved in front of the secretary. From the admiral's point of view, a neophyte who insisted on being at the helm would misapply the strategy, unnecessarily risk the forces, and imperil the mission. "I don't give a damn what John Paul Jones would have done," McNamara responded.[8] Strategy by the book written and revered in the Navy was not, in the secretary's reckoning, designed for resolving crisis.[9]

Beyond the bureaucratic resource implications of McNamara's outlandish claim about the passing of strategy, lay a genuine impulse for strategic reform. Classic strategies such as Germany's Schlieffen Plan before World War I were designed to win a conventional clash of arms. After the near miss of 1962, McNamara's criticism of traditional strategy as obsolescent began to look more reasonable. Winning a general clash of arms became much less feasible and therefore less important relative to avoiding a nuclear exchange in the first place. At the same time, the imperative to avoid war did not erase the need to defend US interests against Soviet blackmail.

In the aftermath of the missile crisis, academics developed a line of research to investigate a special class of mixed-motive games: "situations involving international conflict, resolution of which ought to be accomplished without either a compromise

5 Quoted in George (1991: 377).

6 Miller, Jones, and Van Evera (1991); Betts (2000).

7 Lord (2003: 201, 203).

8 The story is recounted in Allison (1971: 131–2).

9 For more on the connection between crisis management and civil-military tension in the US case, see Feaver (2003: Ch. 6). For a prominent example of analysis focusing on crisis processes as distinct from war, see Lebow (1981).

of vital interests or a resort to major warfare."[10] One of the controversial implications of mixed-motive games against the Soviet Union was that presidents and secretaries of defense experienced strong temptation to deploy the military for sending messages rather than winning battles, but this unsettling news for civil-military relations was not the only insight. Mixed-motive situations continue to emerge after the demise of the Soviet Union and the bipolar world order. The old models for crisis from the 1960s and 1970s can be applied, again, as the United States contends with simultaneous conflicts around the globe. Its superior forces can defeat any adversary separately, but physical limitations on committing the military everywhere at once mean that, at least on some occasions, America and an adversary will share a strong common interest in avoiding war.[11]

As in the case of today's statesmen who grapple with dramatic improvements in information systems, Cold War leaders contended with a form of revolutionary technology. The novel speed and low cost with which the superpower nuclear arsenals could devastate another society prompted analysts to scrutinize bureaucratic and psychological phenomena that might complicate rational decision making.[12] Nuclear weapons technology provided statesmen on both sides a crystal clear picture of mutual destruction if a superpower crisis should escalate out of control.[13] Yet, as Thomas Schelling (1966a) persuasively argued, it was also rational for both sides to run serious risks of war in order to defend their rational interests. Nuclear weapons helped keep the Cold War cold, but they also made nerve jangling showdowns like those over Berlin and Cuba more likely, at least until norms for a less deadly game were mutually accepted.[14]

Today, crises are less likely to involve nuclear threats, but they acquire their own special brand of intensity due to the revolution in information technology. Burgeoning networks of computers and communications in the commercial sphere create wild cards for less powerful states. They provide operational infrastructure or in some cases additional targets for insurgents and terrorist groups bent on answering US military superiority with an asymmetric threat. In the conventional military sphere, new technologies save on the perceived time and cost for the United States to execute a regime change once it has committed to war.

Because they provide a quantum advantage against conventional forces and accelerate military destruction of the state, transformational information systems constitute a kind of second coming, after nuclear weapons, of technological

---

10 Giffen (1965: 8).

11 American arms easily defeated the Iraqi army, but the consequent stretching of military resources makes genuine crisis bargaining between the United States and either Iran or North Korea a more likely scenario. Sanger (2004).

12 The literature in this case is large, but much of it is cited in Tetlock, et al. (eds) (1989). See especially the chapter by Ole Holsti on "Crisis Decision Making," pp. 8–84.

13 Joseph Nye termed this the "crystal ball effect." For example, see Nye (2005: 139).

14 Depending on the interpretation, this was what the Nixon, Ford and Carter administrations had in mind as they pursued détente in the 1970s. Around the collapse of détente, normally linked to the Soviet invasion of Afghanistan in 1979, a debate ensued about whether it was more dangerous to preserve a regime in which the United States might be lulled into complacency or return to the crisis-prone competition of the early Cold War (Lynn-Jones 1987).

intrusion on crisis management. In order to follow the logical implications of crisis management in the information age then, there are good reasons to explore concepts from the nuclear age. Similar behavioral questions emerge. For example, in the earlier era, scholars questioned whether crisis stress augmented or handicapped perceptual and rational faculties of state leaders attempting to navigate their way through the mixed motive game.[15] During contemporary crises for the United States, in addition to the high stress factor, researchers now wonder whether new collection and communication technologies make rational decisions more likely and whether these systems can diffuse psychological and bureaucratic traps that drew so much concern in Cold War studies.[16]

This book hearkens back to the old Cold War definitions of crisis in order to explain why the advent of transformational technology, not unlike the realization of swift and sure destruction thirty or forty years ago, brings with it new challenges for crisis management. During the bipolar standoff of the late-1960s, several scholars working in the behavioralist tradition defined crisis as a technical term to guide their empirical research. Ole Holsti (1972), in *Crisis, Escalation, War*, offered three criteria: high stakes, limited time for decision, and the element of surprise. By this definition, the July Crisis before World War I and the Cuban Missile Crisis were quintessential cases for studying the effects of stress on decision processes.

Similarly Charles Hermann (1972) incorporated all three elements in order to simulate crises in the social science laboratory created at the Great Lakes Naval Training Center. A crisis; 1) threatened one or more important goals of a state, 2) allowed only a short time for decision before the situation was significantly transformed, and 3) occurred as a surprise to the policy makers.[17] The specificity of this definition guided researchers in devising experiments. Over multiple trials, the inputs of threat, decision time, and surprise could be manipulated while systematic changes in decision-making among the participants—such as contraction of the management team for crucial deliberations—could be tracked.

During these simulations, only one leadership team, or one "state", experienced decision making under crisis pressure. Some scholars questioned whether it does not take at least two parties to make a true crisis, and a standard way of noting the difficulty in establishing a single research definition for crisis has been the bifurcation between "decision-making" and "systemic perspectives."[18] In the context of the Cold War, analysts wondered how crises affected the stability of the international system. These contests might provide an opportunity to release built-up tension and improve conflict resolution norms for future problems, or they might breed resentment and dissolve the trust necessary for peacefully resolving future disputes.[19] Michael

15 Jervis (1976).

16 Snow and Brown (2000: 314); Feaver (1998).

17 Hermann (1972: 187).

18 Roberts (1988) organized his review of the crisis management literature according to this question. His "decision making" approach required only one leadership team to perceive a crisis whereas the "systematic" approach reserved the term to describe a particularly volatile condition of multi-state interaction.

19 Diehl and Goertz (2000); Leng (2000); Gelpi (1997).

Brecher and John Wilkenfeld's long running study of crisis over the years created a bi-level database spanning events from 1918–2002.[20] In light of the resistance to a single definition for crisis, it is interesting to note that their definition, which applies to both system-level and actor-level cases, resembles the ones used for studying Cold War decision-making. According to *A Study of Crisis* (2000), the criteria are; 1) a threat to one or more basic values; 2) finite time for response to the value threat; and 3) a heightened probability of involvement in military hostilities.[21]

This definition eases the burden of outside observers if their task is to sift crisis events from a long historical record. It does, however, create inconveniences if the object is to show how, given a plausible level of skill among national crisis players across the decades, the introduction of new technology alters the game. The difficulties are most severe in criterion number three: a heightened probability of military hostilities. This restricts the domain considerably from Charles Hermann's "significantly transformed situation," and there is no reason to think *a priori*, that information-age lessons derived from political-military crises could not apply to an international financial crisis in which debt default, a credit collapse, or capital flight could stand in, analytically speaking, for descent into war.

Criterion three also eliminates surprise as a necessary element of crisis. Again, this makes coding of a large number of cases more convenient. However, it removes important considerations when it comes to technology and crisis decision making. At the height of the nuclear standoff, analysts warned about potential errors in the rational calculus that kept the superpowers from initiating general war. The conditions of surprise—though difficult to measure—addressed both bureaucratic and psychological concerns.

Surprise makes it likely that political leaders as managers would be set at odds against their own bureaucracy's standard procedure. In the context of the Cuban missile crisis, a standard blockade or a regularly scheduled U-2 reconnaissance flight could inadvertently provoke the Russians and lead to disaster.[22] The psychological stress of maneuvering without adequate plans and of not knowing to what extent the adversary might be miscalculating or panicking also made irrational devastation seem like a much more plausible outcome. In the information age, as in the nuclear age, surprise remains central to crisis management.

Technologies for data collection, analysis, and communication hold out the promise of adaptable organizations that can anticipate threats before they pose an acute danger. The horrific example of September 11 nevertheless indicates that

---

20 Recent updates of Brecher and Wilkenfeld's codebooks for system-level and actor-level data are available at http://www.icbnet.org/Data/ICB1-2005-final.pdf and http://www.icbnet.org/Data/ICB2-2005-final.pdf, respectively.

21 Brecher and Wilkenfeld (2000: 3, n. 16, Part I).

22 Both of these standard operating procedures managed to inspire profanity from principals in the crisis. McNamara's frustration is recorded as previously noted in Allison (1971). Kennedy himself wryly remarked after the wayward U-2 flight, "There is always some son-of-a-bitch who doesn't get the word." A detailed chronology of the Cuban Missile Crisis is available at http://www.nuclearfiles.org/hitimeline/cmc.html. The Kennedy remark appears under October 27, 1962.

strategic surprise persists.[23] Maintaining the element of surprise in the definition of crisis serves, then, as a direct challenge to one of the optimistic presumptions behind defense transformation—that the problem of tactical surprise collapses under information dominance.[24] One of the keys to understanding crisis management in the age of transformation is recognizing how surprises continue even after new technologies permit detailed chronologies of an adversary's actions.[25]

Before finally deciding upon an updated definition for crisis, it is worth making one last stop in the literature. In a recent forum on "Managing Crises in the Twenty-First Century," Arjen Boin of the Crisis Research Center at Leiden University (Netherlands) offered an interdisciplinary conceptualization of crisis: it can be "defined more precisely as a 'serious threat to the basic structures or the fundamental values and norms of a social system, which—under time pressure and highly uncertain circumstances—necessitates making critical decisions.'"[26] As Boin mentioned, the definition is broad enough to encompass emergency response as well as interstate contests, and it still contains basic elements of the Cold War definition: threat and limited time, with uncertain circumstances substituting for surprise.

Still, there are major differences between executing a decision sequence under uncertainty and playing a mixed-motive game with a deadly adversary. A natural disaster can be made worse by inappropriate response but it cannot be provoked or intimidated—or persuaded through reason. In some ways, this makes it easier to model "acts of God" ahead of time, including the uncertainties of the aftermath for response teams. Probabilistic outcomes by themselves do not bring on the same bureaucratic and psychological challenges as an unanticipated strategic threat. Surprise, not uncertainty, forces policy managers outside their standard menu of options. Moreover, in a situation like the Cuban Missile Crisis, the interaction of the game more than any force of nature imposes a time constraint on decisions to acquiesce or escalate. Crucial differences underscore the need for a refinement of Boin's suggested definition, one that excludes some important decisions that are commonly called crises, but one that also moves us to the heart of the explanation for why crisis management demands its own chapter in the annals of defense transformation.

A true crisis in today's international security environment, for example pitting North Korea or Iran against a US-led coalition, would combine; 1) a serious conflict of interests recognized as such in the international system; 2) the coming, in limited time, of a final arbiter that all sides seek to avoid; and 3) elements of surprise for key decision makers. Under these circumstances, the United States faces a choice about how to use its advantage in information technology to resolve the crisis on favorable terms. For the purpose of exploring crisis dilemmas in which superior imaging, signals, and communications could come into play, the next section describes the logic behind these mixed-motive situations.

---

23 Betts (2002).

24 Lamb (2005).

25 All-weather tracking of moving objects across the globe summarizes the ambition of the US Air Force new Space Radar project (Fabey 2005).

26 Boin (2004: 167). The definition is taken from Rosenthal, Charles and 't Hart (1989).

The Logic of Crisis

Tracing through the logic of crisis accomplishes two basic purposes. First, it provides the theoretical basis for understanding why international crises have and probably will continue to present policy management challenges that defy easy solutions in spite of improved information technology. Second, while crisis dilemmas and combat decisions often intermingle in practice, the modeling perspective makes a clear case for a meaningful conceptual difference, a gulf that is bound to grow wider as warfare approaches the ideal offered by defense transformation. The series of examples that follow mark an evolution of thought from the missile scare of October 1962 to quasi-imperialist concerns, especially on the part of the United States, in the aftermath of the September 11 attacks. Despite many innovations and refinements, the crisis game still comes down to the problem of missing information—less acute with respect to disposition of forces than the nature of the adversary that controls them.

The Game of Chicken

Many treatments of crisis as a distinct class of international conflict begin their inquiry with the simple two-person game of chicken, illustrated by the 2 x 2 payoff matrix in Figure 2.1.

		Player 1	
		C	D
Player 2	C	(0,0)	(1, -.5)
	D	(-.5, 1)	(-1, -1)

Figure 2.1 Chicken game example

The payoff matrix records the incentives for players in the game to cooperate or defect. "Cooperation" in the crisis context means standing down or conceding in order to reach a settlement that avoids costly conflict. "Defection" represents escalation or firmness to the point where, if the other side does not back down, both sides suffer disaster—the dreaded final arbiter that helps define a crisis situation. The exact numerical values and the precise symmetry in the model matter less than the mixed motives it sets up for the participants.

Both sides have incentive to cooperate in order to avoid the large losses exacted by costly fighting. Yet, in keeping with the definition of crisis, there are severe conflicts of interest as well. Focusing on the ordered pairs along the ascending diagonal, both players are competing to see if they can make the other side cooperate, or stand down, while defecting themselves. The reward for cowing the other side far exceeds the payoff for cooperating with them on some sort of equitable settlement. Moreover, in the language of game theory, the cooperative outcome is not an equilibrium because from each individual player's point of view, if the other side appears disposed to give way, then the player has a large incentive to win more by defecting on the deal.

The remaining element from the crisis definition, limited time, does not appear explicitly in the model. However, the matrix purports to show all available options, so it lays out a situation in which players cannot just wait: they cannot decide not to play. Much of the Cold War speculation centered on what typical people would do in such circumstances with whatever time they had. The metaphor behind the quantified payoffs was two automobiles racing toward one another to see which driver would swerve away first to avoid collision. Harvard economist Thomas Schelling (1960; 1966a; 1966b) was particularly adept at imagining strategic responses that seemed relevant to geopolitical competition between nuclear powers.

Perhaps the most famous insight explained the shifting role of brute force in great power competition. To be sure, influential strategists such as Bernard Brodie (1959) had already questioned the utility of nuclear attack. Even in the realm of conventional strategy, Basil Liddell Hart (1954) realized that regular army forces would be used in the nuclear age and sought ways to catch opponents off balance rather than bludgeon them with frontal assaults. Still, Schelling went beyond changing tactics in the traditional Clausewitzian wrestling match between militaries. The strategic competition between great powers transformed into something more akin to high stakes poker.[27] The analogy made for a perverse understatement since "calling a bet" in the international game could mean millions of casualties. Nevertheless, enormous geopolitical stakes might hang on a bluff, and this notion captured the almost mystical combination of reputation, intuition and resolve required to win the "competition in risk-taking" that materialized between the superpowers.[28]

Among the most intriguing strategies of this competition during the 1950s was brinkmanship. In keeping with Secretary McNamara's later testimony, it hardly merited the distinction as strategy since it discounted the value of traditional means for marshalling force. In fact, the way to bring about the adversary's cooperation was to invent "signals" that would preclude any outcome of the chicken game in which one's own concessions were required. In terms of the metaphor of the teenagers' duel, this meant throwing one's own steering wheel out the window, so the other driver understood he had "the last clear chance" to avoid a crash. For leading powers in the international system, it meant weighing the counterintuitive advantages of ceding control against the inclination to optimize combat assets for defeating the other side's physical capacity to resist. Rather than cool efficiency, the real possibility of irrationality would force an adversary to stand down.

Of course, in the teenager's duel or in superpower relations, a version of the security dilemma still applies. Just as two can respond to a defensive arms build-

27 Gartzke (1999) explicitly referred to the poker analogy as he explained the logic of a sophisticated descendant from the chicken game of the 1960s.

28 Schelling (1966a: Ch. 3).

up and thereby make an attack more likely, two can play at inventing actions to jeopardize self-control. If both sides provoke crises to expand their influence and both figuratively throw out their steering wheels around the same time, Armageddon becomes inevitable. That disturbing conclusion persuaded several strategic thinkers that the chicken game matrix was too simple to capture the essential elements of crisis management.[29] Schelling himself noted that out of their mutual interest in avoiding nuclear holocaust, the great powers might find a way to institute mutual cooperation in resolving crises, perhaps a way to veer from a head-on collision in alternating baby steps without losing face or trust in the other side.

Dissatisfaction with the basic chicken game led some scholars to reject it in favor of approaches that placed greater emphasis on the psychology of crisis leadership. It led other theorists to refine the original game. As several of these refinements reinforced the original insights coming out of chicken, they clarified the conceptual distinction between warfare and the demands of crisis.

Crisis Game Refinements

Particularly in the past two decades, tools from the study of economics have been applied to make the crisis game far more flexible. Rather than a simple matrix with four possible outcomes, for example, today's models feature continuous bargaining offers. Rather than speculating about the risk propensities of players confronting the chicken payoffs, "resolve" has become an important parameter explicitly included in the models. In fact, the salience of this characteristic in determining whether states in crisis go to war highlights the most relevant difference between the two forms of conflict, including during the age of defense transformation.

To see why this is so, it is useful to consider the continuous offer game presented by James Fearon (1995) in his seminal article on "Rational Explanations for War."[30] The basic argument that resort to costly warfare by rational actors did not make sense had been made, but Fearon's formulation set a standard for elegance, and it cut to the heart of elaborate prose explanations on why crises sometimes end in war.[31]

Fearon began with a simple notion of the world as a playing field. The mathematical description of territory and influence at stake resembled a football field with two states trying to control as much real estate as possible between the goal lines (see Figure 2.2).

In the abstract, this rendering of international "space" invites us to imagine that all the things states fight over—territory, economic concessions, political influence—for which a gain on one side imposes a loss on the other can be represented as potential settlements strung along a line of ascending utility. In Figure 2.2, for example, State A's utility ascends to the right while State B would like to control more and more to

29 Rapoport (1966).

30 Several articles, both theoretical and empirical, built upon Fearon's 1995 piece, including Schultz (1998), Gartzke (1999), Wagner (2001), and Gelpi and Griesdorf (2001). Subsequent reviews of the literature on game theory and war often include it; see Powell (2002) and Rieter (2003). For a criticism of the simplifications in Fearon's model see Kirshner (2000).

31 Bueno de Mesquita and Lalman (1992: 57–69).

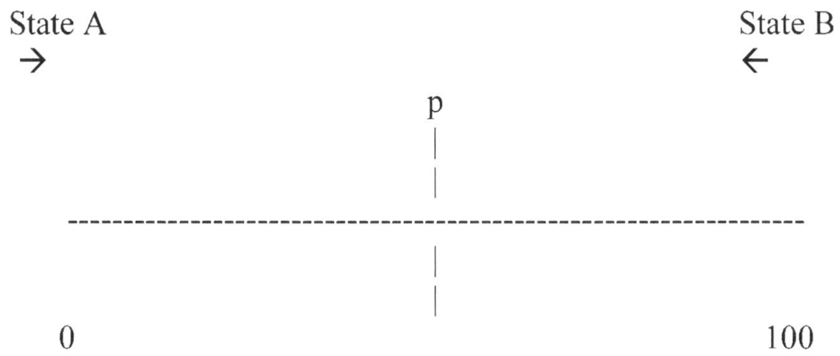

Figure 2.2 Fearon's Field of International Conflict shown with the "Peace Line" of division for two equally powerful states

the left of the line at "100," again, something like a football game. No discontinuity disrupts the field of settlement values because the number of parameters and combinations in international negotiation is so vast that for every conceivable value along the line between 0 and 100, there exists at least one settlement package (supplying utility x to State A and 100-x to State B).

Without too much trouble, one can see how this mathematical abstraction applies to our criteria for crisis. The zero-sum football field represents the stakes in a serious conflict of interest. The lack of institutions or protocol for dealing with this conflict stands in for surprise. The question of the final arbiter after limited time leads us to think about how states might use their power to end this dispute in the absence of mutual agreement. Fearon answered, after realist fashion, that if no settlement were reached after a certain time, states would fight, consuming economic and military resources in order to take all the disputed stakes off the table.[32]

If we consider many states facing crisis decisions over hundreds of years, then successful actors would tend to choose their battles wisely. It is at least plausible that leaders would take expected costs of fighting and their chances of winning into account before rejecting a settlement offer. The lower the expected costs of war and the greater the probability of winning, the greater the share of stakes upon which wise states would insist before sheathing the sword and ceasing their demands.

A powerful insight from this simple model is that if both states have complete information about war capabilities, they ought to agree on a division of stakes without resort to a costly final arbiter. Better to accept a partition that reflects each side's known chances of prevailing in a violent conflict than to pay the blood price of actually carrying it out.

32 In Fearon's model, the status quo, or leaving the stakes in limbo, is not an option; there simply is no utility amount associated with avoiding a decision. States must either accept a demand to surrender their claim or fight. In this sense, Fearon's states work under the limited time criterion of crisis.

Fearon's model directs special attention toward the role of incomplete information. If negotiators doubt the other side's resolve or surmise on the basis of private information that their state has a higher chance of victory in the event of war, they may find themselves in a position to accept greater risk for greater reward. That is, they could press their demands, increasing the risk of war and its attendant costs but as compensation increasing the value of settlement if the other side should acquiesce. When dramatic details are stripped away and crisis phenomena are brought down to their essence, missing information thwarts successful management of the situation, with success defined as maximizing demands in the national interest while escaping punishment from a trial by combat.

Fearon's crisis model does connect to criticisms of defense transformation. The kind of evidence most needed to win the peace under his approach unfortunately does not match very well with the sort of data new electromagnetic devices on aircraft or satellites provide. As Fearon pointed out, in many cases, states will have incentive to prevent secret flaws in either their capabilities or resolve from becoming generally known. Under conditions such as those faced by the Japanese during their preparations for Pearl Harbor, revealing a capability could lower a country's chances for victory in the event of war. Unlike peacetime arms control when a state can deploy its missiles according to existing treaty provisions or permit on-site inspections, so cameras can record all pertinent weapons, crises tempt participants to win by bluffing the other side. Rather than build confidence that seals strategic arms treaties, information systems during crisis permit the kind of surprise that magnified, for example, political fallout from India's abrupt nuclear tests in May 1998.

Fearon's story of how crises deteriorate also challenges transformation because his explanation for bargaining failure requires flawed information on just *one side* of the conflict. Even if the United States could intercept the signal that revealed its adversary's contingency plans, the peaceful resolution of crises demands more symmetry: the weaker party needs to be confident about US calculations as well. When it comes to combat, of course, American forces prefer to avoid symmetry in favor of information superiority. In crisis negotiations, though, a weak adversary may seek concessions of the United States, counting on the US desire to escape the costs of war. In calibrating its demands to gain as much as possible without pushing the United States into war, the weaker party will make fewer errors if it has better information about US capabilities and resolve.[33] As defense transformation increases US technological superiority, this will likely complicate the intelligence work for lesser-equipped adversaries. Unlike conventional war, crisis bargaining becomes more difficult to manage as the United States approaches information dominance.

Finally, the specific type of uncertainty emphasized by Fearon is not easily resolved with more data collection. In order to play the game rationally, each state in the crisis must see the destruction of war as comparable to its utility derived

33 In his critique of contemporary balance of power theory Jim Wirtz believes that weak states frequently have problems estimating the resolve of great powers. One explanation for why US compellence against Iraq failed in 1991 is that Saddam Hussein misjudged US resolve and consequently the capability that the United States could bring to bear in Kuwait (Wirtz 2004: 142–4).

from territory and influence. Even more demanding, a state must comprehend how its adversary compares war costs against the territory and influence at stake. All of this would seem to require a thorough comprehension of leader psychology and collective decision making over and above physical data on the adversary during crisis.[34] The literature on national intelligence and strategic surprise offers little hope that, even with 21st century information collection, physical traces can reliably map to state intentions.[35] Not before the day when technicians acquire this sort of mapping ability, will the art of crisis management finally give way to computer analysis.

After he discussed the role of private information in the breakdown of crisis bargaining, Fearon's next theme took up the nature of commitment problems.[36] Even with full information, states might not make the necessary concessions to reach a settlement superior to war if the concessions themselves could cause a power shift that would, in turn, breed even greater demands. In the extreme, a link between crisis concessions and relative power could make it impossible to back out of the chicken dilemma in incremental steps. Perhaps within the complex, multi-dimensional space in play during international bargaining, trade-offs might be found, or institutions built, to get around the commitment problem.[37] Yet, there is at least some chance that improved information technology could exacerbate the difficulty of crisis bargaining by clarifying the connection between a proposed settlement and a power increase for the adversary state.[38]

In probing Fearon's assumptions about crisis bargaining, especially the notion of war as a one-shot lottery, scholars hit upon other theories to explain costly fighting. For example, limited engagements interspersed between negotiating rounds could serve to improve participants' estimates of each other's capability and resolve.[39] More creatively, fighting could be part of a punishment protocol that locks competing states into an equilibrium of mutual intimidation.[40] Yet, none of these model refinements resolved the greatest obstacles to an information technology solution for crisis management: two reasonable statesmen could examine the same disposition of forces as revealed to them by multi-spectral imaging systems and read the same signal intercepts from an adversary but still arrive at opposite conclusions about whether to escalate.[41] The more sophisticated models for the outbreak of war only reinforce the idea that winning the game of chicken depends on subjective estimates of an adversary's hidden capabilities and preferences. These estimates have as much to do with empathy and intuition as data integration.

---

34 It is far from clear, for example, that a state's resolve—the manner in which it compares war costs to war stakes—remains fixed throughout a crisis so that interlocutors might apply Bayesian updating during diplomatic maneuvers to figure out a state's type (Kydd 1997).

35 Compare Roberta Wohlstetter's (1965) *post mortem* on the awful surprise at Pearl Harbor with Richard Betts' (2002b) review of the 9/11 attacks. See also George and Hall (1997) and Porch and Wirtz (2002).

36 Fearon (1995: 401); Powell (2002); Smith (1998a); Garfinkel and Skaperdas (2000); Eilstrup-Sangiovanni and Verdier (2005).

37 Eilstrup-Sangiovanni and Verdier (2005).

38 Erik Gartzke of Columbia University shared this insight from his ongoing research.

39 Wagner (2000); Smith and Stam (2002).

40 Slantchev (2003).

41 Jervis (1976).

Simulating War

Generally speaking, the modeling of war follows a different approach from the modeling of crisis. While renderings of crisis often derive from the chicken game, representations of war normally emphasize the process of attrition. Crisis analysis usually hinges on backward induction from potential outcomes, each one hanging at the end of a well-defined chain of decisions. War simulations, by contrast, attempt to play out battles according to myopic decision rules once they have been established by the commanders on each side. The different approaches naturally lead to relatively optimistic projections for combat power versus crisis savvy as superior information comes on line.

Predictions of decisive war victories have seemingly come to pass, particularly in US conventional engagements through the 1990s as official attention shifted toward the Revolution in Military Affairs.[42] Certainly, important simulation programs such as the JANUS system used to study the Gulf War have also generated prudent qualifications. Stephen Biddle's work replaying the Gulf War battle of 73 Easting and his subsequent case studies on Afghanistan and Iraq argue for the lingering possibility of low-technology, skill-based counters to America's information age tactics.

Using the JANUS system to aggregate small-unit properties, Biddle ran his tank battle under a variety of initial assumptions. Changing parameters down at the brigade level of engagement, he found that relatively straightforward concealment strategies incorporating professional army doctrine on defensive deployment—along with a bit of knowledge on the functioning of US weapons systems—did indeed increase US casualty ratios by a factor of twenty. A similar increase taken across the board would have brought Gulf War ratios from an astounding 1:3000 up to 1:150, far closer to the historical range for industrial-age victories. Some technology may be necessary, but even a lot of technology cannot vanquish a savvy foe without substantial US casualties.[43]

Despite these findings and despite further anecdotes from Operations Enduring Freedom and Iraqi Freedom, the best arguments for technological pessimism have a hard uphill climb. Even the pessimists like Biddle are not exactly Luddites. They rather seek prudent qualifications to otherwise stratospheric expectations for the new war machines.[44] Of the three services, the Army is arguably most concerned that defense transformation does not lose its way in technology. The Army has the most people, and not unlike organized labor, it harbors legitimate concerns over the pace of substitution for current personnel and over the skill set of future soldiers. These recruits will not only be called upon to make the new technologies function day-to-day, but they will have to work around the glitches on those occasions when the devices

42 Admiral William Owens championed the combat potential of the new information technologies and became the first high-profile vice-chairman of the Joint Chiefs of Staff (1994–1996). In 2001, Secretary of Defense Donald Rumsfeld created the first Office of Force Transformation, headed by former vice-admiral Arthur Cebrowski.

43 Biddle (1997); Biddle (2004: 181–9).

44 Biddle (1997); Press (1997).

fail to live up to their promise.[45] All this, however, does not mean that senior service members want the Army to face its enemies without a technological advantage. The multi-year, 120 billion dollar Future Combat Systems (FCS) program, which offers a more complete, albeit more complex, collection and communications capability for the individual soldier, has garnered general enthusiasm from the civilians within the Office of the Secretary of Defense and from the Army commanders obliged to rethink doctrine in anticipation of the new systems' arrival.[46]

Following the success of technologies such as the Tomahawk precision-guided cruise missile and the JSTARS ground surveillance radar during the Gulf War, all the services, but again, especially the Army, commissioned studies to envision how demands of combat might evolve in the 21st century. Given the availability of machines that would allow US forces to fire on and kill enemies at greater stand-off distances and the prohibitive cost of transferring or maintaining heavy, industrial age ground units in remote theaters, much of the political heat in the late-1990s, and recently after the Iraq War, surrounded the question of "right-sizing" the Army. The service could operate with many fewer men if lighter and faster forces could block or better yet topple opposing states using tactics designed around modern day information superiority.

One model adopted by RAND's Arroyo Center (Darilek, et al. 2001) provided a theoretical rationale for exponential improvements in Army combat performance with better information management. Conventional engagements spread across a theater of operations can be simulated using some variation on Lanchester's Square Law to calculate force lethality with respect to the number of shooters.[47] RAND analysts argued that information age battles would more likely follow a linear law. This was because, in the new era, individual infantrymen, empowered by the inputs from a vast array of sensors could, in the limit, perform as an "Army of one". Whereas before, individual soldiers might sweep a restricted sector of the opposing line in a combat environment of roughly constant force density, the 21st century "wired" soldier could survey the area of the entire opposing force independent of its density.[48]

In the age of increased battlefield awareness, kill levels would depend not simply on the number of blue forces (B) and their individual efficiency at clearing assigned sectors (p) but also on the number of red forces (R) in the combat zone. In simulation terms, this meant that the operative formula for detection and kill increased from (p x B) in the conventional era to (p x B x R). Army planners could anticipate a double-

45 Davis (2003).

46 Global Security (2005); Tiboni (2004).

47 Leppingwell (1987).

48 In World War II, force densities varied—by a factor of three if measured by troops per kilometer of frontage, by an order of magnitude if measured by troops per square kilometer. To save the Lanchester Square Law from this empirical variation, additional assumptions about information processing limitations for industrial age soldiers could apply. The square process occurs when conventional soldiers cannot significantly improve their detection or kill levels even when more enemy targets enter their individual sectors. By contrast, the information age soldier is expected to engage and kill multiple targets across the enemy force in a single cycle, so as enemy numbers increase, the information age kill also increases.

bang from information improvements: efficiency for each engaged target should climb and so should the number of targets engaged. In the limit of the linear law, each army of one engaged the whole of the other force.[49]

The RAND analysis was similarly optimistic with respect to the combat advantages of asymmetric information between equally massive forces. If the Blue force could kill (p_b x BR) in a single cycle while the Red force was stuck at (p_r x R), then in order to have equally effective forces, or forces with equal kill rates, $(p_b \text{ x BR})/R = (p_r \text{ x R})/B \rightarrow p_bB^2 = p_rR$.

In the asymmetric, mixed-Lanchester world, each additional Blue force member would be exponentially more effective than each Red force increment.[50] To put it in policy terms relevant to defense transformation, the Lanchester family of attrition models indicated that, with information superiority, the Blue "Army of one" force could neutralize traditional Red forces with far fewer people.[51]

As the complexity of weapons systems and military operations increases, simulation becomes a more lucrative proposition for defense planners. The Department of Defense established a Modeling and Simulation Information and Analysis Center to educate members of the defense community about new simulation opportunities—and requirements—pertinent to their wide-ranging missions. The Joint Chiefs of Staff, eyeing the rising cost of live training, recently established a goal to "move more electrons and fewer troops."[52] DOD estimated that as the size of units involved in training or planning expands from crew level to battle group to theater level forces, time and money incentives to substitute computer programs for live bodies grow exponentially. Since the essential task for the software is to calculate how much damage an inferior force can accomplish before it succumbs in combat, simulation formulas are bound to reflect the performance gap—whether at the aggregate or small-unit level—demonstrated by superior technology in terms of velocity, survivability, and fire power on the operational proving grounds.

Although Biddle did show in a simulation with relatively high verisimilitude that terrain and force employment can blunt the overarching advantages of favorable

49 In the industrial age, Blue force's kill rate is modeled as (p_b x B)/R. Blue force and Red force are equally strong when $(p_b \text{ x B})/R = (p_r \text{ x R})/B \rightarrow p_bB^2 = p_rR^2$, hence the notion of the square law. Similar reasoning for information age kill rates leads to equally strong forces when $p_bB = p_rR$, hence the notion of the linear law.

50 Darilek, et al. (2001: 37–44).

51 Similar optimism about the effects of information superiority resulted from RAND's joint-choice models. The idea was to show how reducing the fog of war for one side, step-by-step, improved chances of victory. A 10 x 10 matrix sampled 100 possible outcomes from a uniform distribution U(0, 100), representing the clash of equal size forces. Blue sought to maximize points, and Red wanted to minimize. The engagement result was determined by Blue choosing row number (1–10) while Red chose the column number (1–10). When both sides had equal information about the 100 possible outcomes, each side won 50 percent of the time. As Blue acquired superior information about the "real" value of the 100 scenarios and then advanced intelligence on Red's strategy, Blue's selections improved so that it won over 90 percent of engagements (Darilek et al. 2001: 21–6).

52 Modeling and Simulation Familiarization Course, DOD Modeling and Simulation Information and Analysis Center, US Air Force Academy, July 21–25, 2003.

technology coefficients at the small-unit level, the JANUS/73 Easting program also showed that those coefficients exact a dreadful price against an inferior enemy that slips on force employment. As Biddle warned, "against advanced technology, partial modern-system implementation is not enough."[53] For combat, which is to say, the context of killing another complex of killer men and machines, superior technology for directing fire upon the enemy offers a huge advantage. On consideration of historical experience and simulations, US planners understandably hesitate to share transformational technology with other states—unless there has been established with military partners a relationship of trust and long-term confidence through tactical and strategic levels.[54]

Simulation versus Game Theory

Thus far, the United States has also been reluctant to share information with adversaries or allies during the prewar bargaining phase of international conflicts. The protective behavior with respect to superior information technology, however, masks crucial differences between crisis and war. With good reason, simulation models usually incorporate significant advantages for information enhanced combat units that allow them to shoot faster or farther and raise their likelihood of victory. For at least two reasons, the best analyses of crisis bargaining do not confer similar benefits to parties with material or information superiority.[55]

First, as discussed in the section on crisis games, the adversary's willingness to fight and impose additional costs on the United States does not merely rely on capability but also resolve. Estimating another government's willingness to incur risk or accept sacrifice requires empathy, or an understanding of leadership psychology and group processes. These are not the kinds of insights to be gained from satellite images or pattern recognition software.

Communications intercepts could indicate intent, but the amount of requests for information from various sources across the government bureaucracy tends to increase under crisis conditions while crucial conversations converge around an inner-circle of decision makers. The release of the so-called Downing Street memos of July 2002 illustrates the problem. Even with three years of hindsight, these direct reports from British intelligence on meetings with the Americans merely stirred more controversy. Detailed "intercepts" from deep inside policy councils could not close the issue on just when the Bush administration decided to abort WMD crisis bargaining and invade Iraq.[56]

A second reason that information superiority, or more precisely, superior information technology, cannot pave the way to favorable settlements recalls the

53 Biddle (2004: 187). See the 73 Easting simulated casualty charts with and without US advanced technology as discussed in ibid.: 185–9.

54 Here, transformational technology is used to include specialized training as well as advanced electromagnetic systems (Feith 2004). Sullivan (2002: 153–5); Gertz (2005); Mitchell (2006: Ch 4).

55 Fearon (1994).

56 Sanger (2005).

madman theory of crisis management. Attempts to coerce or intimidate the weaker party in crisis bargaining are less likely to be effective and more likely to lead to an undesired war if the target's rationality is fragile. North Korea, for example, faces yawning deficits vis-à-vis the United States on about every dimension of natural power. It has, however, limited the United States' ability to exploit information and material superiority.

A war on the Korean peninsula would of course cost both sides dearly. The United States has been reluctant to use its superior power in order to corner Kim Jong Il between a disastrous war and meaningful nuclear concessions because once the American ultimatum and the acute stress of a true international crisis arrived in Pyongyang, US officials could not be sure how Kim would weigh his options.[57] The real possibility that American technology would be tracking his force movements and probing his electronic communications might close Kim's perceived window for negotiations and deflate any optimism for an acceptable settlement with the United States, making an irrational spasm of violence under crisis conditions even more likely.[58]

Beyond what might be called the two-player limitations of information technology for crisis management, new difficulties await as the situation shifts toward multi-player games. Given the current distribution of power and the strategic ambitions of the United States, models that take into account coalitions along with mixed-motive incentive structures and asymmetric technology will have high relevance. As a first cut, the emergence of n-player crisis teams is more likely to transform the way international crisis games are played if the various players in a coalition can interact synergistically so that the multilateral crisis actor is more effective than the sum of its parts.

We might, for example, initially predict the bargaining position of the coalition confronting Saddam Hussein in 2002 by averaging each independent member's position along a hawk-dove continuum, weighted by national capability. If, however, these same members could engage in democratic deliberation, the social choice, that is, the crisis strategy for a coalition of democracies might float more freely from internal power differentials. The final product could approach synthetic empathy—a mix of Mars and Venus—more attuned to the adversary and to unique circumstances of the conflict at hand. Information technology could indeed promote a higher quality of deliberation between democracies. Yet, this role would center not so much on expanding the total pool of raw information generated by the coalition but on streamlining information dissemination and building a climate of trust.

---

57 *Economist* (2003); Hirsh (2003).

58 Similar logic soured Cold War analysts' views of decapitation strikes in the opening stages of a nuclear exchange. This type of threat would encourage delegation of critical nuclear response decisions further down the Soviets' bureaucratic chain and movement of their nuclear forces closer to hair-trigger mode. As a result of doctrinal interaction, US preparations to deter through the credible threat of decapitation could have made nuclear war with the Soviets *more* likely. Feaver (1998); Feaver (1992); Bracken (1983: 232–7).

Democracies, Information, and Crisis

Examining the differing strategic incentive structures between crisis and war highlighted reasons why exclusive information obtained from electromagnetic devices would provide less advantage in the chicken game than in a battle of attrition. Under prevailing conditions of strategic competition in the international arena, the lower an asset's value the easier it ought to be for the United States to share it with coalition partners. To complement this argument, the United States should also find it easier to share as the benefits of common information processing increase.

These benefits come into play most significantly when mature democracies enter crisis bargaining together against a common adversary.[59] As demonstrated by the US operations to overthrow regimes in Afghanistan and Iraq, a strong lead by the information superior force in a largely democratic war coalition maintains the efficiency and coordination of offensive strikes to deadly effect. In order to see why unilateralist information operations are less effective in the prior stage of crisis management, it is revealing to begin with the interaction of democracies in a more extreme situation when they are divided by serious conflicts of interest.

Conflict Resolution between Democracies

Fundamental to the integrity of liberal internationalism, indeed to the present grand strategy of the United States, is the finding that democracies respond differently to the competitive pressures among nation-states than non-democracies.[60] For many, this notion has been confirmed by the remarkable record of relative peace between the democracies over the last few centuries.[61] The reasons for this peculiar behavior generally fall within three categories: accountability, consistency and transparency.[62]

Accountability refers to the opportunity for multiple constituencies to access, check, or alter foreign policy decision processes within democracies. Given the scope of their international activities, the United States and Britain provide many prominent examples. During the build-up to the Iraq War, both the American president and the British prime minister were expected to explain the nature of the Iraqi threat and estimate the costs of escalation for their respective legislatures, and at a more general level for their national media. The need to neutralize domestic objections and forge consensus prompted the United States and Britain to combine intelligence resources and present the case against Saddam Hussein at the United Nations before going to war. It was also an important reason why Bush administration officials reacted so strongly

59 On the difference between emergent and mature democracies, see Mansfield and Snyder (1995).

60 Snyder (2004); Doyle (1997: 205–12); Van Evera (1990/91).

61 Doyle (1986: Appendix 1); Chan (1997); Russett and Oneal (2001).

62 A potential fourth category, extractive capacity, emphasizes democracy's ability to mobilize free individuals once the polity has finally decided on a course of action. The so-called powerful pacifists argument is not taken up here. It faces recent empirical challenges and does not apply directly to short-run crisis bargaining under conditions of surprise. Lake (1992); Schultz (1999); Gelpi and Griesdorf (2001); Reiter and Stam (2002); Reiter and Stam (2003).

to rough estimates from the Army Chief of Staff during an open Senate hearing in March 2003 that several hundred thousand troops would be required to reconstruct Iraq after the war.[63] The legal responsibility under the 1986 Goldwater-Nichols Act of military chiefs to provide information to Congress, Congress' formal capacity to conduct investigative hearings or deny funding requests from the executive, and the influence of media reporting on public opinion worked to make the crisis management process in the United States, now criticized as too closed, far more open than it was in non-democratic state actors such as Saudi Arabia, Syria, or Iraq itself.

Though many crises last long enough for institutional checks on the executive to have their effect, even in those cases where key choices must be made in the space of hours rather than weeks, democratic accountability still matters.[64] Skeptics note that war initiation by democracies has frequently occurred without wide consultation or opportunity for veto: the Israeli attacks against Egypt in 1956 and Lebanon in 1982, for example, the 1983 US invasion of Grenada, or the quarantine decision during the Cuban missile crisis.[65] In each of these cases, though, the executive weighed escalation with history and the electorate in mind. Paralysis in the face of real danger, or for that matter headlong leaps into war, could come to light soon enough to harm the incumbent in the next election cycle. President Kennedy is said to have rejected passive acceptance of the Soviet Missiles because of how weak that would make him, especially given his previous positions on the missile balance before conservatives in Congress. President Clinton hesitated to use force against the genocide campaign in Rwanda in part because of congressional objections after a bloody battle in Somalia seven months earlier was widely perceived as outside the scope of US national interests.

As the costs of post-war stabilization in Iraq mounted in 2003 and 2004, the three executives of the pro-war democracies paid an electoral price. President José María Aznar's Partido Popular in Spain lost the national elections in spring 2004 after mishandling the investigation of a large-scale terrorist attack by Islamists in Madrid. The party's fragile position was due largely to public rejection of Aznar's war policy. Later in 2004, President Bush lost all three presidential debates and barely survived a bruising re-election campaign despite being a wartime president in a recovering economy. Some of the strongest blows against him referred to his closed deliberations, unilateralism, and shortsightedness in leading the nation to war. Finally, in early 2005, Britain's Tony Blair suffered a drastic reduction in Labour's parliamentary majority during a period of economic prosperity. Again, one of the more telling criticisms was Blair's trustworthiness in managing the crisis with Iraq.[66]

Scholars are still testing whether and how audience costs guide democratic behavior during foreign policy crises.[67] The chicken game model emphasized in this

63 Schmitt (2003).

64 Bueno de Mesquita and Siverson (1995); Gaubatz (1999); McGillivray and Smith (2000).

65 Desch (2003).

66 BBC (2004b; 2004a; 2005a).

67 Reiter and Stam (2003); Desch (2003).

book points to private information about resolve as a major obstacle to successful crisis management. If audience costs can be used to cement executive commitments as well as punish leaders for poorly considered initiatives, then this mechanism should allow democracies to more clearly communicate and stick by their reservation price in international showdowns—thereby discouraging democracies from establishing commitments they cannot fulfill and dissuading adversaries from overreaching in their demands.[68]

With respect to the largest and most widely examined data sets on modern warfare and crisis bargaining—the Correlates of War, Militarized International Disputes (COW-MIDS) data and the International Crisis Behavior (ICB) data—scholars have found indirect evidence for the selection and communication effects.[69] Together domestic access and audience costs form a structure of accountability that belies the stereotype of democracies as noisy and volatile actors in foreign affairs.[70]

Open decision processes, competitive elections, and frequent leadership changes may all generate crosscutting messages for the outside world, but once a consensus has been established behind the democratic executive, that commitment enjoys legitimacy reinforced by the faith and credit of the people. To abandon a long-term venture with democratic *bona fides*, in other words, requires the changing of many minds. From democracies, then, accountability breeds consistency. Consistency, in turn, provides a basis for long-term cooperation.[71]

However important these factors are in general, all of them become more powerful when the interactions occur among democracies.[72] Given their own experience, democracies are more likely to grant the necessary patience for seeing through the messy consensus building of democratic partners. Open processes with several veto points and opportunity for public dissent will command more legitimacy for interactions among democracies, and the audience cost seal of commitment will carry more weight.[73] A concert of democracies also has options

68 Smith (1998b); Guisinger and Smith (2002); Ramsay (2004).

69 Fearon (1994); Reiter and Stam (1998); Partell and Palmer (1999); Gelpi and Griesdorf (2001); Schultz (2001); Slantchev (2004).

70 Gaubatz (1996); Smith (1998b); Leeds (1999); McGillivray and Smith (2000); Choi (2003).

71 Consistency is here used in the sense of low discounting for future benefits. It does not imply blind devotion to the point of imprudence. Several studies indicate that established democracies benefit from safeguards to help them avoid consistency in the extreme: following obsolete doctrines off the precipice (Snyder 1991; Kupchan 1994). On the prudent quality and moderating influence of public opinion in the US case, see Jentleson and Britton (1998) and Gartner and Segura (1998).

72 In their study of the International Crisis Behavior data set (1918–1988), Hewitt and Wilkenfeld (1996: 135) found that as the proportion of democracies on either side of a crisis increased, both the likelihood and severity of violence during the crisis period declined. This result indicates that democratic-on-democratic interaction can have its effects within or across crisis coalitions.

73 Leeds (1999) explicitly makes the case that accountability and consistency mechanisms will work better with like regimes, especially fellow democracies. She finds empirical support in the COPDAB data set, a multiyear accounting of cooperation and conflict between

at the systemic level to reinforce and intensify cooperation that are not as feasible for coalitions of mixed regimes.[74]

Democracies can afford to make conflict management—a term intended to cover all the phases of prevention, crisis, intervention, and post-war stabilization—more transparent for democratic partners. By virtue of being mature democracies, such partners can rely on broad agreement across substantive values. For example, compatible notions about the scope of freedom and opportunity ordinary citizens should enjoy limit the competition between French and American diplomacy. As a fellow democracy, France is less likely to identify its own interest in wielding access to American military infrastructure as a dagger to inflict a mortal wound on the United States.[75] In any case, common procedural values relating to popular sovereignty and the rule of law make it possible for fellow democracies to observe the policy process, warts and all, without endangering its credibility. The reduced risks associated with transparency among democracies make the major benefits all the more attractive, including a reserve of trust between states that can underwrite lasting cooperation.

All the democratic factors—accountability, consistency and transparency—build upon one another. Transparency vis-à-vis other democracies, however, is the real point of entry for information technology in the context of coalition crisis management. For democratic states deciding whether and how to cooperate with the United States against a threatening adversary, multi-spectral cameras, ultra-sensitive antennae, and advance signal processing will only rarely provide the type of information that could illuminate a correct solution for the crisis. Yet, sharing the technology in a way that allowed transparent collection, analysis, and distribution of the same information among allies could make a dramatic difference. As democracies simultaneously reached for the same standing infrastructure to formulate their next moves, any immediate danger would be thrown into long-term relief, where the value of future cooperation among democracies is difficult to ignore. When it came time for critical judgments about the challenger's intentions and resolve, the collective intuition would emerge in a climate of greater mutual respect and trust. Common technology, by instituting transparency and reinforcing bonds of accountability and commitment familiar to democracies, would prepare the ground for a deeper synthesis of state views. As in the case of domestic representative bodies, quality deliberation within a coalition of representative governments generates social choices, including to escalate or not, that are less vulnerable to internal defection and more reflective of practical wisdom under the ambiguity and unremitting stress of crisis games.

---

state-dyads in the international system. Reviews that make the case for monadic effects of democracy still concede the special properties of democracy-on-democracy interaction (Macmillan 2003).

74 Russett and Oneal (2001).

75 In Secretary of State Condoleezza Rice's Paris speech at the opening of the second Bush administration, an agenda that reached beyond common threats and consequent limits to diplomatic competition underwrote her appeal to Europe for greater transatlantic cooperation (BBC 2005c).

Chapter 3

Testing Information Effects on Crisis Performance

After considering incomplete information games used to model bilateral crises and the record of cooperation between democracies, there are several reasons to suspect that advanced information technology might have more significant effects on deliberation within democratic coalitions than on usable knowledge for coercing crisis adversaries. Several model variations of the "chicken game" and case studies from the Cold War point to resolve rather than capability as the key unknown for determining an opponent's reservation price. New information systems capture or analyze subtle disturbances in the electromagnetic field for physical not psychological presence. While knowing the physical disposition of the enemy—and wielding precise control over one's own kinetic effects—provide a dramatic advantage in conventional engagements, transformational information systems are much less central to generating optimal crisis bargaining strategies. In crises, even a physically weak adversary can impose costs on the superior party.

At the same time, militarily inferior partners in crisis can provide benefits disproportionate to their physical capabilities if their bargaining positions and their cooperation with leading states persuade an adversary to rethink its resolve. If it is the case that a revisionist state has more difficulty mobilizing and expending resources to wring concessions from the international community as opposed to the United States alone, then the backing of likeminded nations has value independent of the precise number of tanks or ships they bring to the dispute.

The question arises whether there is a way that a leading state like the United States could utilize superior information systems to encourage higher quality cooperation among its allies without compromising conventional military advantage over crisis foes. The answer may be to change the institutions that govern information sharing among allies. Currently, in order to protect sources and methods at the national level, allies are read into information at different designations for classification. It is as if each partner had a separate key, and each key opened only certain compartments in the US information vault. Britain, France, Germany, Italy, and Spain, in the 2003 case of Iraq, each had a different picture of US intelligence. Even though they were all working closely together as members of NATO and the European Union, they could not share what they gleaned from US products for fear of losing their bilateral privileges with respect to the American intelligence structure.[1]

An alternative information sharing institution would move away from the lock-and-key principle to a common information infrastructure where systems for the

1 Nomikos (2005); Linzer (2004).

collection, analysis and dissemination of data were operated jointly by NATO partners. Instead of sharing products which were masked or tailored to protect US national systems, close democratic and military allies would be sharing processes using intergovernmental technology and organization. Although representatives working in a parallel, common intelligence network might conceivably develop techniques that could expand the pool of information beyond what would be achievable through a simple aggregation of national products, the real gains to be anticipated from common infrastructure would come in the quality of cooperation for coalition crisis management.

In this bargaining situation, coalition demands constitute social choices. For several reasons, deliberative democracy is often preferred to aggregative, or pure majoritarian, democracy to reach collective decisions.[2] In the same vein, procedural details are found to affect inter-party trust in collaborative policy making as much as outcomes.[3] Common collection and analysis of information, as opposed to tailored exposure of finished intelligence products, directly addresses accessibility, equality, and procedural fairness for a social choice among sovereign partners. In the case where the policy at issue is a crisis bargaining strategy, greater coordination and commitment behind a truly joint policy, rather than an imposed preference from the superpower, can inspire more compliance from an adversary. The prospect of deeper concessions, in turn, reinforces coalition unity, for the gains accrue to both aggressive and more risk averse allies.

As plausible as the argument for deliberative crisis management sounds, particularly among the transatlantic allies, it is a difficult one to test. Despite the turbulence in the international system after the Cold War, intense international crises drawing in several NATO allies and threatening regime change against a defiant state adversary are still rare events.[4] In addition, if information sharing institutions are in fact a crucial variable driving crisis outcomes for the Atlantic Alliance, it is impossible to demonstrate this with historical evidence. There is no way to select cases for comparison that would provide variation in the independent variable.[5] For all crises involving the United States and its European allies, in which the United States had an overwhelming advantage integrating imaging, computing, and communication technologies, the superpower always chose to share through traditional lock-and-key arrangements. The information-sharing thesis proffered here makes claims for a system that does not yet exist.

Even without a laboratory or a reservoir of cases, though, we can still build confidence in the proposal by pursuing its subsidiary logic: what else has to be true for a common information infrastructure to work as advertised?[6] The remainder of

---

2 Elster (1998); Gutmann (2004).

3 Hibbing and Theiss-Morse (2001).

4 Rosenau (1990); Holsti (2006).

5 King, Keohane, and Verba (1994: 140).

6 King, Keohane, and Verba (1994: 217) discuss this testing approach for situations when the number of applicable case studies is seriously limited. Stephen Biddle (2004) delved into this testing strategy in order to disentangle the effects of skill versus technology on conventional military power.

this chapter justifies and explains how to test two propositions that, if they turn out to be true, support the case for a transatlantic crisis information system.

Proposition 1: Advances in technology for collection, analysis, or dissemination of information do not significantly alter the bargaining problem or the quality of crisis outcomes for a state attempting to find its optimal crisis strategy.

Proposition 2: Higher quality deliberation among coalition partners could improve crisis outcomes without an increase in technical information about crisis adversaries.

The first of these propositions, if true, would make it easier for the United States to share advanced technology in the context of crisis management at the same time that allies would find it easier to accept NATO technology perhaps less capable than that of US military systems. In short, common infrastructure would not require that the leading state, or trusted guardian, declassify its state-of-the-art sources and methods. Less advanced technology, available for joint development and deployment, would also attract allied crisis managers. Given Proposition 1, the second proposition identifies the driving mechanism for better outcomes: for the new, less sophisticated, crisis information system to be viable, there must be reason to expect that the process of deliberation toward a single social choice among asymmetric allies matters more than any technical losses due to joint construction.

The Logic of Common Information for Crisis Management

In order to get a better sense of the plausibility of our propositions, it makes sense to extend James Fearon's 1995 crisis bargaining model, referenced in Chapter 2, to a situation of three players negotiating under conditions of asymmetric information. As was the case in Fearon's "Rationalist Explanations for War," the simple bargaining model serves as a kind of check on prosaic arguments about what causes crises to break down into war.

As discussed in Chapter 2, the basic crisis model has rivals bargaining over a finite, continuous domain, depicted almost as a football field with real values ranging from 0 to 1. In this zero-sum formulation, State A, moving from left to right, desires to acquire the entire field, and the same holds for State B, moving from right to left. Should the two parties resort to war, each one can expect to gain the entire stake with probability based on relative power. For example, if State A were more powerful than State B and judged twice as likely to win a war between them, its expectation of victory should factor into the sort of settlement that would be satisfactory in lieu of war: (probability of victory) x (value of stakes) = (2/3) x (1). In this example, the more powerful state should expect something on the order of two thirds of the stake in a negotiated settlement.

Fearon goes on to say, though, that State A might gain even more out of the crisis because State B will suffer losses in a fight to avoid unconditional surrender. Those losses in men and materiel can be expressed in the currency of the territory at stake. If the territory is sacred, many losses indeed would have to be suffered before they registered as a significant distance along that scale. Even so, Fearon pointed out that these losses created a window of opportunity for a state willing to risk war. Using our running example, powerful State A could demand concessions beyond the 2/3 line, a territorial distance in exchange for the benefit to State B of avoiding the destructive fallout of war.

The problem is that State B's willingness to pay is inherently subjective and therefore difficult for State A to know with high precision. State A might have an idea of how far would be safe to push State B back behind what its war power merits. In the mathematical model, State A's beliefs appear as a probability distribution over the contested domain. As State A's "final demand" increases, the cumulative probability under that distribution represents an increasing chance that State B's true reservation price has already been crossed and war is imminent. Fearon showed that for a wide variety of distributions, State A's optimal demand entailed a non-zero risk of war.

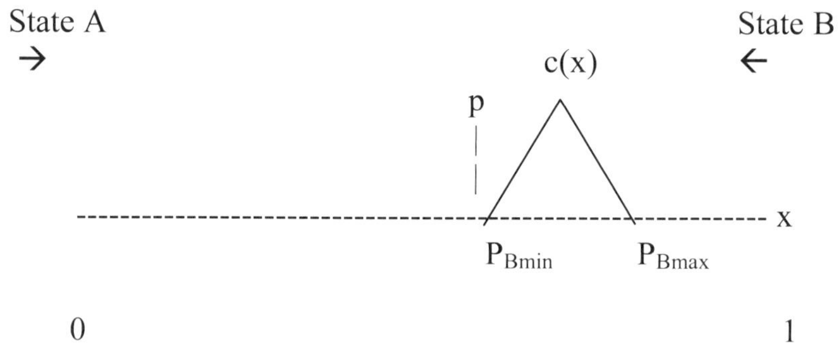

Figure 3.1 Crisis bargaining situation with State A's beliefs about State B's reservation price depicted as a triangular distribution

Note: p represents expected gains from waging war (not counting destruction costs) and also the probability of winning war. Here, State A is slightly more powerful that State B. Because war involves losses—win or lose—State B's reservation price for avoiding war lies somewhere behind p, between P_{Bmin} and P_{Bmax}.

In the simplified account of crisis bargaining illustrated by Figure 3.1, State A's uncertainty about the location of State B's reservation price can be due to other concerns besides State A's lack of information about State B's resolve. Fearon used the example of the Russo-Japanese War of 1904–1905 to show how disagreements about relative power could also lead to war. Russia's unwillingness to accept Japan's ultimatum of December 1903 appears related to Russia's only vague knowledge of rising Japan's military modernization and Russia's underestimation of Japan's sea and land forces. Before the war, even if Japan had patiently explained the details of why Russia's leaders were overrating their own defenses against a Japanese attack, the Russians had every reason to suspect that Japan was bluffing, and of course, if

Japan revealed too much about its plans, it could forfeit war power by instructing Russia on how to prepare forces in East Asia. In terms of the crisis bargaining model, private information about relative power along with incentives to keep that information secret implies that the challenging state, or the state seeking concessions, cannot precisely anticipate its probability of winning a war with State B. This, in turn, contributes to uncertainty about State B's true reservation price.

Between uncertainty over resolve and uncertainty over power, Fearon argued that he could think of no known case where participants updated beliefs about each other's capabilities during crises, but there were plenty of examples when governments revised estimates of an opponent's resolve. One case supporting Fearon is the NATO air campaign against Serbia in Kosovo. Lessons Learned monographs after the 78-day operation recorded how the Phase I target list of the Allies did not cover more than three days of bombing since Serbian leader Slobodan Milosevic was expected to fold early.[7]

On the basis of a judgment over historical cases, then, Fearon focused on modeling the uncertainty over resolve. Given agreement on relative power between crisis participants, logically, there always existed a settlement that both sides preferred to war. This buttressed Fearon's main point that rationalist explanations had to explain why strategic actors would ever accept inefficient resolutions to conflicts of interest. Nevertheless, examples such as the Russo-Japanese War or for that matter the 1991 Gulf War challenge Fearon's (1995) exclusive focus on resolve. Even if updates on relative power did not occur during crises that preceded these conflicts, revised estimates of power seem to have occurred during and after the battles, including by states observing the conflict from the outside. This would indicate that private information about war capabilities and differing estimates of relative power are not uncommon after all.[8]

For the purposes of modeling crisis bargaining and specifically for thinking about how allied cooperation could affect coalition demands, it may be sufficient to argue that many factors create uncertainty about an adversary's reservation price. Some factors may be related to circumstantial information about capabilities while others speak to level of resolve. Together, all of these factors generate something like a continuous, single-peaked distribution for where an adversary's final concession might lie. In order to gain intuition and allow for back of the envelope calculations, we might illustrate the uncertainty using the triangular distribution of Figure 3.1.[9]

7 Lambeth (2001: 20–6).

8 Models emphasizing uncertainty over power include Reed (2003), Slantchev (2003), and Powell (2004). These arguments assume that variance over adversary resolve can be eliminated using some efficient signaling mechanism, leaving uncertainty about power to generate conflict. Anecdotally, at least, Fearon's point still stands: these hoped for resolve mechanisms do not seem to operate consistently across historical cases.

9 I am inclined to agree with Fearon that most of the uncertainty about an adversary's reservation price is more often due to lack of information about resolve rather than power. Private information about secret weapons or novel tactics may be quite significant for winning individual battles, but learning on both sides occurs during the course of a war fought until unconditional surrender. Unclassified estimates of national capability give reliable indications of which side will win such a war (Bueno de Mesquita 2000: 217–24, 234, 413). The cases

Successful crisis bargaining from this simplified perspective becomes a question of formulating an optimal demand given one's own costs for war and uncertainty about the other side's reservation price. Coalitions of states complicate this task in at least two ways. Partner states may have very different notions about the costs of general war—denominated in currency of territory or issues at stake—compared to the lead state involved in the bargaining. Secondly, transformation optimists might argue that the variance of estimates over the adversary's reservation price depends on the quality of crisis information system serving a given government. If so, then the lead state with more and higher resolution imaging platforms and more intrepid collection antennas would also have a more precise belief about an opponent's costs for going to war.[10]

Advances in Information Technology

The second complication goes away, or is at least mitigated, if there is some logic to justify Proposition 1: information technology advances do *not* alter the bargaining problem or greatly improve crisis outcomes. It has already been discussed how, in the Fearon crisis model, much of the bargaining strategy depends upon knowledge of the other side's intentions and that those intentions run quite independently of known capability, historical behavior patterns, or actual deployments. In the language of the model, one crucial factor in the adversary's reservation price is that party's subjective evaluation of its costs from fighting and general war. The kind of information gleaned from satellites and listening devices does not reveal much about how important one thousand or one hundred thousand citizens are compared to the issues at stake; the data from these technologies reveals a limited amount about the psychology of the moment.

One way to quantify this disconnect focuses on the frequency with which state-of-the-art technologies collect information.[11] Admittedly, frequencies are not the sole constraining factor on obtaining strategic assessments. In the aftermath of the Iraq Crisis, Lieutenant General Michael Hayden, then-director of the US National

---

when a less powerful state such as North Vietnam triumphs over a great power may be explained in terms of bargaining while fighting. The more powerful state balks at the cost of engaging a larger share of its forces—the strong state is not resolved to sacrifice the men and materiel it would take to overpower a highly resolved opponent.

10 The bargaining model captures differences in subjective utility among coalition and opposing states through differences in subjective war costs. For states in coalition, u(x) = x, and for the adversary u(x) = 1-x in this constant sum game. Each player, however, pays its own penalty for crisis breakdown and war. If all parties were expecting to lose 100,000 men in a general war, for example, reservation prices behind Fearon's settlement line from the probability of victory could still be very different if the territory meant something different for each player.

11 Other possible technical limitations might come from data storage or computer processing, but the empirical context here is strategic information collection, where most of the storage and processing can take place at fixed domestic locations. In this application of information technology, the most challenging step is more likely to be illuminating or tracking targets on the other side of the world.

Security Agency, remarked that often excellent human intelligence was required in order to tell the image and signals analysts where to look.[12] This implies that at least on some occasions, plenty of data may be collected at sufficiently high frequency, but it is still difficult to write analysis software for finding the proverbial needle in a haystack unless a reliable human agent has supplied hints to narrow down the search. Even so, operating frequencies may be taken as a kind of technological index when specifying a relationship between technical advances and precision estimates for a crisis adversary's reservation price.

Frequencies for information collection are conveniently described as variables on a Cartesian plane. On the x-axis, we might record time frequency, say, bytes per second from a target location or a suspicious communications link available for analysis. This could be configured to provide a rough measure of how close a crisis information system was operating to data collection in real time.

For example, in Alexander George's (1991: 229–30) account of the Cuban Missile Crisis, Nikita Khrushchev was nearly able to corner President Kennedy into a *fait accomplis*. With the weather, the limited access to Cuban airspace and the delays inherent in transporting and developing photographic film, days passed between observable construction at the Cuban sites and the receipt of actionable intelligence in the president's hands.[13] By contrast, during the attempted decapitation strike to open the 2003 Iraq War, US intelligence, the US Air Force, and the president converted (flawed as it turned out) information passed by a human agent into approved targets at Dora Farms within a matter of hours.[14] The obvious increase in information speed and precision does not imply that the president or his advisers always know where to look, but when they do decide to look somewhere, they can receive actionable intercepts or images much faster than forty years ago, primarily due to advances in information technology.

In addition to advantages in time frequency, the United States has also developed electromagnetic devices to reduce the spatial interval of collected information. Spatial frequency, with a few caveats, may be thought of as a measure of resolution. The details of an image become clearer as the pixel size, the size of the color dots making up the image, becomes smaller. To put it in familiar terms, the video games of the 1980s featured low resolution, large-pixel graphics relative to the virtual reality games of 2006 that offer television quality pictures of knights battling dragons. In part, what makes the images of modern graphics so lifelike is the high spatial frequency, which permits display of gory detail for the object of interest, and the high time frequency of updates to eliminate unnatural pauses in the object's motion.

In order to better understand the measures of time frequency and spatial frequency for quality information, and, indirectly, for quality of information technology, it is worth describing some important limitations of these parameters. First, while spatial frequency has an intuitive interpretation for images on television screens, this is

12 Bamford (2004: 354–7).

13 Rogers (1991: 434–5); Allison and Zelikow (1999: 222–4).

14 Gordon and Trainor (2006). Even faster reaction times, using space-based navigation assets, were indicated in the destruction of al Qaeda in Iraq leader Abu Musab al-Zarqawi (Roeder 2006).

less true for antennas sweeping the airwaves in search of hostile communication signals. Even so, the measurement concept might be sustained if spatial frequency were broadened into a kind of index that took into account both the pixel size of images and the capacity of listening posts to distinguish signal from noise within the geographic footprint of antenna patterns.

This bit of hand-waving brings up other problems, however. Distinguishing different frequencies or different frequency combinations over a given swath of territory is not physically the same as distinguishing one square meter of an imaged surface from another. Both have to do with resolution within a geographic frame, but extracting signal transmissions from background noise has a closer analog in the imaging world. Given a constant pixel size of one square meter, for example, it matters whether the element can take on only two values—black or white—a continuous range of values representing different intensities of reflection and appearing as a gray scale, or ranges across multiple frequency spectra providing infrared, color, and ultraviolet hues. When collecting data for detecting prohibited materials or facilities, fidelity rather than resolution may be the real limiting factor.

In any case General Hayden's remarks imply that even if high fidelity is achievable, it does the analysts little good unless they know where to look, and knowing where requires effective synthesis of human with technical intelligence. James Bamford in the *Atlantic* recently discussed an example of high-level cooperation between Hayden's National Security Agency and telecommunications industry executives that invloves tapping, copying, or otherwise collecting massive rivers of message traffic as they cross switching centers—just a few key gateways that connect international cable and satellite networks to the United States.[15] Once intelligence officials know where to place or where to point their sensors, they still need software to cull data and match torrents of collected information against a file of known signatures in order to confirm what they have been observing. In effect, the appropriateness of analysis tools rather than the fidelity of collection devices may be the most relevant constraint.

We might go on deconstructing the spatial frequency index for information quality in this manner. In fact, there is no single technical parameter that neatly encompasses all the features of technical intelligence. Yet, difficulty with the concept of measurement relates to the reasoning behind Proposition 1, which began this section. Advancing information technology does not have significant effect in easing crisis dilemmas. It does not much matter where the measurement lines are drawn. Let us focus on the temporal and spatial frequencies achievable by the leading US information systems, where spatial frequency takes into account the resolution of satellite imaging and the capability to extract meaningful transmissions from the noise in a given geographic area. Both temporal and spatial frequencies for US systems have increased dramatically over the last six decades, but because so many other things are involved, the US ability to narrow down estimates of a crisis adversary's reservation price has not improved accordingly.

---

15 Bamford (2006: 65–70). For our purposes, the greater the percentage of a country's messages transiting these networks, the higher the probability that US technical intelligence can discern signal from noise for transmissions out of that area.

Proposition 1 may now be stated in a way that is more clearly empirical. Let the quality of information technology for a crisis actor be measured as the product (f x s) of temporal and spatial frequencies generally achieved by its suite of technologies. Proposition 1 states that as (f x s) increases, σ, the standard deviation from the probability distribution of an adversary's reservation price, remains about the same. Practically speaking, it would still be difficult to specify valid measurement procedures for the above quantities and apply them to historical crises. In principle, though, a measurement scheme might work like the consumer price index for inflation, tracking the time and spatial frequencies from a sample basket of a country's technologies over time. Some sort of average across collection systems would be taken at a given crisis year before calculating the product (f x s) for an overall measure of information system quality.

The standard deviation—the breadth of uncertainty about a crisis adversary's reservation price, is even tougher to operationalize. In the original application, Fearon had little specific to say about how crisis leaders generated probability distributions over an adversary's maximum concession. It sufficed that if these distributions were well behaved, rational negotiators would accept limited risk of war in order to stretch their demand for a better settlement. Just how much a challenger would try to squeeze from an opponent depended on how costly material losses from war were expected to be but also on the shape of the distribution, that is, how precisely a challenger scoped out the other side's negotiating position. In the extreme, absolute knowledge with a standard deviation of zero would inspire a demand right up to the adversary's red line for war. Again, in principle, if researchers had access to crisis working groups, say at the level of President Kennedy's Executive Committee during the Cuban Missile Crisis, they might over several instances of crisis negotiation, begin to measure dispersion of beliefs by tracking the variety of proposals before a US demand was officially communicated to the outside world.

My preliminary attempts at developing a concept of measurement show why a quantitative test of Proposition 1 is impractical, but qualitatively speaking, historical cases might be selected to both gain confidence and make use of the claim. Taking the United States as a crisis actor over time, its imaging intelligence moved from U-2 photos to KEYHOLE satellites to digital analysis of multi-spectral emissions and motion tracking radar.[16] In the last decade or so, all this has been supplemented by unmanned aerial vehicles that allow focus on enemy developments at the tactical level. Qualitatively speaking, the product of time and spatial frequencies available for analysis has increased several times for the United States since 1950. Yet, while Americans may have more and better raw data on their crisis opponents, they do not have a precise idea of their opponents' final offer. In accounts of crisis deliberations their remains nerve-wracking uncertainty in terms of how far to push in a situation defined by both sides seeking advantage within some golden range of agreements preferable to war.

Consistent with Proposition 1, before the recent Iraq War, the United States could not be sure of the WMD capability of Iraqi formations or the nature of cooperation between Saddam Hussein's conventional defense forces and irregular terrorist

16 Burrows (1986); Fulghum (2003).

units.[17] As elements of the US Army pushed toward Baghdad, they could not, even then, be sure how hard Iraqi soldiers would fight, how much of the capital they would sacrifice, or how they might reorganize as insurgents, in order to raise costs for the Americans.[18]

The complexity of crisis optimization increases when the United States attempts to bargain as part of a coalition. Parties normally on the same side in a crisis may not push equally hard when the other side's reservation price cannot be nailed down. In addition to staking its international leadership on a deal that may surrender too much, or in the other extreme, trigger an unnecessary war, the United States must also worry about breaking bonds of support from coalition partners.

Comparing Cases

The notion of a disconnect between increasing precision of collection devices and broad uncertainty about crisis adversaries' bargaining positions seems plausible. To appreciate how ingrained this pattern is in the history of US foreign policy, it makes sense to perform a more detailed case comparison. Selected cases should feature the United States in mixed motive situations, where geopolitical interests were in play but pursuing them through war could easily entail more costs than some sort of compromise. Furthermore, the crisis communications should bring in long-time partners or interlocutors with the United States who during the crisis expressed concerns about the US approach. Under these circumstances, the United States had an incentive to persuade allies that its view of the adversary and its view of appropriate demands or concessions were precisely correct.

Considering the record of US crises compiled in the International Crisis Behavior data set and the Militarized Interstate Disputes data, the kinds of crisis where the "trusted guardian" hypothesis really applies involve the United States and its Western European allies after 1945 debating how best to handle threats to Europe. A steady stream of such threats animates the history of NATO between 1949 and 1999. In order to observe maximum variance on our independent variable—in this case technological sophistication of the US collection suite—the method would be to dip into this stream at its two extremes. It so happens that at the birth of NATO early in the Cold War and at the transformation of NATO after the Cold War, there were clusters of crises. In the first group of cases, the allies struggled over how to meet the Soviet threat to Berlin, with France and West Germany advocating a firmer approach against the communists and Great Britain tending to be more pragmatic. The second group, nearly fifty years later, saw several of the same Western allies arguing over how to meet the illiberal threat posed by Serbian policy to a peaceful and democratic European order after the fall of the Soviet Union. This time, France and Germany seemed more willing to constrain the use of force and expand bargaining flexibility while Great Britain desired maximum pressure against Serbian leader

17 US Senate Armed Services Committee (2003); Council on Foreign Relations (2003).

18 Uncertainty during the US military's approach to Baghdad is described in General Tommy Franks' (2004) memoir and in the intrepid jounralism of *Cobra II* (Gordon and Trainor 2006).

Slobodan Milosevic even if it meant sending NATO-member ground troops out of the traditional area for collective defense and into Kosovo.

Between the two clusters of crises, the decades saw the rise of the Space Age and the Information Age—vast improvements in remote sensing and data processing along the lines previously discussed. If in fact we observe continuing difficulties in perceiving the adversary's reservation price and persuading even close allies to reach consensus on Western demands, this is an intriguing result in favor of Proposition 1: information technology improves by leaps and bounds; yet, on the dependent variable, the efficiency with which the appropriate negotiating strategy is cobbled together and the crisis won, there is little apparent change. In short, the Berlin series and the Yugoslavia series of crises offer an opportunity to make just the sort of qualitative observations we would expect to see if Proposition 1 were true.

Of course, similar evidence could also obtain if the proposition were false and other variables were countering, say, the positive effect of new information technology on crisis management success. Two strong candidates for "omitted variable bias" in this sweeping comparison are the balance of power and the institutionalization of NATO.

With respect to the power balance, it changed dramatically between the early Cold War and post-Cold War eras. The Soviet Union wielded much more political influence and presented a much greater military threat than Milosevic's Serbia did decades later. Moreover, US partners in Western Europe were relatively weaker compared to other crisis actors in the 1950s than they were in the 1990s. Traditional balancing theory would suggest that smaller partners would be more inclined to cooperate with the US champion as they faced a more powerful adversary.[19] In other words, the shifting balance between the Berlin and Yugoslavia cases, away from NATO's nemesis and toward junior partners in the alliance itself worked against and perhaps overwhelmed the positive effect of advancing information assets in the United States. Under this logic, possessing more time-sensitive data at higher fidelity over greater swaths of the Earth's surface did make it easier to find the optimal demand for settling a crisis, but strong European partners had less incentive to fall in line with the United States against hapless Serbia than they did before the mighty Soviet Union.

If power shifts indeed wipe out real benefits of information age technology, this would also add risk to major investments in national systems dedicated to prevailing in crisis. The more successfully technical requirements were fulfilled, the fewer friends the United States could expect to have in the next round of conflicts. Intra-alliance balancing could be reason enough to reject pure technological solutions from American defense labs to the kinds of international crises prevalent after 9/11.

On the other hand, analysts should distinguish between balancing behavior under conditions of war versus pre-war bargaining. Once fighting has broken out and near-term survival is at stake, there is a necessary relation between intentions and capability. States concern themselves less with whether to use power and more with how to use their power efficiently. In wartime, the more formidable the enemy, the less maneuvering room junior partners have to push back against their champion's desires. During crisis, though, the adversary has not yet decided to

19 Mearsheimer (1991); Andrews (2005).

wager on national capabilities. A prudent concession or a show of firmness may yet avoid the final reckoning, which is costly for all. Thus, almost regardless of the power distribution among champion, allies, and adversary, reasonable policy makers can disagree about whether it is best to press forward or ease back demands. In fact, because the stakes were higher in the Cold War crises, when the Soviet Union presented an existential threat to Western European allies, arguably, it was *harder* for the allies to resist pressing parochial views about the best crisis strategy upon their American champion. As Milosevic was less of a threat to the post-Cold War balance, partners might actually have been more willing to overlook vague US arguments and accede to a consensus crisis strategy for the sake of the alliance. By this argument, it should have been easier under the less dire circumstances of the Yugoslavia crises for advanced technology information aids to bring about a strategy that inspired coalition unity and forced Milosevic directly back to his reservation price, his minimum demand for peace.

A similar sort of alternative logic attends the second major objection to the Berlin-Yugoslavia comparison. In the intervening decades between the case clusters, institutionalization and enlargement of the NATO alliance made it far easier for junior partners to resist US preferences, even if the United States had during the Yugoslavia years far more impressive information charts to support its policy choice. As in the first objection on balancing, it would be useful to know that technology-based improvements in crisis negotiation could be overcome by an independent influence, evolving rules and procedures in NATO that blunt the leading state's ability to corral junior partners. Still, what is more likely, institutionalization and enlargement of NATO over fifty years have been strategically guided by the United States. At least some procedures like standard requirements for interoperability actually facilitate US influence. This explains why Western European statesmen seeking greater autonomy from American preferences look to European Union projects such as the European Security and Defense Policy as future alternatives, not mere complements to NATO and US systems.[20] In the later series of crises, then, the United States could wield the threat of disrupting heavily institutionalized modes of cooperation in NATO to align allies behind its preferred position, making the task of persuasion through information analysis easier than it had been in the 1950s when collaboration was more *ad hoc*.

In sum, the balance of power and alliance institutionalization objections raise important caveats. However, one of the advantages of qualitative case comparison is that it allows for process tracing.[21] As we observe crisis management dilemmas in the bargaining over Berlin versus Yugoslavia, we can check to see whether new levels of strategic information in the 1990s were crucial for clarifying an optimal strategy, but power shifts among crisis actors or subterfuge using NATO requirements prevented that strategy from being smartly implemented by the Western powers. If, on the other hand, state-actors in the later crises, especially the United States, continue to be divided within their cabinets about the likely response of an adversary, if the loyal opposition—domestic or foreign—makes a case that US policy is self-defeating, these are signs that Proposition 1 may in fact be operating. With all the powerful

20 Howorth (2003); Posen (2006).

21 Van Evera (1997: 64–6).

information tools coming on-line in the 1990s, the United States and its coalition partners failed to assemble a significantly sharper picture of a rival state's ultimate intentions. They were no more certain than they had been decades earlier about their crisis opponents' reservation price.

The Benefits of Sharing

If the new technologies cannot deliver the optimum bargaining offer to win international crises, it seems counterintuitive to think that sharing the technology—in the sense of building and operating it together—would make much difference in crisis performance. Yet, Proposition 2 implies that if the United States sponsored a somewhat less capable crisis information system for use by its allies, even if the resulting data did not quite achieve the time frequency, spatial resolution, or fidelity of US national systems, crisis outcomes for both the Europeans and the United States would improve. The key to better crisis management is not more collection or more analysis to target the adversary's bottom line but transfer of information in a credible way that brings allies together. A common position reached through deliberation among Americans and Europeans can induce adversaries to take a step back.[22]

In order to see the benefits of sharing technology as opposed to mere data, we can return to Fearon's (1995) bargaining model. From his proof, the optimal demand, x, for a crisis actor, with all crisis stakes simplified down to a single dimension, maximizes the following expression for expected utility, $(1 - C(x))x + C(x)P_{US}$. The value x is what the demander receives if there is no war, and the value P_{US} is the expected value—the probability of winning the whole stake—when war ensues. The war outcome depends on whether the demand x is far enough to cross the adversary's reservation price. The demander's belief about that price distributed over x has probability density function c(x) and cumulative function C(x). Again, as Fearon showed, for the large class of probability distributions where the hazard rate, c(x)/(1-C(x)), is increasing in x, the demander's expected utility is maximized when it demands $x^* = (1-C(x^*))/c(x^*) + P_{US}$.

In the right-hand expression, the reciprocal of the hazard rate is only defined when the density $c(x) > 0$, which occurs when $P_{\underline{I}} < x < P_{\bar{I}}$. In other words, adversary reservation price P_I is believed to fall somewhere within two extremes ($P_{\underline{I}}$ and $P_{\bar{I}}$) on the x-dimension. As Fearon pointed out, if relative power between the competing states is known with high degree of certainty, there is a settlement that both "expected value maximizers" would prefer to war: they simply divide the pie according to their power ratio rather than fighting it out for the same expected result less the destructive consequences of war. Even if there is uncertainty about hidden sources of national capability, as long as the anticipated destruction of war is sufficiently costly, there will be a zone of agreement available between P_{US} and $P_{\underline{I}}$ as depicted in Figure 3.2.

22 Rival states with something to lose should find it harder to maintain resolve when they fail to split Europe from America. Terrorist networks might not be as cowed by transatlantic unity. Then again, they are not generally engaging NATO countries in crisis negotiations. The idea would be to make improved crisis management work against terror indirectly by making it harder for rival states to cooperate with extremist networks.

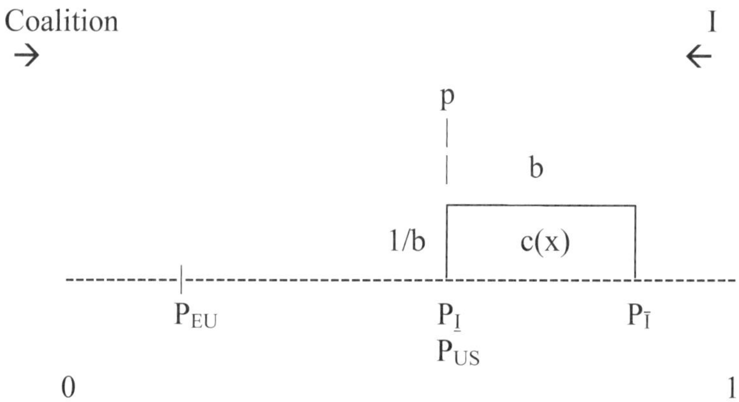

Figure 3.2 Crisis bargaining situation with EU and US in coalition against I

Notes: US is shown as very resolved; the payoff for war is simply the expected value from winning the stakes of the crisis with no negative utility for war losses.

EU is less resolved; even though it is about as powerful against I as US, it feels the pain of war more, so its reservation price is far behind line p.

Uncertainty about I's reservation price is represented as a uniform distribution, c(x), over the range b, with height 1/b.

Fearon's formula for the optimal demand x* demonstrated that the rational demander ("US" in Figure 3.2) risks war, that is, crosses beyond $P_{\underline{I}}$ in order to try and obtain an even better settlement. For our purposes, it is interesting to remark that a less resolved partner, say EU, who could count on the power of US in a fight with I, will appear on the same Figure 2 with a reservation price $P_{EU} < P_{US}$.[23] EU's preferred demand will be $x^{**} = (1-C(x^{**}))/c(x^{**}) + P_{EU}$, which is less than x*.[24]

Exactly how much less depends on the dispersion of beliefs about P_I. If, for example, beliefs were focused on an impulse function right at P_I, a dispersion of zero, players EU and US would make the same winning demand, $x^* = P_I$: the reservation price of I, the best settlement for US and EU, and no risk of war.[25] On

23 In Figure 3.2, the capability ratio between EU and I is depicted as about the same between US and I, assuming the US would also participate if EU acted, but the destructive costs of war are felt much harder by EU than by US.

24 The expression $(1-C(x))/c(x)$ is defined on x when $c(x)>0$, that is, between $P_{\underline{I}}$ and $P_{\bar{I}}$. In the region where it is defined, $(1-C(x))/c(x)$ is decreasing in x for continuous, single-peaked distributions, until its value crosses below x at the level of equilibrium demand x*. For EU, the expression does not need to fall as far as it does for US before the equation for optimal demand is satisfied. If P_{EU} is quite small relative to $P_{\underline{I}}$ (if the destructive costs of war are too great) it is possible that $(1-C(x))/c(x)$ is never large enough to justify risking war, in which case EU's optimal demand would remain at $P_{\underline{I}}$.

25 Reed (2003: 637).

the other hand, if beliefs are highly dispersed as shown in Figure 3.2, there can be a difference. This is easier to see if we translate the x-axis so that $x' = x - P_I$, where x' is only defined for $x > P_I$.

For a uniform distribution with base b, we have to solve

$$x = (1-C(x'))/c(x') + P_{US}.$$

$$x' + P_I = (1 - x'/b)/(1/b) + P_{US}.$$

$$x' = b - x' + [P_{US} - P_I].$$

$$x' = \{b + [P_{US} - P_I]\} / 2.$$

By a similar calculation, the demand for EU will be

$$x' = \{b + [P_{EU} - P_I]\} / 2.$$

Now, for a highly resolved US, $[P_{US} - P_I] \approx 0$, and $x' = b/2$. Translating back to the x-domain,

$$x^* = P_I + b/2.$$

For a very unresolved EU, $[P_I - P_{EU}] > b$; there is no defined x' that satisfies the equation; and EU must retreat to

$$x^{**} = P_I.$$

Unlike US, EU makes a minimal demand under uncertainty about the adversary's reservation price that does not risk war. Given the highest variance of beliefs across base, b, then, EU and US crisis demands may differ by as much as b/2.

Lock and Key Transfer

From the above calculations, there are some types of beliefs about a crisis adversary's reservation price—imprecise to be sure—that result in quite different negotiation strategies for a highly resolved United States versus more reluctant European allies. In the simplified model, these differences are driven by divergent views on whether the costs of war are worth the stakes at issue. It is another way of saying that potential partners labor without a common threat assessment and thus disagree about the utility of the use of force—precisely the problem cited for the breakdown of transatlantic cooperation, with devastating consequences before the Iraq War of 2003.[26]

On several occasions during the winter of 2003, the United States attempted to transfer information collected primarily on its exclusive, national systems in order to sway potential partners toward its view of the Iraqi threat. In the language of the model, US allies had to weigh the utility of accepting the information transfer at face value. Keeping Proposition 1 in mind, the allies would evaluate the American circumstantial

26 Feith (2004); Gordon and Shapiro (2004).

evidence in the context of their own beliefs, which despite their lower technology level generally looked much like the American estimates of adversary capability and resolve.

In our running example, if the allies (EU) accept the leader's information claims and back a demand of $x = P_I + b/2$, they can expect, based on their prior beliefs, a 50 percent probability of war: $C(P_I + b/2) = ½$ for the uniform distribution beginning at P_I. EU's utility for accepting is then ½ $[P_I + b/2]$ + ½ $P_{EUfight}$, where $[P_I + b/2]$ is the peace payoff, and $P_{EUfight}$ is a war payoff reflecting EU's decision to fight and bleed alongside US.

Yet, if EU does fight under the "accept" scenario, it does not do so enthusiastically. The very fact of the fighting after lock-and-key transfers indicates that US misled, that its superior information technology did not translate into precise knowledge of the adversary's reservation price or better crisis outcomes. EU would have been better off letting US make the demand $x = P_I + b/2$ on its own. During the events of 2003, the United States tried to exclude some European allies from the spoils of victory, but to the extent that US cannot exclude EU from the benefits of winning a crisis, EU might as well free ride on US resolve: ½ $[P_I + b/2]$ + ½ $[P_{EUside}]$ would be the expected payoff for rejecting the US argument. As long as sitting out the war, that is, $[P_{EUside}]$, brings more benefits than fighting alongside US, that is, $[P_{EUfight}]$, EU has an incentive to remain unmoved by lock-and-key information transfers during crisis.

Common Information Infrastructure

How might sharing equipment and processing information together work out differently? Proposition 1 implies that even if coalition information systems are not quite up to the technical standard of US systems, beliefs about the adversary's reservation price—based on the adversary's relative capability and resolve—will remain about the same. What might change, however, is EU and US resolve. In the process of collecting, analyzing, and deliberating together, it would be harder for a lead nation such as US to claim that assets outside the common suite had led it alone to precise knowledge of the adversary's minimal demand. Instead, the common endeavor would lead to a collective, probabilistic assessment of the threat that did not deviate far from classified national estimates. Independently verifiable, quality work at the coalition level could lay the foundation for mutual trust and further cooperation. For formerly reluctant partners, the prospect of future benefits alongside US would tend to increase resolve.

In the model, increased resolve brings increased utility for EU because EU does not have control over US's demand on I and therefore cannot avoid the risk of war. EU's utility under the old lock-and-key approach is ½ $[P_I + b/2]$ + ½ $[P_{EUside}]$. Under conditions where EU is very unresolved, $P_{EUside} < P_I - b$, so the maximum utility under lock-and-key is $P_I - b/4$. Without US in the picture, EU would demand $x = P_I$, the best settlement possible while clearly not crossing I's reservation price. US aggressiveness places a burden on EU, and for the uniform distribution discussed here, the greater the dispersion of beliefs—in laymen's terms the greater the uncertainty about the adversary's bargaining position—the greater the burden for EU.

By contrast, under the use of common information infrastructure, one of the expected fruits of deliberation would be to raise the resolve of EU closer to the level for US; in other words, $P_{EUnew} > P_{EUside}$. In addition, deliberation would be expected to redefine differences among allies assembled in a congress so that parochial perspectives were resolved into an alliance view; in essence, $P_{EUnew} \approx P_{USnew}$. Under conditions where the threat assessment process was shared and EU managed to water down US's demand until $P_{EU} \approx P_{EUnew} \approx P_{USnew}$, EU would at least enjoy an expected utility of P_I. Once EU and US views of the situation were moving together, the Fearon concept of crisis bargaining would follow Thomas Schelling's earlier notion of crisis as a competition in risk taking: a side would expect to do better as it was more willing to countenance the costs of war. If, through collection and interpretation using common information infrastructure, P_{EUnew} and P_{USnew} ended up looking very much like $P_{US} \approx P_I$, EU's expected utility would approach the US utility for a demand at $x = P_I + b/2$: $P_I + b/4$.

Of course, it might not be politically safe for EU leaders to advocate that their populations stoically accept losses of men and materiel alongside US when negotiations fail and war ensues. From a state-on-state perspective, though, it is I's ability to frighten EU, or EU's unhappiness at the disruptions of war—however reasonable those sentiments might be—that reduces expected crisis performance. If there were a crisis over Iranian nuclear weapons procurement, for example, and both sides were unwilling to wage all-out war, mutually destructive economic sanctions might well stand in as the final arbiter for the crisis. The more European states faced the hardships of imposing an embargo or boycott, the worse they would be expected to do in stopping Iran's progress toward nuclear power status. In part, this is because those allies cannot just defuse the situation by serving up Iran's minimum demands. A more resolved United States stands in the way of such accommodation. Even though the allies would like to escape, they may yet face collateral damage from higher US demands and resulting economic war against Iran. The same sentiment that saps Europe's resolve also makes destructive side effects of aggressive US leadership more painful.

It is that pain that common information infrastructure could help relieve. Rising European resolve is difficult to measure scientifically, but it would likely manifest itself in whether and how leaders girded their populations to assist the United States at the most difficult times. The basis of the alliance relationship, the manner in which advanced technologies are shared and operated together, may affect partners' willingness to trust the United States and support US positions in a crisis despite short-run costs. In fact, this dynamic has likely affected British policy after reinstatement of a US nuclear technology sharing agreement in 1958, Australian policy after a similar rapprochement involving intelligence sharing in the Reagan years, and—most important in the current NATO context—participation of countries such as Spain and Italy in the Iraq conflict.[27]

27 Hubbard (2005: 16–7, 45–7, 115, 124). Unfortunately for the United States, the dynamic can work the other way as well. Breakdowns in intelligence cooperation at the tactical level, particularly in Italy's case, made allied participation in the US-led coalition more difficult to sustain politically (Ludden and Poggioli 2005).

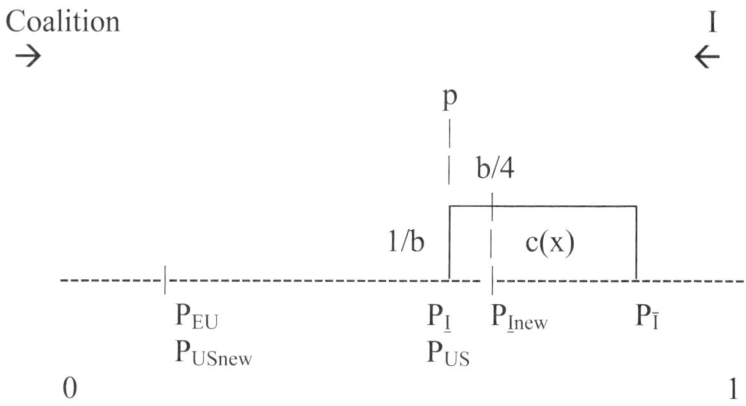

Figure 3.3 $P_{\underline{I}} - P_{USnew} > b$; US still fares better with common information infrastructure

Note: With Common Information Infrastructure and genuine deliberation involving EU, US has lost resolve, taking a new position on the costs of war close to the original of EU. US loses appetite for risking war, but may still perform better in the crisis if new coalition unity makes adversary I less resolved. I need only step back a small amount (b/4) to compensate for larger loss (>b) in US resolve to move unilaterally.

On the other hand, if common infrastructure encourages real deliberation among a congress of allies, positions may end up coalescing somewhere below $x = P_{US}$ in the model, that is, below what US would have demanded as a unilateral actor (see Figure 3.3).

From deeper discussion and mutual learning, the United States at war could come to feel Europe's pain. Under logic parallel to that just laid out for Europe, decreasing US resolve would actually reduce the utility of expected outcomes from crisis bargaining. If US in the model is going to benefit from common information infrastructure, the utility gains will have to come from somewhere else.

As previously discussed, highly resolved US can expect to receive $P_{\underline{I}} + b/4$ from its optimal strategy of demanding $x = P_{\underline{I}} + b/2$. If after deliberation and arrival at a common threat assessment with EU, US's reservation price drops by an amount $\varepsilon < b$, then US's new optimal demand will scale back from $P_{\underline{I}} + b/2$. In fact, from the solution for x′ on page 18, the new demand is $P_{\underline{I}} + (b\text{-}\varepsilon)/2$, where $0<\varepsilon<b$, and the new expected utility is $(1 + \varepsilon/b)/2\ \{P_{\underline{I}} + (b\text{-}\varepsilon)/2\} + (1 - \varepsilon/b)/2\ \{P_{\underline{I}} - \varepsilon\}$. As ε approaches zero, this expression reduces to the familiar $P_{\underline{I}} + b/4$. As ε approaches b, the value of US's utility expression drops toward $P_{\underline{I}}$, which is associated with a coalition concession that does not cross I's minimum possible reservation price. If US, as a result of deliberation with EU, loses its resolve, there is zero probability of war with I, but US's expected utility for the crisis outcome drops; essentially, US ends up approaching crisis adversaries from a weakened bargaining position.

Though our model is very simplified, it does capture a concern Bob Woodward reported in his inside Washington exposé *Plan of Attack*. Hawks in the Bush administration resisted Secretary of State Powell's recommendations to try for a United Nations enforcement resolution against Iraqi WMD programs, and they balked again when America's most important coalition partner, British Prime Minister Tony Blair insisted on returning to the Security Council for a second, more explicit resolution on the use of force against Iraq.[28] Each opportunity for additional deliberation, the hawks feared, was an opportunity for US resolve to melt into European hand-wringing, making it harder to compel or enforce concessions against Saddam Hussein.

At the same time, Hussein appeared keen to keep the Permanent Five in the Security Council from gelling to form a unified crisis strategy. During the months of the crisis, he cooperated just enough at the key decision points to give both the French and the American side enough ammunition to continue on their separate paths. Conceding everything to the French, taking the United States out of the debate might have given the game away for the Iraqi dictator, either because his enemies close at hand would have concluded that he did not have any WMD and was attempting to maintain his rule from a weak position or that information gleaned from intrusive inspections would be exploited to weaken him further.[29] Partial cooperation left most everyone with serious doubts about the extent of Hussein's disarmament, and as important, if the United States responded with force, it would have to come alone—without UN or NATO sanction.

Hussein's apparent interest in breaking up the coalition against him in the actual Iraq crisis points to an intriguing possibility for lead state crisis negotiators in the model: yes, open deliberation toward a robust consensus could sap some of the lead state's resolve, but this potential loss in performance could be compensated by a favorable shift in P_I, the minimum in the range of uncertainty about I's reservation price. In the unlikely scenario where US's reservation price retreated to the point where $P_I - P_{USnew} > b$, P_I would have to shift by b/4 to P_{Inew}, in Figure 3.3, to make information technology sharing attractive for US. The parameter, b, in the model specifies the range of beliefs about I's reservation price. Roughly speaking, it is also a measure of I's resolve.

Given the context of actual state-based challenges against the United States in the post-Cold War era, it is quite plausible that adversaries would perceive material losses differently depending on whether they occur in heroic resistance against the imperialist United States or vainglorious refusal to accommodate the will of the international community. For many among both elites and masses of today's revisionist states, the former is self-affirming while the latter is self-deluding. Lives wasted could well cost more than lives sacrificed for an appropriate cause. Holding territory or influence against NATO or the United Nations may be less important than holding it against the United States, which is to say that common information processing and common position taking among allies could affect intangibles so that adversary resolve shrinks back toward its minimum value.

28 Woodward (2004).

29 Woods, Lacey, and Murray (2006).

Variables such as crisis resolve and crisis stakes are difficult to quantify and measure across historical cases. There is no guarantee that if US partners operated common satellite networks, a challenger's resolve would decline by the right percentage to compensate the risks of interdependent crisis management. Yet, the Fearon logic does provide theoretical grounds for optimism. Given conditions of highly uncertain beliefs about an adversary represented in our model by the uniform distribution, it does not take much second thought on the adversary's part, in terms of the range of potential settlements, for coalition unity to pay off. This is so even if deliberation with less resolved allies fuels anti-war sentiment in the leading state.

The causal mechanism driving Proposition 2, that shared information systems improve crisis performance over shared information, lies in plausible expectations for shifting the other side's resolve. Junior partners benefit from fearing war less, which predisposes them to change once they can trust a lead state. More productive for the lead state, before assembling a high-tech profile of adversary intentions or trumpeting national toughness, is darkening the adversary's vision of war by encouraging crisis allies to accept war's costs.

Testing the Counterfactual

Careful comparison of crises involving the Western allies over Berlin versus Yugoslavia can help to evaluate empirical support for Proposition 1 that fundamental political-psychological dilemmas of international crisis management recur with about the same intensity despite dramatic advances in the technical collection and analysis of intelligence. Unfortunately, for the purposes of testing theories of crisis information sharing, structured focused comparison is less applicable for Proposition 2.

Just two international crises have occurred with the US high-bandwidth network in place that involved intensive information sharing among coalition partners: Kosovo 1999 and Iraq 2003.[30] Considered together for case comparison, these crises do not offer variation on the independent variable—the dominant mode of sharing information stays constant at lock-and-key. In order to construct an additional case about the consequences of switching to common information infrastructure, we must resort to the counterfactual: what would have happened in terms of allied cooperation if crisis information had been processed jointly at all stages from collection through dissemination.[31]

30 For the breakdown of the Israeli-Palestinian negotiations at Wye River Plantation in 2000, the United States was mediator rather than a crisis actor. During the EP-3 spy plane crisis with China in 2001, few partners were intensely involved on the US side. More importantly, information sharing during these crises like in the cases of Kosovo and Iraq was primarily lock-and-key, not via common infrastructure. Potential crises brewing over nuclear proliferation in Iran and North Korea have already seen intelligence sharing among allies, but these conflicts have yet to run their course, and all signs point again to reliance on the lock-and-key mode (Linzer 2005a).

31 As James Fearon put it in his early article on counterfactuals, "when the degrees of freedom in the actual world are negative, a causal claim requires argument about counterfactual cases for its justification" (Fearon 1991: 180).

Of the two alternatives, the Iraq crisis is more interesting at this point because the United States as the lead country was less successful at keeping the coalition together. Admittedly, from the perspective of case study methodology, Iraq is "easier" than Kosovo for showing that common systems could have helped in a situation where close allies rejected each other's intelligence products and followed antithetical policies. Confirmation in Iraq does not guarantee that typical crises engaging transatlantic partners will provide similar golden opportunities for improvement.

On the other hand, some important aspects of the Iraq case that were not prevalent in the Kosovo crisis may reappear in future WMD conflicts. Iraq forced the NATO powers to weigh concerted action far outside of Europe, which meant even greater reliance on US lift and planning capabilities in the event of war and higher material and political costs for forces created to operate in Europe. The adversary's ability to hurt coalition partners—which would raise the magnitude of objective losses in a war yet conceivably reduce their subjective value relative to long-term benefits for prevailing in the crisis—depended on the status of underground weapons programs that were difficult to penetrate using either human or technical intelligence.

Iraq, like Kosovo, presented a salient challenge with implications for NATO allies about whether and how they would cooperate against subsequent threats to world order. Unlike Kosovo, however, the outcome in Iraq could easily alter the balance of power for its region in ways that helped some allies while hurting others. Consequently, in addition to differences in their domestic political environments, allied leaders viewed Iraq through competing geopolitical frames that aggravated initial differences in crisis resolve. Because allied resolve may also lag behind that of the United States in future conflicts and resolve drives the argument supporting common information infrastructure, circumstances of the Iraq case call for further study.

While in some sense, it is hard *not* to imagine a better transatlantic performance than the one that occurred, the Iraq case features three additional compensating advantages. First, the case has already been studied thoroughly. The lack of a historical record on common infrastructure should not automatically paralyze investment in better crisis technology, including better crisis organizations. Tracing the breakdown of cooperation on Iraq provides some clue as to how investment for future crises might be managed wisely. Second, the Iraq venture has consumed vast resources worth hundreds of billions of dollars for the United States alone. If closer allied cooperation at the crisis stage could have reduced suffering on the part of the coalition or innocent Iraqis, a small percentage reduction on a very large expenditure is still of significant policy value. Finally, other aspects of the Iraq case make it a suitable candidate for analysis according to the criteria for plausible counterfactuals established by specialists in the study of international relations.[32]

The dependent and independent variables in this design are clear. Allied cooperation in terms of military and financial assistance could have been greater than what it was, after the war as parts of Iraq decayed from disorder to insurgency, and before the war in response to US overtures at the United Nations and especially from

32 Fearon (1991); Tetlock and Belkin (1996); Lebow (2000).

Security Council members who were major partners in NATO.[33] On the other side of the equation, the independent variable is the method of information sharing among NATO allies. In the case of the Iraq crisis, the United States did transfer significant intelligence back and forth with France and Germany and even more with the likes of the United Kingdom, Australia, and Spain. Much if not all of this information was in the form of tips or pre-screened products passed across bureaucratic barriers of national intelligence organization. Conceivably, this method could change to resemble more of a combined military operation in which NATO allies were working together using the same systems for strategic intelligence collection, analysis, and dissemination.

This change in the independent variable—from lock-and-key sharing to common information infrastructure (CII)—is realistic. To be sure, the construction of a common system could require tens of billions of dollars and several years, but even this amount is below what the US Army alone contemplates for its Future Combat Systems architecture.[34] CII would involve more hardware and launch costs for operations in near Earth orbit, but crisis management platforms would not have to be designed like Future Combat Systems vehicles to survive under combat conditions or destroy hardened targets. The overall number of nodes and variety of environments for the CII network would likely be less than that for Future Combat Systems. Rather than technological or financial, the highest hurdles before a CII system would be political.

Even in the political realm, though, certain historical precedents indicate at least some interest in attaining the level of cooperation CII would require. NATO, after all, boasts a fifty-eight year record of strategic and operational cooperation on matters of collective defense. The transition to out-of-area crisis management has not been free of setbacks, but it does continue in the bureaucratic form of NATO Transformation Command, to which the United States and France have contributed enthusiastically. The transition also proceeds in the willingness to expand NATO's International Security Assistance Force to dangerous regions such as southern Afghanistan.[35] Moreover, preliminary examples of CII—NATO's Alliance Ground Surveillance (AGS) program and the European Union's Satellite Centre—demonstrate political will on the part of states in the Atlantic Alliance to jointly develop assets for tactical and strategic intelligence. The F-35 Joint Strike Fighter and US offers for international subcontracting on missile defense systems show genuine American respect for European technological prowess in fields relevant to information collection, analysis, and communications.[36]

In the NATO context, there are sufficient precedents to justify the plausibility of CII for crisis management, and there are reasons to think that the causal pathway

33 Gordon and Trainor (2006: 457–60). It is important to note that cooperation could vary in the other direction. Financial pledges for rebuilding Iraq at an international donor's conference in October 2003 actually exceeded what many officials expected (Lansford 2006: 164). The surprise Group of Eight letter from European states in support of US policy that mortified France at the end of January 2003 was apparently the brainchild of Spain's Jose Aznar, not someone within the Bush administration (Gordon and Shapiro 2004: 133).

34 Gilmore (2006).

35 BBC News (2006).

36 Wayne (2005).

from common processing to greater transatlantic cooperation is "cotenable" with the mass of historical information about this case. In his review of counterfactuals for studying world politics, Richard Ned Lebow specified eight criteria for judging the persuasiveness of an alternative history that highlights the importance of some proposed intervention that never actually took place. Most of these criteria relate to the notion of cotenability, broadly defined.[37]

Lebow's historical consistency and theoretical consistency, for example, apply when the proposed changes in information infrastructure encourage allied cooperation in ways that are consistent with known policy disagreements going into the crisis and with recognized patterns in state behavior: Are the purported benefits of CII, for example, consistent with France and other powers each following a national interest defined by geography, culture, and ideology of the governing party? Sustainable antecedents, plausible conjunctions, and tolerable second order counterfactuals refer in one way or another to whether the causal logic flowing from CII is cotenable with all other historical consequences likely to play out from the original change: the birth of a new strategic intelligence organization within NATO.

The Lebow criteria demand judgment calls. There is no way to observe alternative histories as in a laboratory with a few treatment variables tweaked from their original values. Yet, these judgments can be enhanced by a technique familiar to practitioners of quasi-experimental case comparisons. Process tracing is supposed to dig down into case details in a way that correlation testing cannot to verify underlying causal mechanisms.[38] In this case, we can use step-by-step knowledge of the deterioration in transatlantic cooperation to check whether details of the failure on Iraq are consistent with the existence of a causal process linking information sharing and policy cooperation. That same process should operate regardless of whether the independent variable is set at its historical or counterfactual value. To paraphrase King, Keohane, and Verba (1994), we can expand our useful observations by asking what other variables should be affected if our causal logic is indeed operating and our independent variable is set for failure, that is, at lock-and-key rather than CII.

Such ancillary questions are key to testing at least the feasibility of a new information system before political and financial commitments are made to build CII. When it comes to predicting effects of technology changes—and here we are envisioning relatively modest systems integration and organizational management rather than new devices based on different physical principles—reliance on the counterfactual is not as radical as it might first appear. Various political scientists with an eye toward crisis management have already employed the technique to ask what might have been if technology had been different: if U-2 aircraft had been less capable during the Cuban Missile Crisis; if military mobilization and transportation systems had been more flexible during the July Crisis before World War I; and if there had been no nuclear weapons for the intervals of crisis and détente that composed the Cold War.[39] One could hardly cite a trio of cases more central to theorizing about international relations. The counterfactual, here, appropriately extends this tradition

37 Lebow (2000).

38 Van Evera (1997: 64–6); Yin (2003: 40–2).

39 George (1991); Trachtenberg (1990/1991); Mueller (1989).

to the pivotal crisis period of the Second Iraq War, probing how the propensity for international conflict or cooperation would have changed had some information collection and analysis systems been shared among NATO partners rather than compartmentalized into national classified assets.

As in previous studies, our technology-based independent variable competes with other candidate explanations for the lack of allied cooperation on Iraq. These are covering law explanations as referenced by Philip Tetlock and Richard Ned Lebow.[40] For the Iraq case, two approaches stand out.[41] Perhaps the most prominent, stemming from international realism, is the notion that after the 1991 Gulf War, the Kosovo campaign, and Operation Enduring Freedom in Afghanistan, it became increasingly clear that power in the international system was concentrated in the United States, so even long-time allies began to consider balancing against their erstwhile security guarantor. This structural focus on the distribution of power has been the source of pessimism among some transatlantic experts who compare against intra-alliance disputes during the Cold War and conclude that because the rift over Iraq cuts more deeply to incompatible views about future world order, it will be harder to repair.[42]

From the liberal school of international relations comes the idea that several NATO allies could not stand with the United States on Iraq because public opinion in these democracies was so vehemently against the Bush administration's war policy, essentially backing French Foreign Minister Dominique de Villepin's view that Iraq should be afforded some sort of due process through deliberate UN inspections rather than a precipitous invasion. For many legal scholars and United Nations advocates, the transatlantic breakdown happened due to flawed American leadership. Relying so completely on hard power to eliminate the Iraqi threat, the United States abandoned principles of domestic and international legitimacy it had done so much to champion after the great wars of the 20th century.[43] From this perspective, the rift will not and should not heal until the United States once again recognizes the vital link between public opinion, international organization, and foreign policy in democracies. In so many words, mass opinion in the transatlantic community will exact a price unless America renews its commitment to the liberal principles underpinning international law.

Both the realist and liberal frameworks can help build compelling causal accounts of the Iraq crisis as they have in many previous international conflicts. In the spirit of "poking counterfactual holes in covering law explanations," a well-appointed what-if scenario can remind us of alternative outcomes that were plausible in the heat of decision making but were subsequently erased by disciplined realist or liberal analysis.[44] Once we resign ourselves to one of the covering law explanations,

40 Tetlock and Lebow (2001).

41 In testing explanations for divergence between the United States and traditional European allies on Iraq, Schuster and Maier (2006: 223) select three approaches corresponding to neorealism, utilitarian-liberalism, and liberal-constructivism. Following the tradition of E.H. Carr's (1964, c1946) classic *Twenty Year's Crisis*, I find it more convenient, here, to combine the last two covering law accounts under "liberal idealism."

42 Kagan (2003); Pond (2005).

43 Secretary General of the United Nations (2005).

44 Tetlock and Lebow (2001).

accepting Iraq 2003 as just another case of realism or liberalism at work, we discard more imaginative approaches to transatlantic reconciliation. Neither the realist nor liberal versions of the story allow much room for missed opportunities. For each theory, the important independent variable is frozen in place: neither the distribution of national capabilities nor neoconservative ideology can vary for this crisis. As soon as Iraq topped the United Nations agenda in September 2002, transatlantic breakdown was a foregone conclusion.

Asking a technology-based counterfactual brings more fluidity to the problem. It opens the possibility for transatlantic cooperation in high-stakes crises even without the rise of a common great power rival or a change of political party in Washington. Most importantly, the method spotlights moments during the crisis when things might have gone differently, when old NATO allies could have worked together despite differences in power and ideology to thwart a common danger. Before too long, transatlantic democracies may find themselves in a similarly difficult situation. Understanding counterfactual moments that are missing from the established covering law accounts of Iraq may lay the foundation for a better crisis outcome next time around.

Chapter 4

Changing Technology, Enduring Dilemmas: Comparing the Berlin and Yugoslavia Crises

The integration of information systems for strategic intelligence would not necessarily improve the amount or quality of technical data available to the leading power. The United States already possesses constellations of air-breathing and space-based sensors. The size of its investment in intelligence, surveillance, and reconnaissance technology far outstrips that of its European partners, and the United States military would object to integrating assets at a level of fidelity that enabled unique offensive capabilities. With regard to European partners, they might receive a higher volume of data under a NATO system, but in some cases, the take from the alliance's proprietary technology, built with common investment funds, might, again, be inferior in quality compared to advanced national systems such as France's Helios II project.[1]

Without technical gains, the most visible kind of benefit, alliance members would likely drag their heels when it came to paying the entry costs of closer cooperation: pooling national funds to build a system for NATO, setting aside the necessary political capital to grant NATO a voice in strategic intelligence estimates. Even so, a less visible but more profound benefit weighs toward completion of such a project. Common collection and analysis—even if it produced a less sophisticated product, would contribute to the deliberative quality of an allied crisis position that could be trusted by all sides, regardless of their power position in the partnership. Today, leading states as well as junior partners face a situation in which technical capacity at the margin can be traded cheaply for something more precious—process legitimacy that fortifies commitment to a common position.

Legitimacy is harder to measure than the technological parameters for information collection, but, more effectively than bandwidth or bytes per second, it binds sovereign parties to a social choice, it convinces them to stick with an alliance position that national leaders must still sell to their domestic audiences as a necessary compromise. That stickiness, that strength of multilateral commitment to NATO's position, matters more for successful crisis bargaining with so-called states of concern than, say, the marginal difference in imaging resolution between US classified satellites and proprietary satellites that could be built for the Atlantic Alliance.

1 Hitchens (2006).

The appeal of a shift toward Common Information Infrastructure rests on the proposition that higher quality technical intelligence does *not* dramatically alter the crisis problem for national decision makers. This proposition is somewhat controversial. A standard textbook on international relations, Donald Snow and Eugene Brown's (2000) *The Changing Contours of Power*, made the opposite claim. Major conflicts such as among the European powers in 1914 "were allowed to fester into full-blown crises because the parties had incomplete, differing views both of the situation and of the intentions of other parties."

> With modern global television, such situations are more difficult to imagine. Outlets such as CNN and ITN ensure that all parties have generally the same information about situations as they begin to unfold, providing a greater ability to solve problems before they escalate.[2]

The section on the "impacts of high technology" went on to discuss how strategic surprise and covert action along the lines of Pearl Harbor or the CIA coup in Guatemala in 1954 is largely prevented today by modern surveillance and television coverage.[3]

In light of the strategic attacks of September 11, 2001 and the evolution of a powerful Iraqi insurgency under the very nose of modern surveillance and the global media, such high tech optimism may appear quaint. Both before and after September 11th, though, scholars recognized the non-linear relationships between advancing technology and improved warning.[4] In almost all cases, the rub lies in an irreducible complexity at the interface between human beings and large organizational or technological systems. The bureaucracy may be reformed and the technology may become more capable, but certain cognitive and psychological limitations of individual users of these systems inevitably, it seems, compromise performance.[5]

The same sort of thing occurs when it comes time to judge the other side's resolve in a crisis and formulate a demand. Even with more voluminous and precise data on physical traces, the information on adversary intentions, *contra* Snow and Brown, is never complete. Even if the intelligence support across bureaucracies within and among alliance members is somewhat homogenized by the work of global media or supranational organizations like the United Nations, different decision makers routinely "connect the dots" in different ways, drawing divergent conclusions about the appropriate crisis response.

---

2 Snow and Brown (2000: 314). See, also, Cold War historian John Lewis Gaddis (1986: 123–5) on the "reconnaissance revolution" as one of several causes for the long peace between the superpowers, especially after the Cuban Missile Crisis.

3 Snow and Brown (2000: 314–5).

4 Betts (1978); Chan (1979); Handel (1984); Betts (2002). For more optimistic views, see Levite (1987) and Parker and Stern (2005).

5 Parker and Stern's (2005) analysis of the September 11 surprise is instructive here. Their three cuts at the problem of intelligence failure are Psychological, Bureaucratic-Organizational, and Agenda-Political. The last two can be related back to the first since they all address distortions of prioritization or perception among analysts and decision makers.

The idea that better technology does not track with more effective crisis strategy may be illustrated systematically by comparing low technology versus high technology crisis cases. The previous chapter discussed reasons for selecting the series of crisis decisions over Berlin for comparison with crises over the break-up of Yugoslavia some forty years later. The following sections establish rules of evidence for evaluating the cases then lay out the historical findings. In fact, the many innovations for collecting and analyzing strategic information between the Berlin and Yugoslavia episodes—though they greatly advanced combat options—did not markedly improve crisis performance.

Regardless of the available technology, there were heated debates about adversary intentions and appropriate responses to counter Khrushchev in the 1960s and Milosevic, still, in the 1990s. The implication is that crisis systems, if they can be separated from combat systems, are easier to share among allies: no state surrenders meaningful advantage with respect to partners in crisis strategizing by moving toward joint technology. At the same time, sharing of finished intelligence products from a more sophisticated technology suite is not very impressive when the advanced technology cannot coordinate and align competing estimates of adversary resolve.

Structuring the Case Comparison: Berlin versus Yugoslavia

Both series of crises have been thoroughly studied by historians and political scientists. In the more remote case of Berlin, they benefited from declassified archives out of foreign and defense ministries, including the meetings of key decision makers.[6] For Yugoslavia in the 1990s, memoirs and exclusive interviews fortified explanations for why protagonists escalated or conceded at particular moments.[7] Following George and Bennett (2005), the objective of historical comparison, here, is to demonstrate how well a political theory is likely to work in practice. The proposition relating rising technology level to flat crisis performance has already been put in abstract terms. In order to be useful for informing policy, variables in the theory must have a transparent connection to facts in the available record.

George and Bennett (2005: Ch 3) suggested structuring comparison around a series of questions that pull relevant material from the cases and clarify variation in key variables. Under the circumstances, our independent variable is straightforward: between the crises over Berlin, occurring from the late 1940s to the early 1960s, and crises over Yugoslavia during the late 1990s, US instruments for collecting, analyzing and communicating intelligence advanced. Undeniable, dramatic variation of the independent variable is a principal justification for selecting US cases that took place decades apart.

---

6 See, for example, Shlaim (1983) and Press (2005). Examples of recent archive collections include the National Security Archives at George Washington University, Washington, D.C. (www.gwu.edu/~nsarchiv/nsa/publications/berlin.crisis/) and May and Zelikow (1997).

7 For example, Stigler (2002/2003) based his evaluation of the NATO air campaign over Kosovo in part on interviews with former Yugoslavian officials.

On the other hand the dependent variable—crisis performance—poses more of a challenge. Questions for "interrogating" the histories of Berlin and Yugoslavia concentrate therefore on operationalization of this dependent variable. These questions are divided into two sets; the first focuses on capturing the uncertainty of decision makers on the US side while the second examines the technological basis for finally settling on a crisis demand.

SET I: Describe dimensions and seriousness of allied disagreement over the adversary's reservation price.

1. What were the divisions—within the United States or between the United States and key allies such as the United Kingdom, France, and Germany on crisis demands that went too far (or not far enough)?
2. What were the expected consequences—within the United States or within the NATO alliance if the wrong crisis position were taken?
3. On what occasions did surprises for the allies or updating of adversary resolve occur during crisis bargaining?

SET II: Trace process links from information technology to crisis demands.[8]

A. What was the technical intelligence basis for various points of view on the appropriate demand, or the best response, for the crisis?
B. What was the role of individual character and skills in formulating demands during the bargaining?
C. Were there instances of omission or overload tied to decentralization of the information search or centralization of crisis authority?

The first set of questions identifies and establishes the seriousness of disagreement over what to do about the crisis. For this study, the normative motivation is to improve crisis performance. Previous projects by Cold War crisis scholars such as Alexander George (1974) and Irving Janis (1989) wrestled with scoring crisis outcomes. Research by Herek, Janis, and Huth (1987) was particularly interesting. The political scientists asked a panel of historians to judge on a list of nineteen Cold War crises which ones redounded to US interests. As a validity check, they also asked their panel to judge whether the chances of war between the superpowers had risen or declined as a result of the crisis, the idea being that such a war was not likely to contribute toward any party's welfare. Indeed, the final coding showed a strong relationship between successful US crisis management and a lower chance of war after the episode.[9]

Of course, the correlation was not perfect. From the perspective of this study, heavily influenced as it is by Schelling's competition in risk taking and Fearon's

---

8 Keeping the model of Chapter 3 in mind, a crisis demand, here, contains within it an estimate of the adversary's reservation price. An optimal demand for the alliance would land right on the reservation price, pushing the adversary as far back as possible without provoking a war.

9 Herek, Janis, and Huth (1987: 217).

efficient bargaining model, well-managed crisis episodes would not necessarily progress smoothly toward a permanent settlement. As power ratios or resolve over immediate stakes changed due to exogenous developments, the risk of war could spike upward. In the chicken game approximation to a crisis, optimal behavior links closely to an analogy with poker: are the players appropriately navigating the dilemma between escalating the stakes of a potential victory and containing the risk of catastrophe? In the international context, are they pressing for the national interest while leaving sufficient opportunity to avoid war?[10] Indeed, the primary purpose of Fearon's model was to lay out plausible conditions under which the optimal crisis strategy entailed positive risk of war.[11]

As discussed in Chapter 3, balancing probabilistic costs and benefits becomes more risky as uncertainty grows about the opponent's power and resolve. A direct way to improve outcomes in terms of utility for the United States would be to zero in on the opponent's reservation price. The first set of questions in our structured comparison of the Berlin and Yugoslavia series invite us to detail whether US or allied leaders could in fact nail down this crucial parameter. The finding that they could not—at least not for a very large portion of the bargaining during both the 1948–1949 airlift and the 1999 air strikes—should raise doubts about a technological fix for the challenges of crisis management.

Even so, we cannot be entirely confident in the precision of our measurements. There are few cases to draw from, and no instrument can quantify how much uncertainty there was among US and allied leaders as they sized up crisis opponents across the decades. In response to these limitations, the second set of questions focuses on process tracing. The non-relationship between advancing technology and continued uncertainty about reservation prices is supported as the case analysis sheds light on how estimates were formed. In the latter cases, when modern information technology was employed, alternative approaches such as personal diplomacy continued to shape final estimates of the other side's resolve and surprises during bargaining continued to force updates on this parameter. These process based indicators reinforce the idea that advanced technology cannot support crisis bargainers through well-defined steps that lead to accurate appraisals and optimal crisis demands. Instead, the cases show that the same techniques as before—marked by psychological and bureaucratic factors—drive crisis strategy, despite the emergence of newly capable information systems.

For purposes of analysis, each case breaks down conveniently into three crisis decisions. The Berlin series featured three prominent showdowns: the blockade of roads and rail lines to the city in 1948–1949, the erection of the Berlin Wall in

10 Gartzke (1999).

11 Reed (2003) plays off Fearon's argument in order to relate various power ratios to the probability that optimal crisis behavior leads to war. In his view, as power ratios approach 1:1, uncertainty increases. Not knowing where their opponent's reservation price is, even with similar "mean estimates," rational challengers press into the unknown, trading probabilistic gains from a more favorable settlement against increased risk of war.

August 1961, and the Soviet insertion of nuclear-tipped missiles into Cuba in 1962.[12] Similarly, the complex history of the Wars of the Yugoslavian Succession becomes manageable if we focus on three turning points toward the end of the story: the Serbian counterinsurgency campaign against Kosovar militants in October 1998, the Serbian invasion and ethnic cleansing of Kosovo in March 1999, and the Serbian decision to withdrawal short of a ground war with NATO in June 1999.[13]

The following case studies begin by summarizing historical contexts for each of the series and confirming that each of the decision points under examination in fact meet the criteria for crisis discussed in Chapter 2. After these preliminaries, each study proceeds to answer from the historical record our six analytical questions for evaluating crisis performance. In evaluating the historical record it was necessary to lay out a method for dealing with the massive archives on the Berlin case. Obtaining comprehensive access and translations for all of these collections would be prohibitively costly, and even if I were to assemble all the documents relating to allied assessments of Stalin and Khrushchev's bargaining positions during my three Cold War decision points, there is still the issue of interpretation, or coding reliability, for these documents.

A vivid illustration of the interpretation issue appeared in a recent, iconoclastic treatment of the "Crises over Berlin" in Daryl Press' (2005) *Calculating Credibility*. His chapter marshaled archival documents to demonstrate that US assessment of Soviet credibility rose as the strategic balance shifted toward the Soviets between 1958 and 1961.[14] Press' argument countered the idea that Soviet reputation for fulfilling threats on Berlin should have declined after several lapsed deadlines for turning over access routes to East German control or cancelling Western privileges with respect to Berlin. Important evidence for determining the direction of American attitudes came from a series of preserved communications by US Ambassador Llewelyn Thompson in Moscow back to superiors in Washington. "In a third telegram, he (Thompson) argued that a Soviet treaty 'would probably lead to developments in which chances of war or ignominious Western retreat are close to 50–50.'"[15]

Read one way, this excerpt seems to show that the US government in spring 1961 was rapidly reaching the conclusion that Khrushchev would accept extraordinarily high risk of war over Berlin. Yet, in another way, Thompson's telegram of May 27, 1961 is more important as a demonstration of serious disagreement between government officials placed at different vantage points for the crisis. Thompson's telegram from Moscow responds to a previous telegram to the State Department

12 The last example may be stretching the scope of the series, but American participants at the time and subsequent scholars saw a clear connection. If the United States moved too aggressively in Cuba, rather than responding with a nuclear strike, the Soviets could respond in Berlin where they had conventional superiority, perhaps leaving the Americans the last clear chance of avoiding catastrophic general war (Allison and Zelikow 1999: 104).

13 Again, this selection of episodes from the drawn out Yugoslavian wars is not preordained, but taking the sample from late in the series does have the advantage of maximizing the changes in technology, and the American military campaign in 1999 generated quality unclassified sources on crisis decision making.

14 Press (2005: 97–9).

15 Ibid. (p. 97, my parenthetical).

from Berlin. While Thompson agrees "in the main" with Berlin's analysis, he also wants to communicate crucial differences. US officials in Berlin are suggesting a "completely negative stand," something appropriate only if Khrushchev were *less resolved* than Thompson believes.

For the American Ambassador to the Soviet Union, caution and flexibility are the order of the day. Hesitation from the West will not invite Soviet aggression. Khrushchev, in Thompson's estimation, does not need "progress on Berlin" in order to consolidate his domestic position. "Both sides consider other would not risk war over Berlin." The danger is in being too firm, or pressing the other side as some advisers to President Kennedy wish, in a way that would link Berlin to the "Soviet Empire in Eastern Europe." Serving in Moscow since 1957, Thompson is counseling Eisenhower-like patience for a new American administration.

In a sense, the May 27 telegram represented a wise man's case for continuity against impetuous calls for change. None of the factors Thompson cited—Soviet nerves, imposed cohesion of Soviet allies, geography, and local balance of power—changed since 1957. Even though Khrushchev renewed his Berlin threats for the freshly inaugurated Kennedy, and even though the strategic balance was dynamic, as Press detailed in his book, Ambassador Thompson saw no reason to treat the 1961 threats differently than those that passed before.[16]

The point of reviewing the Thompson telegram at length is that despite the discipline imposed by structured case analysis, researchers will situate primary documents multiple ways in the historical context. As a way of addressing this limitation, we can leverage the fact that several historians have already reviewed primary sources for both the Berlin and Yugoslavia series. Often, they explained why certain crisis decisions were made, but typically, like Press, they were not highlighting the level of uncertainty involved in estimating an adversary's bargaining position. Surveying the record and making sense of it, they were predisposed to arrive at some final judgment: the adversary was in the end revisionist, defensive, or flexible for the crisis according to the weight of evidence but usually not all at once. To take a quantitative analogy, historians coded particular values for a variable like adversary resolve; they fixed the location of its mean rather than the extent of its variance.

Given this tendency, it is both feasible and worthwhile to review secondary sources to see if across the accounts there emerges disagreement among actors about their crisis opponents' minimum demands. To settle on a crisis response, of course, such uncertainty at some point needs to be overcome. The secondary literature can help by revealing how available information was processed and how personal, organizational, and political factors, as opposed to information technology, influenced final decisions on crisis strategy.[17] In the interest of replicable results, where historians disagreed on crisis perceptions related to my argument on the ineffectiveness of information technology, I attempt to trace the conflicting interpretations back to a primary source—a memorandum or an interview—so that in principle a historian, perhaps with newly released documents, could someday revisit that source and settle

16 Thompson (1961).

17 The three categories correspond to Graham Allison's (1971) three models in his classic work on the Cuban Missile Crisis, *Essence of Decision.*

the controversy. After these lengthy preliminaries setting the case structure and the rules of evidence, the next section begins with three crisis decisions over the status of Berlin during the Cold War.

The Blockade (1948–1949), the Wall (1961), and Cuba (1962)

For much of the Berlin era, systems for collecting analyzing, and communicating information about strategic adversaries were built around technologies developed early in the 20th century. In 1948, remote images had to be taken by cameras mounted on aircraft. Fourteen years later, during the last of our crises in the Berlin series, both the aircraft and the cameras had improved significantly, but the basic principles were the same as before. Despite the development of radar during World War II, in October 1962, there was still no computer coordinated synthetic aperture for improving image resolution over broad areas or multispectral analysis that could penetrate cloud cover.[18] In terms of communications, before the advent of satellite networks, crisis managers in Washington, D.C. relied on transatlantic cables sent by their representatives in the field, often the ambassador or military commander at the scene. On occasion, Washington summoned top officials in Berlin to "teleconferences." These were teletype affairs rather than real time voice communication. Time delays compared to modern electronic mail messaging made it impractical to call such transatlantic conferences on a daily basis. Even during intense crisis periods, cables ferried the bulk of information between remote crisis actors.[19]

In the case of military deployments, forward units from the Navy or land forces relied on radio contact back to headquarters when it would not compromise security.[20] Limitations in collection and communication methods meant delays and extended uncertainty as central decision makers grappled with whether to escalate or attempt concessions in order to push crises toward a favorable conclusion. Under such stressful circumstances different personalities on the crisis management teams reacted differently. Often, the crisis outcome hinged upon who the president decided had the best feel for the situation—not necessarily one with the most information or expertise—but one with the best instincts.

What made the drawn out conflict over Berlin so prone to crisis was its salience for indicating which of the two remaining powers after World War II might be running ahead. As the Cold War historian John Lewis Gaddis pointed out, the status of the German capital city after the war was anomalous in geopolitical terms.[21] According to the Potsdam agreement, the United States, Britain, France, and the Soviet Union each had responsibility for separate sectors of Berlin, just as the four powers governed separate sectors of Germany itself. Berlin, though, sat nearly one hundred miles inside the Soviet zone. With respect to the military tactical situation during the Berlin era, none of the protagonists gave the Western allies any possibility

18 Allison and Zelikow (1999: 221–4).

19 Shlaim (1983: 410–11).

20 George (1991: 261, n.34); Allison and Zelikow (1999: 231–4).

21 Gaddis (1986: 138).

of physically protecting the Western sectors of the city, the corridors from Western Germany, or for that matter, Western Germany without resort to nuclear weapons.[22] As has been emphasized in our crisis model, capability was not so much the issue, but resolve was. However much the West was willing to pay, or to risk, before accepting the inevitable and allowing Berlin to fall, this would be the most visible indication of how hard the West would fight to keep other territory, in Europe and beyond, out of Soviet hands.[23] The very improbability of successfully defending the two million Germans in West Berlin made the city a convenient focal point to demonstrate the extent of Allied unity and resolve, which was crucial for Cold War bargaining.

Berlin was never far from the thoughts of Allied or Soviet leaders after the four-power arrangements of 1945. Between 1958 and 1962, Soviet Premier Nikita Khrushchev put first the Eisenhower then the Kennedy administration under nearly continuous pressure to resolve the US, British, and French status in Berlin. In his history, Jack Schick (1971) termed all these years, simply, *The Berlin Crisis*. Alexander George and Richard Smoke (1974) also included the deadline episodes of the late-fifties in their award winning analysis, *Deterrence in American Foreign Policy*.

For our purposes though, three more narrowly defined episodes in the "low information technology" era most clearly fit the criteria of crisis—including high conflict of interest, elements of surprise, and fear of an *ultima ratio*—lending a chicken game quality to the interaction. By contrast, in 1958–1959, Eisenhower simply waited, calling Khrushchev's bluff and allowing the Russian deadline to fade away. The kind of bargaining that places insurmountable demands on information technology does not permit this sort of escape: in the chicken game, players either reach a settlement or face a catastrophic final arbiter. Our crisis picks up when the protagonists have already lost the option not to play. In the context of Berlin, crisis dynamics most clearly emerged during; 1) the blockade and airlift of 1948–1949; 2) the building of the Berlin Wall in 1961; and 3) the Cuban Missile Crisis of 1962.

Berlin Blockade and Airlift

The first major crisis between the victorious powers over Berlin was difficult to code in terms of distinguishing the initiator and the defender.[24] Certainly, Western authors for years portrayed the Soviets as diabolical challengers.[25] The move to cut off Berlin in their eyes was as cynical as it was strategic. Threatening millions of innocent civilians with starvation could never alter the ultimate balance of power in favor of the as yet non-nuclear Soviet Union. The menacing tactic simply completed a pattern of Soviet expansion into areas left vulnerable by the West, which had recurred in Czechoslovakia as recently as February 1948.

---

22 George and Smoke (1974: 393–4); Shlaim (1983: 183–7); Press (2005: 84).

23 Shlaim (1983: 252–3).

24 Senese (1997: 416); Gelpi and Griesdorf (2001: 646); Leeds (2003: 431).

25 Davison (1958); Smith (1963). Blaming the Soviet Union exclusively for the dangerous and costly arms race became less automatic after US missteps in Third World crises (Gaddis 1983).

On the other hand, the Soviets did not experience an unbroken run of successes in efforts to expand their influence after the war. Western countermeasures in Iran, Greece, and Turkey—and in the elections of France and Italy—could be viewed as part of a pattern to balance against Soviet power. In the fall of 1947 and spring of 1948, the Soviets were increasingly isolated from four-power talks on the future of Germany. It appeared as if the United States, Britain, and France were finally going to agree on an economic program uniting the three Western sectors of Germany. In fact, the triggering event for the Soviet blockade on June 24 was probably the decision to introduce a single currency for the three Western sectors.[26] Moreover, immediately before the Soviet move, American Military Governor Lucius Clay announced that the currency would indeed circulate in the Western sectors of Berlin. By the end of June 1948, Stalin could claim with some plausibility that it was the Americans and their Western allies who were doing the most to break down four-power cooperation on Germany, the post-war European order, and the prospects for world peace.[27]

With respect to our structured analysis of this low technology crisis, geostrategic competition between the communist bloc and the capitalist allies after World War II and the likely consequences of general war were sufficiently grave to concentrate the minds of the Berlin protagonists. Even with enormous incentives to correctly assess the enemy's resolve and find the negotiating strategy that would concede the least possible on Berlin while avoiding war, Allied opinion still split in significant ways.

General Clay faced the first major decision on the day the Soviets imposed their ground blockade. Obvious options were to await instructions from Washington, lodge a verbal protest, or take action against the restrictions. Washington preferred to wait a day or two to give President Truman opportunity to consult his national security team.[28] This delay in an attempt to manage risk made sense on a number of levels: several pairs of eyes not just in Washington but among the Allies would have time to study Soviet statements and actions to implement the blockade; the overall strategic situation—inferiority of allied conventional forces in Germany—was not going to change; and the force equation in terms of US or allied redeployments might actually improve in a number of days.[29]

General Clay, however, preferred not to wait. Part of the difference in approach owed to his proximity and his experience in directly dealing with previous Russian ploys against Berlin. Clay and Colonel Frank Howley, American Commandant in Berlin, also did not wish to wait quietly while the Allies and Berliners made up their minds. "On June 24, at 2:00pm local time," Howley "went on the air…'We are not getting out of Berlin…The American people will not stand by and allow the German people to starve.'"[30] That same day, before President Truman had the opportunity to

26 Shlaim (1983: Ch. 2, esp. p.44).

27 A United Nations commission originally sanctioned by the Security Council eventually took a neutralist stance, holding both the Soviet and Allied sides responsible for the 1948 Berlin crisis. The commission's proposed concessions from both sides reflected this even-handed principle, which was roundly rejected by the Truman administration (Smith 1963: 124; Young 1968: 150; Shlaim 1983: 374–6).

28 Shlaim (1983: 200).

29 Ibid. (p. 204–5).

30 Ibid. (p. 199); cited from Frank Howley's (1950: 200) memoir, *Berlin Command.*

meet with his cabinet or issue an official US position, Clay, despite divisions on his own staff with respect to Russian intentions, told reporters at US Army Headquarters in Heidelberg that the Russians "cannot drive us by an action short of war as far as we are concerned."[31]

When Truman did intervene on June 26, directing that the "improvised 'air lift' be put on a full-scale, organized basis," there had not been time to collect definitive information on Berlin.[32] The cabinet meeting of June 25 had served mainly to place Berlin in the context of the US global position against the Soviets. Neither conventional war nor economic warfare was justified by the immediate provocations. Truman's choice was to rein in Clay's more aggressive impulses while snatching the Soviet gauntlet for a Berlin contest short of war.[33] Because nobody knew how long an airlift might succeed in supplying West Berliners or how far the Soviets would go in eliminating East-West exchanges or harassing the air corridors, Truman simply stepped into the vacuum created by his divided cabinet and backed Clay.[34]

As the airlift neared its first month of operations, questions remained about whether Truman's doubling down on Berlin had been the right move. The Soviets might wait until the US Air Force pulled its transport aircraft from other commands, disrupting supplies and force mobility around the globe, before administering the *coup de grace* on the city. Even if the Soviets simply stood pat, the prospect of the German winter cancelling flights into Berlin and forcing prioritization between food containers and coal shipments seemed to put time on the Soviet side.

In response there were a few options to accelerate the pace of the crisis and force the Soviets to lay their high cards on the table. Clay favored, once again, an aggressive, militarized approach: send an armored convoy toward the blockaded roads in order to demonstrate, when the trucks passed though to Berlin, the Soviets' unwillingness to enforce their position with measures that would almost certainly start a general war.[35] A second, political-economic approach also favored by Clay was to forge ahead with elements of the London Program, building an independent and productive West German entity from the Allied zones. Even if the Soviets managed to starve out the West from Berlin, they would forfeit an enormous prize, the four-power agreements that gave them access to political developments on their western flank. Finally, for those officials in the United States and its allies who occasionally questioned the strategic wisdom of rescuing the tiny enclave of Berlin at enormous cost, there was the possibility of a face-saving settlement that would lift the blockade in return for Western concessions.[36]

---

31 Shlaim (1983: 200); quoted from *Newsweek* July 5, 1948.

32 Shlaim (1983: 208); from the *Memoirs* of President Truman (1956) Vol. 2, p. 130.

33 Young (1968: 182).

34 Shlaim (1983: 207–9). Following the June 25 cabinet meeting, Jean Smith reports that Secretary of Defense James Forrestal, Secretary of the Army Kenneth Royall, and Under Secretary of State Robert Lovett remained behind to urge caution and restraint. Three days later, after Truman in a follow-on meeting brusquely reiterated his determination to stay, Secretary Royall "incredulously inquired whether he (Truman) had 'thought through' the situation" (pp. 108–9). Smith relies on the Walter Millis edition of the Forrestal Diaries (NY: Viking Press, 1951).

35 Smith (1963: 117).

36 Shlaim (1983: 348 and n. 117).

The second and third measures eventually garnered more enthusiasm than the convoy option, but in fact none of the strategies were implemented in pure form. All generated intense controversy; no one side, hawk or dove, triumphed in these debates completely. Even President Truman at times found his options constrained by initiatives of subordinates responding to the demands of the moment, as Clay and Howell had done in the first days or as the Joint Chiefs did before a pivotal National Security Council meeting on July 22.

Truman recalled Clay and his political advisor from the State Department, Robert Murphy, to make their case in person for cracking open the Soviet barriers. If time and the local balance of forces were on the Russian side, the strategic balance was not; moreover, B-29 Superfortresses, armed with the atomic bomb, were available for deployment to Britain. Clay and Murphy felt that if the Russians really wanted war over Berlin, the ultimatum would have come directly. Wishing to avoid war, the Russians would not attack an escorted convoy, knowing the United States would have to respond with force, any more than they were impeding the relief flights already in progress.

The Joint Chiefs of Staff, on the other hand, took a different view. Berlin was not the place to fight the Soviet Union. Even if Allied forces could concentrate there in time, they would not do so without leaving other points around the globe vulnerable. The Chiefs resisted Clay's convoy idea as an unnecessary provocation, and Air Force Chief of Staff Hoyt Vandenberg further criticized the plan for stripping other commands in order to send 75 additional transport planes to sustain the airlift.[37]

President Truman, in his decision to send the Berlin crisis into another round, did not entirely agree with either the bold escalation of Clay and Murphy or the caution of the Joint Chiefs. The Russians might not swallow the humiliation of a US convoy passing through their checkpoints, but neither were they eager to upset the status quo and plunge the world into war. The President rejected the Clay-Murphy convoy, in part because it was not endorsed by the Chiefs, but he also supported reinforcement for the airlift against the recommendation of his Air Chief. The choice of crisis management strategy made sense in the context of a sophisticated portrait of Russian resolve, what Alexander George and Richard Smoke (1974: 132) would later term the image of the opponent.

Truman and Stalin with some allowance for the vagaries of bureaucratic control established rules of the game for Berlin.[38] These rules survived on the basis of estimates for one another's resolve, and these estimates were the stuff of psychology and human insight. The details of crisis rules would have been different if radar or computers had been more advanced, but there still would have emerged some convention for each side to demonstrate its willingness to risk war and to confirm beliefs about the intentions of the other.

From the standpoint of coalition crisis management, the United States, despite its disproportionate military power among the Western allies, nevertheless adjusted

---

37 Ibid. (p. 262–4). Shlaim's analysis of the July 22 National Security Council meeting was based on official minutes and firsthand accounts, including that of President Truman (1956) in his *Memoirs* Vol. 2, pp. 131–3.

38 Young (1968: 268–70).

its policies to accommodate allied preferences. Once the convoy was rejected, an agreement with Stalin—some version of option three, above—was the only way to escape the mounting costs of the airlift while avoiding defeat. Avoiding defeat meant holding out for as few concessions as possible and exploring another dimension in the contest of resolve. Stalin would be in a weaker position if the Allies could present a united front on Berlin, which they agreed to do after the Americans' July 22 National Security Council meeting, but entering joint talks also guaranteed that Stalin would fight back with tactics designed to split the Allies.[39]

His modest success in this endeavor probably prolonged the crisis, and it showed, again, the importance of a common "image of the opponent" for maintaining a coherent bargaining position. The joint approach to Stalin produced serious negotiations through the month of August. When the principal negotiators sent an agreement lifting the blockade back to the four military governors in Germany for implementation, however, the devil was in the details. Appropriately enough, the Western governors would not consent to a single currency in Berlin issued solely by the East.[40] The military governors of France, Britain, and the United States understood that Western currency reform had been the proximate cause of the crisis and that agreeing to a Soviet-controlled currency, without guarantees of Western input, as the sole legal tender for Berlin would essentially confer success on Russian blackmail. Beyond that assessment though, the three Allies diverged in significant ways, with the United States caught in a dilemma, desiring a harder line than its junior partners but not wanting to move alone against Stalin.

In early September, with Stalin's terms looking less viable, Britain and France still wished to continue talking in Moscow.[41] Most of the officials on the American side, by contrast, understood General Clay's reluctance to continue with settlement talks. Implementation of the August 30 agreement had broken down with the Russians clearly expecting the West to bend toward Stalin's interpretation. Although the West could compromise its interest by seeming too eager, Secretary of State George Marshall preferred tripartite unity over a unilateral ultimatum to break off negotiations, and he acceded to the European's wishes.[42] Ten days later, Marshall met in Paris with the foreign ministers of the United Kingdom and France. Again, they insisted on identical notes to the Soviet Union with another last opportunity to lift the blockade before referring the matter to the United Nations, and again, Marshall agreed.[43] The move also corresponded with President Truman's domestic reelection strategy since running away from the Allies or the United Nations might have appeared as impatient and reckless in its own way as rushing back to another settlement with the Soviets.[44]

At all events, solidarity with the allies came at a cost. The UN arbitration, unlike the US analysis, treated both sides in the Berlin dispute as equally legitimate,

39 Shlaim (1983: 310–1).
40 Ibid. (pp. 326–33).
41 Ibid. (p. 336).
42 Ibid. (p. 342).
43 Ibid. (pp. 349–50).
44 Ibid. (pp. 355–7).

including Soviet complaints about US–led assaults on four-power cooperation in Germany. At the end of the official UN inquiry, the United States still had to step away from its partners, rejecting with some embarrassment a solution crafted by ostensibly neutral parties.[45]

In another important instance, as the United States probed ways to wrest time from the list of Soviet advantages, and before the Western counter-blockade, or embargo, could pose serious inconveniences for the East, General Clay wanted to make the westmark *sole* currency in the Western sectors of Berlin by November 1. Britain and France again reacted cautiously, fearing that forcing the Soviets to negotiate on currency from a position behind where they were when they imposed the blockade was, at the onset of winter, a needless provocation. In fact, the Western currency did not become exclusive tender in West Berlin until March 20, 1949, months after Truman's reelection, with the delay attributable mainly to Allied objections.[46]

William Stivers (1997), in a revisionist article called "The Incomplete Blockade: Soviet Zone Supply of West Berlin, 1948–1949," concludes that Allied obstructionism and US sensitivity to its junior partners helped the Western cause in this case. Particularly, during those foggy months in late fall, there are no records confirming how the airlift tonnage in those days could have kept West Berliners fed and warm unless the Soviets were discreetly permitting leakage.[47] This means that during November-December 1948, the Russians had maneuvering room to counter any American "currency offensive" by squeezing Berlin harder on the ground, threatening the slim margin remaining to the airlift without the necessity of actually attacking the air corridors.

In sum, at important decision points during the Berlin airlift, when no party had an information lock on Soviet resolve, meaningful differences separated the allies as to whether the West should conciliate (send additional notes to Moscow, accept the results of UN brokering) or press (eliminate eastmarks in West Berlin) against the Soviets. In at least some instances, the most powerful player—the United States—benefited by deferring its initial strategy preferences in order to keep the allies together until a favorable settlement could be reached. Individual psychology of key officials involved in the bargaining rather than information dominance governed the course of the crisis. Accordingly, when the final deal came in May 1949, Philip Jessup and Jacob Malik were UN representatives working outside UN forums and procedures. The most technically knowledgeable but politically implicated officials from the Defense Establishment, even the hero of West Berlin, General Clay, were not apprised of the negotiations until mid-April, when a common position among allies, now NATO allies, had already been hammered out.[48]

---

45 Ibid. (pp. 375–6).

46 Stivers (1997: 601–602).

47 Ibid. (pp. 579–80, 598, 600—n. 70) references among several other sources a mid-November report from the CIA, "Is Berlin Blockaded?" The Soviets may have desired pressure on the West but without the spectacle of starving Berliners under their responsibility—not just because Soviet authorities had shut down the ground access routes but because the Soviet Union was still signatory to the four-power arrangements for the city, arrangements they were supposedly defending against Western secession.

48 Smith (1963: 129); Shlaim (1983: 384–6).

Berlin Wall

The Berlin Airlift demonstrated that the Soviets could not coerce the Western allies out of the city by cutting off the access routes in East Germany, but it did not end tensions over the Cold War enclave. The victors after World War II had not envisioned a permanent division of Germany but had disagreed over the terms under which it would be restored. Through the 1950s, the Western sectors consolidated political institutions and economic policies laid out in the London Program, follow-on to the failed four-power talks in December 1947.[49] The Federal Republic of Germany (FRG) approved its constitution just weeks after the lifting of the Berlin Blockade on May 23, 1949, and elected its first national government under Konrad Adenauer in September. By 1955, under the pressure of economic and political competition against the Soviet Union and its proxy in East Germany, the FRG was sufficiently sovereign to control its own arms and sign to the formal commitments of the North Atlantic Treaty Organization.[50]

During the late-fifties, the last few years of the Eisenhower administration, the Soviet Union under Nikita Khrushchev responded to the threat posed by the remilitarization of Germany. This threat included the deployment of intermediate range missiles on West German territory with American-controlled nuclear warheads as part of Eisenhower's "New Look," itself a response to the communists' conventional superiority in Central Europe. The culmination of the Marshall Plan and decisions reached by Western foreign ministers at the end of 1947 was coming to pass. Permanent rejection of four-power cooperation led inexorably to two sovereign Germanies, each one embodying the values and interests of diametrically opposed superpowers.

In this context, when German sovereignty could be manipulated as a diplomatic weapon against the other side, Khrushchev in December 1958, threatened to negotiate an agreement with the sovereign German Democratic Republic, ceding control of the Western access routes to Berlin, which crossed through East German territory. Since the Soviets under the old, much deteriorated four-power agreements guaranteed free passage along the routes, implicit in Khrushchev's move was a temporary interruption of legal access while the West entangled itself in detailed negotiations with the new, sovereign guarantor.[51]

As it turned out, the Eisenhower administration managed the situation as a crisis in slow motion, refusing to acknowledge the Soviet six-month deadline. Offers to begin serious talks on the future of Germany and Berlin came and went. Hopes were placed in the 1960 summit, but in the end, that diplomatic opportunity became a casualty of Soviet success in shooting down an American U-2 spy plane in Russian air space. The whole episode lacked the urgency of a classic crisis. Neither side mustered the will to invoke an ultimate contest. Neither concession nor settlement

49 Ibid. (pp. 31–2).

50 See the United States Diplomatic Mission to Germany website at http://usa.usembassy.de/garelations4555.htm.

51 George and Smoke (1974: 390–1, 399–401).

on Berlin occurred as both sides deferred play, but with a new US president taking office in 1961, the intensity of the conflict would ratchet upward.[52]

By the time John Kennedy met Khrushchev in June 1961, at least the perceived bargaining position had changed. Kennedy's resolve in the context of taking back communist outposts could be called into question after the poorly planned and aborted Bay of Pigs invasion against Fidel Castro in April. The young administration had revealed hesitancy also in its backing of royalists against communist Pathet Lao forces in Southeast Asia, a region where Khrushchev had called for "wars of national liberation."[53] In the course of his strategic review, Kennedy was frustrated by the lack of American options to deal with emerging Soviet threats: the idea that the United States could bluff its way through the Cold War by alerting its nuclear forces at every minor setback in a struggle that spanned the globe was quickly losing its appeal.[54] The Soviets of course, were busy attempting to reverse the strategic balance, and the Cold War was never simply a contest of superpowers. The strategy of a leading power, if it were to succeed, had to take allies into account.[55]

Even Khrushchev felt this maxim operating on the Warsaw Pact. In addition to the threat against Soviet interests represented by consolidation of West Germany and the NATO alliance, the Soviet Premier had to consider the predicament of Walter Ulbrecht's collaborationist government in East Berlin. The frontier between the Federal Republic and the Democratic Republic of Germany, created as an early improvisation of the Cold War, could be guarded by the new East German authorities. The line between the eastern and western sectors of Berlin was another matter. In accordance with the old four-power agreements, citizens in either zone could travel freely throughout the city. As the competition between East and West intensified, Ulbrecht and therefore Khrushchev faced the growing humiliation and economic drain of mass migration from East to West through the portal of Berlin.[56]

When Khrushchev issued his *aide-memoire* to Kennedy and the Western allies in June 1961, threatening a unilateral treaty with East Germany if the two Germanies could not agree on a permanent arrangement for reunification within half a year, it was increasingly clear that somewhere in that timeframe, he would have to move the West out and away from Ulbrecht's capital or find some other way to staunch the refugee flow. In the end, Khrushchev accepted and more or less won the gamble of a *fait accomplis* against the Allies.[57] Smith (1963: 262) in his analysis surmised that the Allies actually anticipated closure of the eastern sector boundary during their foreign ministers meeting in the first week of August and decided to accept a barrier against refugees from the GDR as long as Allied access to West Berlin remained unobstructed.

52 Schick (1971: 118–21); George and Smoke (1974: 391, 414).

53 Ibid. (pp. 414–5); Halberstam (1992: 72, 76, 90–3); Freedman (2000).

54 Schick (1971: 141–2); Gearson and Schake (2002: 29–31, 36–8, 183–9).

55 This was the premise of a recent edited volume by Gearson and Schake (2002), which demonstrated how each of the major allies influenced US policy and how US decision makers sometimes divided on whether and how to accommodate European partners.

56 Schick (1971: 158–61).

57 George (1991: 550–1).

Yet, there are compelling reasons to believe that President Kennedy was genuinely surprised by the first barbed wire barricades, which appeared on August 13 while he was vacationing in Hyannis Port.[58] Despite the fiery rhetoric of Khrushchev's speeches in July, he had been ambiguous about what exactly he would do to change the status quo in Berlin or when. His bluster could easily have been an attempt to improve the Soviet negotiating position, with no risky actions planned before the *aide-memoire* deadline at the end of 1961. If Kennedy and the allies felt they had more time to plan, this explains why they had no contingency policies in place for fast moving events after August 13.[59] The Allies may have concluded beforehand that sealing the border was an East German problem and not worth a major war, but that was a far cry from developing countermeasures to demonstrate Western resolve in the wider contest against the Soviet Union.

Tactical surprise made it more likely that Khrushchev's gamble would succeed. He was undeniably breaking precedents set under the four-power accords, taking away the free movement of East Berliners and greatly restricting the access of Allied officials and West Berliners to the eastern sector. When Khrushchev relented to Ulbrecht's demands, he could not have known for sure whether or how the West would intervene to support an uprising of ordinary people trapped in the GDR, to enforce the free movement principle in the four-power accords, or to preserve the chances for reunification of all Germany on Western terms. The fact of the surprise demonstrated that even the intelligence services of the leading power could not precisely anticipate major coordinated actions from the Soviet side. Kennedy is reported to have asked incredulously, "With all that cement and stone going up, why didn't we know about it before?"[60] Not knowing meant less time for the Americans and their allies to formulate an optimal, unified response. The real answer to Kennedy's question, though, was that the diplomats and professional services underestimated Khrushchev's willingness to accept a calculated risk, and this error colored the abundant evidence from human sources and technical observations out of Berlin.[61]

Khrushchev's initial victory put the Allies on notice that the status of Berlin and greater Germany was again in play. Although they unified around the idea of defending Western access, they split on the appropriate response to the GDR's walling off East Berlin. In some sense, the crisis exacerbated existing divisions among the Allies, many of these not surprisingly related to different views on the strength and resolve of the Soviet Union. Britain along with France and the FRG had worried about the consequences of following Kennedy's strategic lead, raising the nuclear threshold in Central Europe from where Eisenhower had left it.[62] The Allies felt that the Soviets would simply scoop up concessions everywhere the United States

58 Smith (1963: 272). Schick (1971: 173) quotes Kennedy from Edward Weintal and Charles Bartlett (1967) *Facing the Brink: An Intimate Study of Crisis Diplomacy*. NY: Charles Scribner's Sons, p. 211. "Is this our first knowledge of their action?"

59 Schick (1971: 161–73, *passim*).

60 Ibid. (p. 173, n. 46).

61 Smith (1963: 258–66); Schick (1971: 161–2).

62 Ibid. (pp. 154–5); Gearson and Schake (2002: 184–7).

held back nuclear weapons for "flexible response" and replaced them with inferior conventional forces. On the other hand, Britain, still under Prime Minster Harold Macmillan, who had led the diplomatic effort for a permanent four-power settlement in the 1950s, favored the Kennedy administration's interest in 1961 for a new round of negotiations—against the preferences of Paris and Bonn.[63]

In the weeks following the sector closure in Berlin, there was a fresh set of disagreements on how to check the Soviet advance against the four-power rights and obligations without stumbling into a nuclear exchange. To be sure, the Allies unified on August 23 as the military commandants in West Berlin dispatched troops to defy a declared 100 meter ban by the GDR and defend Western rights up to the wall itself.[64] Still, during those very days, the GDR was systematically reducing the number of crossing points and adding procedural requirements for Westerners to enter East Berlin. Britain, along with France and the FRG wanted firm countermeasures, again to head off the erosion of existing Western rights under the four-power accords, but the Kennedy administration overruled, lumping the crossing points issue with the erection of the Wall as a GDR affair and thus not worth another step toward the brink.[65] As the momentum for East-West negotiations to permanently settle the status of Germany resumed in fall 1961 and winter 1962, Macmillan and Kennedy pushed talks while France's DeGaulle and West Germany's Adenauer warned against them.[66]

The fact of Allied disagreements before and after the Wall does not imply that transatlantic partners also failed to agree on important strategies or that the European countries acted independently of American power, but systemic analyses of the Cold War tend toward the opposite extreme, focusing on Washington and Moscow as leaders of rival alliances and ignoring differences within the blocs that were especially significant during crises. Despite asymmetric distribution of military and economic capabilities across the Atlantic Alliance, Kennedy had to listen to his partners.

First, his allies could publicly oppose his demands or refuse to sign a joint communiqué to the Soviet Union, pointing up divisions within his own government, and ultimately weakening the perception of US resolve. This was indeed the gist of Adenauer's August 29 letter informing the US president of disagreement and neutralist sentiment in the FRG—just weeks before West German elections—as a result of flaccid US response to GDR initiatives.[67] Secondly, given the lack of any technical solution to the mystery of Soviet resolve, there was always the chance that an ally in Paris, London, or Bonn was correct and Washington mistaken about Khrushchev's true bargaining position. Overestimating Khrushchev could mean the loss of West Berlin on the heels of the Eastern sector. Underestimating him could lead to a violent incident and loss of control.

63 Schick (1971: 143, 155–6); Gearson and Schake (2002: 43–9, 88, 141–2).

64 Smith (1963: 300).

65 Ibid. (pp. 300–1).

66 Smith (1963: 302, 316); Schick (1971: 181–2); Young (1968: 131–2). Gearson and Schake (2002: Chs. 4, 5, 7).

67 Smith (1963: 303). Also see Gearson and Schake (2002: 141–2).

Without an air reconnaissance photograph or a telecommunications intercept to settle the issue, the coping mechanism for deciding how hard to push back on Berlin devolved to personal contact and experienced judgment. To some extent this happened following Khrushchev's threat at Vienna but prior to the sector wall. After Kennedy's nationally televised speech of July 25, which laid out a comprehensive strategic response to Khrushchev's moves on Berlin, the Soviet leader pulled American disarmament negotiator John McCloy from meetings in Moscow to talk personally at the Premier's Black Sea retreat. So interested was Kennedy in gauging his Soviet counterpart, that he received cables from McCloy about the conversations with Khrushchev while still at Hyannis Port and quickly recalled his mid-level adviser back to Washington, so they could meet in person.[68]

At the end of August, with mounting concern about how far Khrushchev would exploit the successful division of Berlin, Kennedy called General Lucius Clay, hero of the Berlin Airlift, back into service as his envoy to the once again threatened city. The president sought to "add to our resources of judgment and action," which was to say that Western rights would have to be defended in Berlin, forcing the Soviets to accept less than they bargained for but not so much less that they would elect to fight.[69] Uncovering that fine line depended on evidence, of course, some of which could be collected through professional observation, but the crucial factors for distinguishing strategic preferences were not related to availability of information. Final judgments came down to the skill and character of the person interpreting the data points.

Clay's personal touch did in fact restore the confidence of West Berliners in the Kennedy administration's commitment.[70] By the same token, the frustrations of Clay and the eventual curtailment of his influence after a nerve-wracking tank-to-tank confrontation at Checkpoint Charlie in October 1961, show how perceptions—and the process of resolving perceptual disagreements within a government or within an alliance—guide the choice of crisis strategy and determine the success of crisis outcomes.[71]

Cuban Missile Crisis

On the face of it, the Cuban Missile Crisis of October 1962 might not seem the best choice for studying information sharing and the North Atlantic Alliance. The epicenter of the crisis, after all, occurred some 90 miles south of Florida, and the pace of the crisis, thirteen days from the aerial photos of Soviet installations to the October 27 agreement that forestalled an American invasion, left little opportunity for allied deliberations. From the beginning, President Kennedy took the Soviet challenge as a personal affront against his public pledge to keep offensive missiles out of Cuba.

68 Smith (1963: 252).

69 Ibid. (p. 303); Schick (1971: 168).

70 Smith (1963: 309–15).

71 Ibid. (pp. 319–25); Trauschweizer (2006). Garthoff (1991) discussed how misperceptions of the underlying Berlin strategy on both sides led to intensification and most likely unnecessary escalation of the crisis in 1961.

Several analysts have remarked that regardless of the relatively insignificant change in the strategic balance effected by the missiles, Kennedy—not the Western Allies but Kennedy—could hardly let Khrushchev get away with it.[72]

Yet, there are several other considerations that make the Cuban affair relevant to our questions on information sharing and crisis management. First, the showdown grew out of the Berlin context.[73] Though the allies with the exception of British Ambassador David Ormsby-Gore were not consulted before Kennedy's pronouncement of the US quarantine on October 22, foreseeable reactions of the allies helped stiffen US resolve to reject another Soviet *fait accomplis*.[74]

The high politics of the crisis—the idea that the West's willingness to resist Soviet expansion worldwide was at stake—and the Kennedy administration's reaction to the Soviet initiative, literally drawing a line in the sea and daring Soviet ships to cross it—set up classic crisis dynamics that were not lost on the participants. Secretary of State Dean Rusk after Soviet missile ships halted before the American blockade responded as if the United States had just narrowly won a game of chicken: "We're eyeball to eyeball, and I think the other fellow just blinked."[75] Recorded arguments in the Kennedy administration's Executive Committee meetings and memoirs from both sides of the crisis make clear that at various points the protagonists felt surprise at their adversary's actions, that time for preventing or limiting violence was nearly out, and that the *ultima ratio*, if no agreement could be reached, would be nuclear war.[76]

The crisis' historic importance and the features that make it so analytically tractable have attracted extraordinary scholarly attention, so there is a wealth of information about the inner workings of the decision process, particularly on the American side.[77] Moreover, with respect to our structured comparison, American officials faced decisions about compromise and escalation with a significant link to information technology. The triggering event for the crisis was the successful overflight by the U-2, the United States' premier system for aerial photo imaging. Once the Kennedy administration settled upon the quarantine as a middle option to buy time and avoid either a collapse in credibility or general war, there were also issues of command and control for the line of ships as well as subsequent probes, including additional U-2 flights, against the Russian position. Because October 1962 represents a continuation with some of the same actors and many strategic calculations from the Berlin series, and the crisis introduces more sophisticated technology for imaging and communications, it represents a kind of bridge case

---

72 Press (2005: 125, 140–1); Young (1968: 164, 212); Allison and Zelikow (1999: 339).

73 Schick (1971: 208–12).

74 Young (1968: 164, n. 53). Press (2005: 127–8, n. 43).

75 Allison (1971: 131).

76 Press (2005: 120, 132–3). See also George (1991: 232–5) and Allison and Zelikow (1999: 354–5).

77 Examples include Young (1968); Allison (1971); Holsti (1972); George, Hall, and Simons (1971); George and Smoke (1974); and Janis (1982). A second wave of scholarship exploited the growing availability of American and Russian archives along with new interviews of participants from the Cuban Missile Crisis (Bouchard 1991; Blight and Welch 1998; Allison and Zelikow 1999; Zelikow and May 2002; Press 2005).

between the low tech crisis management of the 1940s–1950s and high tech crisis management techniques available to American leaders dealing with Yugoslavia in the late-1990s.

As other researchers have found the Cuban Missile Crisis to be the quintessential illustration for their arguments on the influence of psychological or bureaucratic constraints on rational decision making, the weakness of rational deterrence theory, or the importance of the strategic balance on calculating adversary credibility, this project sees in those thirteen days vivid confirmation of two patterns for information age crisis management: 1) despite increasing technical intelligence about the adversary, crisis actors disagreed over interpretations of the data in ways that paralleled their divergent, subjective assessments of adversary resolve, and 2) technology was not effective as a cure for crisis dilemmas—it redefined them but did not eliminate the need for personal skill, experience, and instinct for solving them.

A preliminary indication that photographic evidence would not automatically generate a clear strategy for Cuba came during the late summer months before the actual crisis. By the end of August 1962, U-2 pictures seemed to show missile related activity on the island and human intelligence sources also provided chatter consistent with a new Soviet initiative. For CIA Director John McCone, the intelligence data was sufficient reason to order more aggressive surveillance.[78] Yet, the capture of pilot Gary Powers that had so embarrassed Eisenhower demonstrated the U-2's vulnerability to Soviet surface-to-air batteries. Acting on McCone's hunch could bring another humiliation for the United States, something that neither the country nor the CIA could afford after several errors in planning the Bay of Pigs operation some sixteen months earlier. To make the situation more awkward for McCone, he was an isolated Republican voice in a still young Democratic administration facing mid-term elections.[79]

In the end, McCone was right. Many career analysts and essentially all Democratic appointees of the National Security Council underestimated Khrushchev's willingness to betray his pledge to Kennedy on Cuba. As would happen during the crisis itself, for the national security team to assess threats and opportunities correctly, the process of sharing data and deliberating its meaning meant more than technical performance of intelligence systems or the take from human sources.

Secret intelligence redefined the problem, but the policy response depended upon organizational and political norms for transforming these inputs into partial knowledge of the adversary. Even though the preliminary analysis in the summer of 1962 occurred within a single administration rather than across sovereign governments, for crisis information sharing in the NATO context, it is still relevant to note that quality of deliberations about Khrushchev's intentions suffered, in a metaphorical sense, from the shape of the table. It was very difficult for McCone's view to prevail, independent of its correctness.[80]

78 Allison and Zelikow (1999: 331–8).

79 Ibid. (p. 332–3); Holland (2005).

80 For Holland (2005), this conclusion was borne out from retrospectives such as *Eyeball to Eyeball* by CIA image analyst Dino Brugioni (1993), summaries of directives and meetings found in State Department records (*Foreign Relations of the United States—FRUS*) and CIA

Once the Soviet offensive missile sights were discovered on October 14, there ensued another round of discussion, debate really, in the forum of the President's handpicked Executive Committee (ExCom). Now classic retrospectives from the five-to-ten-year period after the crisis such as Graham Allison's (1971) *Essence of Decision*, and Alexander George's (1971) *Limits of Coercive Diplomacy* underscored the genuine danger of the Cuban Missile Crisis. In the first days of deliberation, the ExCom was not decided and indeed drifted toward more aggressive reactions—air strike or invasion—to protect the domestic right flank of the President and the credibility of US commitments abroad before it zeroed in on the moderate quarantine option.[81]

A recent analysis, Daryl Press' (2005) *Calculating Credibility*, pointed out that the nature of the ExCom consensus on moderation, reached within a matter of days, was heavily influenced, not by Khrushchev's repeated hesitation to carry through his maximal threats on Berlin, but by a straightforward shift in the strategic balance against the United States between 1960 and 1962.[82] This insight has sobering implications for the role of reputation in international politics as well as the evolving relationship between the United States and Russia, which remain custodians of the world's largest nuclear arsenals. However, it would be mistaken to take "calculating credibility" too far and imagine that the risk and uncertainty involved in crises somehow evaporates after ordinary, scientific comparisons of military power. Credibility, in Press' terminology was a more flexible concept than the ultimate knowledge of resolve useful for crisis bargaining. It was one thing to know that Khrushchev possessed sufficient missiles and bombers by October 1962 to cripple the United States, but it was no less important, when deciding how hard to push him out of Cuba, to know what magnitude of costs Russia would endure in order to use them.

During the actual crisis bargaining, ExCom members thought more in terms of expected lives: what risk would Khrushchev run of a nuclear exchange that would likely destroy Russia's major cities? The most significant arguments boosting the quarantine over the air strike and invasion options honed in on the probable Soviet reaction. For example, the invasion stood the best chance of eliminating the offending missiles, but American decision makers disagreed about whether the Soviets would 1) launch a limited strike from the island before all the active sites could be neutralized; 2) coordinate a general strike from Moscow; or 3) attempt to saddle the Kennedy administration with the last clear chance to avoid all out war by ordering a counter invasion of West Berlin.[83]

Within a few rounds of ExCom meetings, the quarantine emerged as the favorite option because it communicated firmness without seeming to demand an immediate

---

records (*The CIA and the U-2 Program, 1954–1974*). Holland also benefited from additional documents and records released after 2000 via the CIA Records Electronic Search Tool (CREST) at the National Archives—College Park, MD (NARA).

81 Allison and Zelikow (1999: 338–47).

82 Press (2005: 134–5, 141, 147).

83 The account of Allison and Zelikow (1999: 338–47) was buttressed by transcripts from the first edition of the *Kennedy Tapes* book (May and Zelikow 1997).

counteroffensive from the Russians. For Press (2005), rapid consensus on the blockade rather than a stronger response demonstrated Khrushchev's credibility, but Press' excerpts from the presidential archives also revealed the difficulty of gauging Soviet resolve from image intelligence and human sources. It seems that most of the ExCom members, including President Kennedy and cautious Secretary of Defense Robert McNamara, held out little hope for an American blockade: it would not force Khrushchev to remove missiles already ensconced in Cuba; it would provide time to activate those sites; and it would leave Khrushchev the option of turning the tables in West Berlin where the Soviets enjoyed conventional superiority.[84]

In the end, however, ExCom's grim assessment of Khrushchev's resolve turned out wrong. The Soviet leader was not pushed by Politburo hawks into invading Berlin, and although the Americans did give up their Jupiter missiles in Turkey, this concession was heavily qualified—the liquid-fueled Jupiters were obsolete in any case, and the "missile trade" was kept quiet to spare Kennedy reputation costs with NATO and American public opinion. For Kennedy's crisis management team, the quarantine option unfolded in a surprisingly effective way.

Several influential scholars, including Allison (1971) and George (1991), wished to encourage better crisis management without promoting crisis initiation as an effective tactic of diplomacy. Their analyses implied that Kennedy's team was lucky in addition to being good—that information technology, to include both machines and the organizations that ran them, narrowed options for the ExCom in the right direction. For example, the limits of the U-2 system for obtaining high resolution photographs influenced the timing of the key discovery on Cuba. The spy planes were vulnerable to Soviet surface-to-air missiles, so in order to reduce the risk of another U-2 incident, the aircraft in August and September flew over Cuba at oblique angles, making the Soviet emplacements harder to see. During the paucity of American flights between September 6 and October 14, cloudy weather played a role, and in another debate over risk, the CIA and the Air Force took time to determine which organization's pilots should fly the missions.[85] Insofar as they were characteristic of limits inherent in the U-2 system, these technology-related delays increased the chances that Kennedy would catch Khrushchev's ploy in midstream, after some offensive missiles had arrived in Cuba but before the Soviet force was fully activated. The timing was too late for a clean military strike but early enough that US firmness might convince Khrushchev to reconsider. According to this interpretation of events, the U-2 intelligence system would have guided any American government, not just the Kennedy team, to an option like the quarantine, which balanced willingness to fight and openness to peaceful settlement.

Shortly after Allison (1971) first published his provocative analysis, Stephen Krasner (c1972) offered a rejoinder in the journal *Foreign Policy*, warning readers not to take technological or bureaucratic determinism too far. Most of the delays in the intelligence system during September-October 1962 were due not to weather but the risk propensity of responsible officials, who in most cases tried to remain

84 Press (2005: 120, 130–2).

85 George (1991: 229–30); Allison and Zelikow (1999: 329, 331–8, esp. 336–7); Holland (2005).

faithful to the President's preferences.[86] Had Kennedy been willing to accept a higher probability of another U-2 incident, the CIA-Air Force dispute would have been quashed and the planes would have flown directly over the protected missile sights. Political judgment, not technical performance, was a deep cause, constraining the performance of the U-2. That same political judgment of risks and opportunities predisposed Kennedy toward quarantine rather than strike regardless of whether the offensive missiles were discovered fully or partially deployed.

Krasner went on to say that Allison's bureaucratic constraints were more convincing when it came to implementing the President's crisis strategy. There were limits to the command and control system, which contributed to a U-2 wandering unauthorized over Soviet airspace; to uncertainty on the part of Secretary of Defense McNamara regarding how aggressively the US Navy would enforce a blockade that was intended as a cautionary message for Khrushchev rather than an act of war; and finally to the continued presence of obsolete Jupiter missiles in Turkey.[87]

Krasner's endorsement of Allison on the implementation side is worth remarking on, here. It, also, can be taken too far if we are supposed to conclude that new communications technology with all-weather performance, wider bandwidth, and smaller power requirements would somehow eliminate command and control issues during crisis. First of all, Krasner's two categories—decision and implementation—interact during real life games of chicken. The choice to ascend or descend a half-step on the escalation ladder conditions the command and control challenges, and performance on implementation influences the next decision about escalation. If, as Krasner asserted, risk propensity affects how collection technology is deployed to unveil the initial conditions of a crisis, it also affects how hard communications systems will be pushed during the implementation phase.

Thomas Schelling's (1966a: 94) paradoxical idea to win the competition in risk taking by throwing controls out the window notwithstanding, Presidents Truman, Eisenhower, and Kennedy preferred to retain fine control in a crisis. Rather than irrevocably abandoning their responsibility in one dramatic gesture, they tried to stress command systems by increments, so the Soviet side would have time to see the growing danger of all-out war, time to keep their wits about them and negotiate an escape from deadly crisis dynamics. During the Cuban Missile Crisis, raising the probability of inadvertent provocation—placing extraordinary implementation demands, for example, on the Navy's command and control—became an escalation decision in its own right.

Regardless of the level of sophistication for information technology, the difference between technical constraints imposed by crisis decision aids vice strategy implementation aids is not as stark as Krasner implied. Political judgments of acceptable risk indeed govern how collection systems are employed and how their take is interpreted. Such judgments also determine the degree to which fine control is delegated or central authority is overloaded so that errors become more likely. Even with advanced satellites and supercomputers, crisis politics are such that presidents fret over interpretations of what they are seeing and hearing and whether their emergency implementation demands communicate sufficient resolve to the adversary.

86 Krasner (1973: 316, 317–8).

87 Ibid. (p. 319); Allison and Zelikow (1999: 241–2).

Concerns about the limited capacity of technology to resolve crisis dilemmas encourage the search for special assistants, individuals with the appropriate skills, experience, and personality to help a president size up the rationality and resolve of the other side and at the same time convince these adversaries to accept a settlement before mutual disaster overtakes all parties. As we have seen, General Clay played this role in Berlin during the Airlift and again after the Wall in 1961. President Kennedy, not entirely comfortable with Clay's risk taking, began to rely more on his brother. During the chicken game in Berlin over the fall of 1961, Robert Kennedy was assigned the delicate task of conveying to Moscow the President's intentions to tolerate the Wall and simultaneously resist harassment of Western officials entering East Berlin.[88]

By the time the missile crisis erupted the following year, the Attorney General had become one of President Kennedy's most potent instruments for settling Cold War crises. In both the decision and implementation aspects of crisis management, Robert Kennedy's personal touch loomed large.[89] His most renowned interventions seemed to snatch diplomatic victory from the jaws of nuclear Armageddon. The air strike option collapsed in the ExCom after his note to his brother remarking that he now knew "how Tojo felt" planning Pearl Harbor.[90] Appreciating command and control difficulties on all sides in the crisis, it was Robert who, as a US invasion of Cuba neared, urged his brother to accept Khrushchev's more conciliatory first letter and ignore threats in the second.[91] Perhaps only Robert Kennedy could have convinced Soviet Ambassador Dobrynin that an American invasion with its astronomical risks was actually imminent—well enough to push the Soviets into a settlement that favored the United States.[92] The incongruity of Robert Kennedy's official position against the coercive diplomacy tasks at hand spoke to the premium President Kennedy placed on trust in the setting and execution of crisis maneuvers.

Taking stock of the Cuban Missile Crisis as a bridge case between the old Berlin series and the high tech showdowns that took place over Yugoslavia many years later, certain patterns already suggest themselves. Rising information technology did not directly correlate with improved performance in international crisis bargaining because the basic dilemmas of crisis management did not get any easier as national security teams attempted to cull adversary intentions from collected data streaming in at higher rates and greater fidelity. During the Cuban Missile Crisis as well as earlier conflicts over Berlin, officials within the US Government or across allied governments disagreed about the meaning of incoming evidence from the Soviets'

88 Schick (1971: 180) drew on public actions recorded by the *New York Times*, September 25, 1961. Garthoff (1991) noted Robert Kennedy's communication to the Soviet press attaché (and KGB officer) in Washington, Georgi Bolshakov, on October 27, 1961—from Arthur Schlesinger's 1978 account.

89 Allison and Zelikow (1999: 329, 346–7).

90 Krasner (1973: 318).

91 Allison (1971: 227–8); Allison and Zelikow (1999: 359–60).

92 Ibid. (pp. 128–9, 360–2). Allison and Zelikow note that Khrushchev had all but decided to remove the missiles before Dobrynin's report of his meeting with Robert Kennedy reached Moscow. Still, that report encouraged the Soviets to agree quickly on essentially the terms of President Kennedy's Saturday evening (October 27) letter (p. 362).

opening moves, especially if the information related to this adversary's vision of a crisis endgame. Neither did more sophisticated command and control systems solve the problem of how to demonstrate resolve. Only a human agent could be trusted to decide the appropriate balance between over delegation of decision making power to experts in Washington, or in the field, and information overload at the top. Similarly, it took a personal touch to communicate willingness to run high risks, to wager great loss of life if necessary, while maintaining sufficient self control for avoiding war. Technology, independent of its specifications, credibly expressed crisis resolve when it was operated near the breaking point, when the increasing likelihood of malfunction translated directly to greater risk of war.

Yugoslavia Crises: Bargaining over Kosovo, 1998–1999

The temptation to push technology to its limits carried through more than 45 years of development. Part of the reason fundamental continuity in crisis behavior went unacknowledged was that geopolitical demands changed so radically, from survival against a superpower foe with conventional superiority in Europe to promotion of a liberal order in the last, recalcitrant corners of that continent and beyond. In addition to the ends, the means of geopolitics changed; technical parameters, including the boundaries of information system performance, receded rapidly.

Exponential improvements in information management were illustrated by the revolution in air power, which took place in the last ten years of the long interval between our crisis series. During the Gulf War of 1991, only ten percent of bombs were smart munitions, and those laser guided bombs required a designator, an operator to lase on target until the bomb hit home. Ten years later over Kosovo, joint direct attack munitions (JDAMs) were wired into the space-based global positioning system (GPS), providing precision bombing now with all-weather capability and no need for a laser designator.[93] The new technology worked well: the real problem was not destroying targets but politically vetting new strikes to keep the list populated.[94]

Consistent with a central proposition in support of trusted guardianship, crisis information systems—unlike combat systems—are easy to share with allies in the sense that they do not provide exclusive means for success that must be strictly guarded, even from partners, in order to perform. National information system performance and combat capability went up dramatically during the Revolution in Military Affairs, but optimal crisis management outcomes in the latter series of bargaining episodes over Yugoslavia remained just as elusive as they had been over Berlin decades earlier.

A gap between the trajectory of technology and the flat results of crisis bargaining might not surprise some realist observers who would point to the coincidental structural change in the international system. Without the Soviet menace, why would transatlantic partners with diverging priorities see eye to eye even if the US intelligence establishment could perfectly anticipate Serbian leader Milosevic's next

93 CNN (2001); Clark (2001: 9–10). Hansen (2006).

94 Clark (2001: 224, 235–42); Halberstam (2001: 425, 444–5, 450–1); Peters, et al. (2001: 25–6).

move? This criticism, though, applies more to war torn Bosnia in the mid-1990s than to Kosovo in 1998–1999. In 1993–1994, the Europeans did have a very different view of the threat, not just due to historical grievances or proximity of refugees, but especially because several NATO members had soldiers at risk on the ground where the United States stayed clear. The Americans' "lift and strike" solution—lift the arms embargo for Bosnian Muslims and strike from the air at the aggressor Bosnian Serbs—would leave lightly armed European peacekeepers at the mercy of Serb reprisals.[95] After 1995, far fewer Western Europeans were in the line of fire and air power, even if it was not yet precision guided, stood a better chance of affecting the balance of indigenous forces on the ground.

The success of Operation Deliberate Force after a few weeks of air strikes in Bosnia and the subsequent settlement at Dayton did condition European and particularly NATO's attitudes toward Kosovo a few years later.[96] The outcome of the crisis in Bosnia seemed to reinforce the wisdom of firm resolve and swift action for checking Serb aggression.[97] At the same time, hard lessons learned from the experience of outgunned peacekeepers and frustrated commanders wrestling with the "dual-key" system in Bosnia made it more likely that NATO would accept the formal steps called ACTWARN and ACTORD for mobilizing its air forces and putting them to use over Kosovo even without sanction by the UN Security Council.[98]

By the time of the bargaining late in 1998 for the withdrawal of Serbian police and military units from Kosovo, NATO had established that Milosevic was a threat to stability on the alliance's southern flank.[99] If information technology were key to assessing the limits of Milosevic's position and rallying allies around the most efficient strategy to make him stand down, it did have a fair opportunity to work: the interests of the member states at that point were fundamentally aligned. Yet, just as Europeans and Americans disagreed about how to contain the Soviets during the Berlin series, they disagreed again on how to stop Milosevic during the post-Cold War political transition in the Balkans. Moreover, despite the advantages of real time remote sensing and high bandwidth communications, at important junctures in the conflict over Kosovo, NATO misread opponents' intentions. In the information age, the basic incentive structure for crisis bargaining still left ample room for the information superior party to be surprised.

The Ceasefire, 1998

Three years after the Bosnian agreement at Dayton, the outer wall of sanctions from the World Bank and the International Monetary Fund remained in place until human rights conditions in the Serbian province of Kosovo improved. Oppression of Kosovar Albanians was unlikely to stop, however, until the political status of Kosovo was resolved. Here, the international community, against all intentions,

95 Kaufman (2002: 82, 88–n. 47, 89–n. 56, 57).

96 Ibid. (p. 120).

97 Halberstam (2001: 425); Bellamy (2002: 85–89); Blumenthal (2003: 635).

98 Clark (2001: 135, 144); Bellamy (2002: 98).

99 Bellamy (2002: 88–92).

found itself fueling the crisis. It supported autonomy for Kosovo to restore basic rights to the Albanian majority, many of whose freedoms had been brutally curtailed by Milosevic's government for the protection of minority Serbs in the province and to keep the remaining territories of Yugoslavia unified.

At the same time, protection of minorities—even those such as Serbs in Kosovo or Russians in Central Asia—with powerful patrons nearby, and respect for the sovereignty of United Nations members struck European and American observers in the diplomatic Contact Group for Yugoslavia as valid ends, despite the concern that Milosevic's means were reprehensible. Rather than overwhelming force from NATO, Milosevic could expect a bargaining process, a window for negotiations, in which he would find an agreement, with international imprimatur, to retain Kosovo for Serbia and circumscribe the power of Albanian parties in the province.[100]

Bargaining over Kosovo became more complicated with the rise of the Kosovo Liberation Army (KLA). The ragtag group expressed the fighting spirit of independence minded ethnic Albanians, and it was not above assassination or bombing to harass superior government forces. In response to the KLA's hit-and-run tactics, Milosevic could respond that his use of force, though ugly in the sight of Europe, was necessary to counter what amounted to terrorism against the state of Yugoslavia. For its part, the KLA also operated under a perverse incentive to fight while bargaining. By goading Belgrade's enforcers into a cycle of increasing violence, the KLA would make international intervention more likely.[101] Kosovo might not gain independence, but after the shooting stopped, Milosevic, if he survived, would be much weaker before negotiating the next political settlement.

While the KLA was leveraging Western intervention, Milosevic might be forgiven for underestimating its importance. The lessons of Bosnia were ambiguous. Yes, NATO air strikes had made it more difficult for Bosnian-Serb forces to terrorize Sarajevo, but they had been self-limited in scope and had come only after three years of inter-allied hand wringing. In fact, the Allies, at London in March 1998, united around the goal of preventing another Bosnia in Kosovo but in fall 1998, after fits and starts trying to coax a settlement with ethnic Albanians, still split on how far to push Milosevic.[102] For its part, the United States as the leading member of the NATO alliance found itself buffeted by cross-currents. When it rewarded Milosevic economically for accepting talks with the Kosovars in May, it was seen as excessively flexible. Yet, when the American Secretaries of State and Defense threatened direct force during the over flights of Operation Determined Falcon in June, several allies groused at the lack of a UN Security Council mandate for striking Serbia.[103]

In a move reminiscent of the call for Lucius Clay to return and shore up the Western position in Berlin during 1961, the Clinton administration and NATO summoned Richard Holbrooke, the architect of Dayton, back to conduct final

100 Mertus (1999: 154–8, 175–87, 228–9, 231–4); Bellamy (2002: 59–64); Kaufman (2002: 150–4).

101 Bellamy (2002: 67).

102 Bellamy (2002: 73–88); Kaufman (2002: 156, 158–60).

103 Ibid. Hendrickson (2002: 243–4).

negotiations for averting a Kosovo War in 1998.[104] Despite the high technology sensors available to monitor Milosevic's moves with respect to his paramilitary and police forces, the last minute bargaining was much less formulaic engineering and more improvisational jazz. Holbrooke drew the analogy himself, reflecting on the need for technical competence, a respect for the themes—or the minimum demands of his sponsors—and the creativity to find new solutions with old information. Very often the fresh answers were not in the latest pouch from surveillance but from the choice of expression or the body language of his face-to-face interlocutors.[105]

During the negotiation of October 1998, Holbrooke had to convince Milosevic to pull his forces out of Kosovo, which was legally still part of Serbia. This time the creative solution tapped unarmed observers from the Organization for Security and Cooperation in Europe (OSCE). After six months of frustration, the peace talks between Milosevic and Kosovar Albanian leader Ibrahim Rugova had fallen apart. A relentless offensive in August employed the Yugoslav Army in clearing operations, resulting in an estimated 500,000 refugees out of a Kosovo population of 2.5 million and prompting the UN Security Council to call for a ceasefire.[106]

Yet, as General Clark recorded in his memoir, NATO did not immediately embrace the Holbrooke agreement, sensing that without some sort of NATO presence, Milosevic was unlikely to let the KLA or Albanian civilians off the hook. Perceiving NATO to be far more threatening than OSCE observers to his control over the province, Milosevic stiffened his resistance, and Holbrooke was forced to turn back to NATO for more high cards. Indeed, NATO provided them. After Holbrooke renegotiated the withdrawal agreement to include NATO air patrols, the North Atlantic Council on the evening of October 12 escalated from ACTREQ to ACTORD, meaning that unless Milosevic complied with the new Holbrooke terms, NATO would begin air strikes after 96 hours. General Clark and NATO Secretary General Javier Solana used the force authorization as leverage to pry very specific commitments from Milosevic, down to the redeployment of individual military and police units. In doing so, Clark and Solana did not court war, but they did push Milosevic harder than some in Washington saw prudent.[107]

First, the strategic rationale was controversial.[108] The Contact Group on Yugoslavia, which included Russia, the United Nations Security Council, and the North Atlantic Council, had taken official positions in support of preserving the Federal Republic of Yugoslavia. Though the Yugoslav and Serbian forces were better armed than secessionist forces in Kosovo, violence and atrocities had been initiated by both sides. The cautious faction in Washington, which included the Secretary of Defense, the Chairman of the Joint Chiefs of Staff, and powerful Republicans in Congress, questioned where Solana, Clark, and Secretary of State Madeleine Albright were headed: could the alliance's air assets effectively backstop OSCE

104 Bellamy (2002: 74–5).

105 Ignatief (2000); Clark (2001: 142).

106 Bellamy (2002: 84–5). Chronologies of events surrounding the crisis in Kosovo appeared in Mertus (1999: 307–9) and Kaufman (2002: xiii–xxii).

107 Clark (2001: 144–7); (Halberstam 2001: 399–400); Kaufman (2002: 163).

108 Nye (1999); Rouleau (1999); Carpenter (2000).

verifiers on the ground? Did the mission make eventual insertion of NATO ground troops into Kosovo more likely? Were NATO and Washington diverting forces to essentially fuel a civil war that was not among any member's vital interests?[109]

While it is true that strategic differences existed independent of Milosevic's position, these differences mattered less if NATO could know precisely the nature of the Serbian leader's resolve. The aggressive faction, who wanted to halt Serbia's human rights abuses to the point of threatening NATO ground intervention, might have paused if they understood that Milosevic would fight to the death and pursue a scorched earth policy in Kosovo. Similarly, cautious policy makers could see the benefits of pressing the NATO threat if it was known that Milosevic would quickly fold the way Bosnian-Serb forces around Sarajevo had responded to Operation Deliberate Force in August-September 1995.

In the event, the Allies and the factions in Washington compromised as if they had decided that Milosevic would back away but only when the NATO threat was on the verge of materializing into a NATO offensive. The 96-hour ACTORD of October 12, 1998 has been mentioned. With violence continuing in Kosovo during November, NATO ministers on December 4 announced a build-up in the Former Yugoslav Republic of Macedonia, adjacent to Kosovo, in case the OSCE ground observers needed to be extracted under protection.[110]

Yet, NATO only arrived at this rough consensus after multiple rounds of deliberation, and the members could not be sure how Milosevic might react each time NATO tightened the screws. Milosevic had conceded under pressure before, but despite all the collection and analysis technologies, including a CIA tap on calls from the Yugoslavian deputy prime minister's office, no one could guarantee how the Yugoslavian President might respond in the future.[111] The Western negotiator who knew him better than most, presidential envoy Richard Holbrooke, sweated through several sessions beginning in October, probing various parties in the talks—the Serbs, Washington, the Contact Group, NATO—for some kind of opening. After days of intense bargaining, he still could not pin down whether Milosevic would peacefully accept NATO-run air verification or force the Allies to execute their ACTORD.[112]

Even after Holbrooke left Belgrade on October 12, Clark and Solana were still unsure Milosevic would comply. When they visited Milosevic in mid-October, they arrived with the ACTORD remaining in place and intelligence on individual units operating in Kosovo.[113] Hemmed in by the prospect of NATO bombing and exposed by US intelligence systems, the Serbian strongman could still surprise. His overall police commander, Colonel-General Djordjevic, told Clark, "We were within weeks

109 Clark (2001: 141); Halberstam (2001: 376–7).

110 NATO Ministerial (1999); Leurdijk (1999: 14–n. 19); Clark (2001: 154–6); Bellamy (2002: 106–13).

111 Bellamy (2002: 115–6).

112 Holbrooke returned to NATO and the Contact Group for consultations on October 8 (Clark 2001: 141–3).

113 Clark (2001: 145–51); Bellamy (2002: 97).

of killing them all, when you stopped us. Why did you stop us?"[114] Finally, when details of the Yugoslavian withdrawal of forces were ready for signature, Milosevic shocked the NATO commander over brandy: the only real solution, he said on October 25 as he signed onto NATO air verification, was to kill all the KLA.[115]

Rambouillet, February-March 1999

Given that the surest route to NATO air strikes in Kosovo was a humanitarian catastrophe that would provide legal cover for bypassing Russia's veto on the UN Security Council, Milosevic's preferred solution to the Kosovo problem made a peaceful settlement highly unlikely. Nevertheless, a few months later, representatives from the Federal Republic of Yugoslavia and the constituent republic of Serbia traveled to the French chateau at Rambouillet for "proximity talks" with a Kosovo delegation that included representatives of the KLA.[116] For the cautious faction among NATO allies and the Russian delegation, the thought was that NATO threats of force and an interim political agreement that delivered demilitarization of the KLA without a guarantee of independence for Kosovo would be enough to entice Milosevic at the eleventh hour.[117] The more aggressive General Clark, ready by this time to brandish force and use it in order to stop Yugoslavia's military and police, still felt in early March, well into the talks, that in the end Milosevic would sign to avoid bombing.[118]

In fact, the Yugoslav delegation dragged their feet at Rambouillet, heedlessly risking bombing and diplomatic isolation as it became clear after Secretary Albright's personal intervention that the Kosovars would see it in their interests to accept a compromise. For the follow-up meeting in Paris on March 15, the Kosovars came to discuss implementation details and wrap up the accord. Meanwhile the Serb representatives tried to reopen political issues as a way of unraveling the February 23 text from Rambouillet.[119] On the ground in and around Kosovo, Yugoslav troop levels were on the rise. The Kosovars signed the Rambouillet terms on March 18 but without the presence of the Russian member from the Contact Group's negotiating team. By March 22, the OSCE verification mission had withdrawn from Kosovo, the number of refugees in Kosovo was spiking past 200,000 as it had in October, and Richard Holbrooke was called back into service once again for another last chance session in Belgrade.[120]

114 Clark (2001: 148, 152).

115 Ibid.

116 Weller (1999: 227).

117 Bellamy (2002: 136, 145, 149).

118 Clark (2001: 170).

119 Weller (1999: 234–6). Weller cited an official statement from the Rambouillet co-chairmen on March 19, blaming the Yugoslavian delegation. Posen (2000: 44, 48–n. 21) noted that last minute changes to the military annex granting NATO access to all of Yugoslavia made it politically impractical for Milosevic to accept the final offer in Paris.

120 Ibid. (pp. 217, 236); Bellamy (2002: 146, 149, 151). Lambeth (2001: 9) cited a report from the UN High Commissioner for Refugees.

As an illustration of how little superior information technology mattered for either detecting or eroding enemy resolve, journalist David Halberstam's reporting of the final face-to-face meeting with Milosevic before the launch of NATO operations on March 23, 1999 captured Holbrooke's puzzlement when the usual bargaining methods stopped working.

> Holbrooke thought Milosevic was oddly fatalistic and much less afraid than he was back in October when the Americans had last threatened to bomb. Holbrooke was not sure what had changed him. Perhaps it was the bombing that had taken place during Desert Fox, when the United States attacked Iraq for seventy hours and then stopped, and Milosevic believed that he could withstand that kind of bombing. Or perhaps he had received from sources within NATO some sense of the limited nature of the NATO bombing orders and believed he could withstand that, too. Or perhaps it was simply a complete mood swing—that happened often enough with him. Whatever the reason, he was much less terrified than he had been a few months earlier, displaying an odd cockiness bordering on indifference.[121]

Or perhaps, Milosevic and other Serbian officials had grown more fatalistic about the decision to confront NATO. Troop deployments had ramped up sharply since the end of the Rambouillet process came into view in late-February. A month later, the logistical and morale requirements of mobilizing forces added their own impetus to Serbian crisis management.

Despite the fact that the Yugoslavian army and police movements were detectable around Kosovo, Halberstam went on to note that several important policy makers on the NATO side nevertheless underestimated Serbia's resolve. "White House spokesmen, talking to reporters, made it clear they felt the bombing would last only three or four days." Secretary of State Albright on television judged NATO operations would bring Milosevic back to Rambouillet within a "relatively short period of time."[122]

Post mortem reports on the NATO air campaign indicated the overall assessment of Milosevic's position—that only a little force would be required—conveniently papered over real differences among the allies. Within NATO, even within Washington, there was still empathy for Serbia's and Federal Yugoslavia's claims on territorial integrity and their indictment of violence employed by the KLA. Across the alliance, there was little enthusiasm for striking directly at Belgrade and punishing Serbian civilians. These sentiments complicated NATO planning.[123]

---

121 Halberstam (2001: pp. 421–2).

122 Ibid. (p. 425).

123 *Washington Post* reporter, Dana Priest, authored a revealing series of articles on high-level decision making during the 1999 Kosovo campaign, published on May 30, September 19, September 20, September 21, and December 29. See especially "Soldiering On in a War of Constraints: NATO's Top General Works around Politics" (May 30) and "Bombing by Committee" (September 20). Inter-allied controversies and related intra-governmental disagreements within the United States are reviewed and analyzed in Coletta and Feaver (2006: 116–22). On NATO planning, based on General Clark's memoir and interviews at NATO Headquarters, see Nardulli, et al. (2002; 18–9).

Just one third of the aircraft that would eventually be needed for Operation Allied Force were in place when it began on March 23, and the target lists were only prepared through the first few days of bombing.[124] Expansion of these lists in the first weeks of the war, as Milosevic resisted and the number of Kosovar refugees swelled near one million, would become excruciating for the NATO commanders who labored to obtain unanimous political approval on each new target as they held off calls from certain European capitals to suspend the bombing.[125]

At the initiation of air strikes—despite the evidence of Yugoslavian army dispositions and Milosevic's "mood change"—NATO allies were still divided about whether bombing would be wise strategy and for the most part mistaken about how much bombing would be required to pry concessions from Serbia.[126] Information technology could cope with the physical traces presented by Serbia, it could roughly track the accelerating destruction inside Kosovo, but it could not solve the critical question of Milosevic's determination. Without that answer, NATO did not know how much it could safely demand or how much coercive measures would cost to secure the terms of Rambouillet.

Endgame, May-June 1999

Seventy days later, NATO had blasted through the Phase I and Phase II target set, and there remained questions about how far to expand Phase III, which potentially included targets of value to the Serbian leadership as well as civilians' quality of life.[127] Debates on targeting in this case as well as negotiating points properly fell under the rubric of crisis bargaining and not simply combat operations. The chicken game aspect of limited violence was more prevalent during the Kosovo endgame than, say, the limited war in Vietnam.

Bombing in North Vietnam did remain constrained for fear of disastrous reactions by China or the USSR, and in December 1972, Richard Nixon escalated bombing to force the North Vietnamese government back to the negotiating table in Paris.[128] Yet, the overall thrust of the Vietnam intervention—counterinsurgency in 1966–1967—aimed to search and destroy Viet Cong cells, that is, eliminate them more than persuade them. With Milosevic, use of the military was more akin to Nixon's Christmas Bombing several years later: those attacks had no hope of destroying the enemy. Neutralizing him by that time was too costly, but the violence might still be enough to push him toward a more favorable settlement.

In order to appreciate the contribution of information technology to the Kosovo outcome in May-June 1999, then, it must be placed not just in the context of successful combat sorties but in the frame of crisis management. Air strikes against

124 Halberstam (2001: 425, 444); Lambeth (2001: 13–5, 24–8). See also, Barry Posen's (2000: 59) analysis based on unclassified sources in *International Security* and Nardulli et al. (2002: 24, 32–n. 23) based on an interview with air commander Lt. Gen. Michael Short.

125 Priest (1999a); Clark (2001: 249); Lambeth (2001: 22, 24–6, 29).

126 Posen (2000: 51–n. 25, n. 26, 59–60, 69–n. 68); Bellamy (2002: 161–2, 166).

127 Clark (2001: 364–5); Lambeth (2001: 38–n. 57, 40); Nardulli et al. (2002: 33).

128 Burdick (1984); Clodfelter (1989: Ch. 6).

fixed targets in greater Yugoslavia and military units in Kosovo caused more death and destruction, but their part in crisis bargaining was nevertheless analogous to the Berlin Airlift in 1948–1949, the redeployment of infantry battle groups from West Germany to Berlin in 1961–1962, and the anti-submarine and ship boarding operations of October 1962. The use of force in these cases sent signals about American and Allied resolve while probing for more evidence—or time—to discern the other side's willingness to risk disaster.[129] Under this sort of comparison, Phase III air operations over Kosovo reveal by now familiar limitations on collection, analysis, and communications systems for escaping crisis dilemmas. Employment of these technologies, at least at the national level, did not reconcile competing views on the adversary's intentions.

At the fiftieth anniversary NATO summit in Washington, D.C., the Allies reaffirmed their determination to continue the pressure on Serbia until Milosevic halted ethnic cleansing, withdrew Yugoslavian forces in accordance with the October 25, 1998 NATO accord, and accepted the Rambouillet terms granting autonomy for Kosovo. By late April though, Phase III bombing and intensified tactical operations within Kosovo were creating embarrassing collateral damage for Western governments that had approved the military mission—without UN sanction—for humanitarian purposes.[130] Moreover, the public consensus on objectives masked vigorous behind-the-scenes debate over means. Before the summit, President Clinton and British Prime Minister Tony Blair had argued over the political wisdom of preparing a ground invasion. The French government continued to resist strategic targets such as Serbia's electrical grid, and American airmen questioned the diversion of resources to small concentrations of Serbian troops and equipment in Kosovo.[131] Some of the divisions related to differing technical assessments about the physical consequences of a proposed attack, but far more important were contradictory views on what the political effects would be on each side's determination.

Until the end of Operation Allied Force, which is to say the end of crisis bargaining with Serbia, the Allies vehemently disagreed about ground preparations and bombing strategy.[132] In June, as General Clark agitated to "energize" the air campaign against petroleum targets outside Novi Sad, officials in Washington worried about how Milosevic would respond in the final give and take to achieve a ceasefire and Serbian withdrawal.[133] Javier Solana also warned Clark to "be very careful with the bombing."[134] Again, the question was not whether allied aircraft could destroy refineries and airfields but whether the physical destruction would make it more or less difficult to achieve political acceptance of NATO's terms, in this case via the acquiescence of Russia at the June Group of Eight meeting and at the UN Security Council.

---

129 Blechman and Kaplan (1978: 12–4).

130 Clark (2001: 274, 296–8); Halberstam (2001: 460); Lambeth (2001: 136–43); Nardulli, et al. (2002: 46).

131 Halberstam (2001: 461–2, 468–70); Lambeth (2001: 40, 189–95); Peters, et al. (2001: 28–9); Nardulli, et al. (2002: 33–4, 38).

132 Clark (2001: 343, 351); Peters, et al. (2001: 49–51).

133 Clark (2001: 364).

134 Ibid. (p. 365).

Within the Western alliance, Russia's role was fodder for more debate: would concessions for Serbia won by Russia encourage Milosevic to throw in the towel sooner or would Milosevic drag out the process to further weaken NATO's demands?[135] Months after Serbia signed the military agreement to withdraw from Kosovo and permit the entry of a NATO peacekeeping force, uncertainty on the allied side lingered. Looking back on the air campaign, the ground threat, the Russian influence, and the last minute concessions, no one was quite sure why Milosevic settled when he did.[136] Despite after-action interviews supplementing all the crisis intelligence from human and technical means, the nature of Milosevic's resolve remained mysterious as it was for special envoy Holbrooke on the night before the bombing.

Another aspect in which information technology did not afford the United States an easy solution for Kosovo was command and control. As occurred during naval operations in the Cuban Missile Crisis, advanced communications did expand the tactical space: they widened possibilities for crisis response. Yet, intervening political factors limited how well sophisticated maneuvers, or fine control, could coax the adversary to a favorable settlement. Within the US decision making structure, differences over crisis strategy created incentives for aggressive commanders to strain against the rules of engagement in order to press Milosevic and for more cautious officials to employ state-of-the-art communications in order to drill down into General Clark's organization and monitor the rules of engagement in detail.

Pushing decisions down for flexibility and pulling them up to the highest levels for greater control whipsawed the system. The same information management problems that bedeviled older arrangements cropped up again in the modern American system under the crisis conditions of Operation Allied Force. Despite wider bandwidth and increased connectivity, cognitive demands still strained American pilots. They could not always discern in a matter of seconds as they were preparing to launch weapons whether a civilian bus was crossing a bridge at the wrong time or whether refugees were within proximity of military targets.[137] At the same time, with so many approval levels involved, the Americans struggled to reduce the turnaround time for tactical targets from detection, up the chain, and back down again to attack within three hours.[138]

The flipside of too much information for timely processing was filtering to increase efficiency. Yet, even at the level of strategic bombing, where small errors could bring enormous consequences, vital information never made it into the CIA brief for European Command, resulting in the errant American bombing of the Chinese Embassy, Belgrade on May 7.[139] In terms of public diplomacy to explain the failures and highlight the successes of the campaign, General Clark received

135 Ibid. (p. 365–6). Posen (2000: 51–2, 66–7, 71, 75–6) draws largely from press accounts.

136 Byman and Waxman (2000); Posen (2000); Daalder and O'Hanlon (2001); Hosmer (2001); Biddle (2002); Stigler (2002/2003).

137 Clark (2001: 274, 276); Lambeth (2001: 136–7); Nardulli, et al. (2002: 27, 48).

138 Lambeth (2001: 158–61); Nardulli, et al. (2002: 89–91).

139 Clark (2001: 296–7); Lambeth (2001: 144–7).

timely information for his press conferences, but American leaders, let alone the broader group of allies, argued over the content, tone, and frequency of his public appearances.[140]

Problems of information overload and filtering only worsened with the added political complexity of NATO decisions. In their defense White Paper following Operation Allied Force, the French spoke for several allies when they complained about the Americans' stinginess and reticence in distributing operational information to partners who may not have contributed large shares to the military effort in absolute terms but were indeed important for legitimacy.[141] The Allied critique of the leading power's information sharing on targets and plans would haunt the Americans as they fought, detractors would say unilaterally, in Afghanistan and Iraq after 9/11.[142]

On top of all these information management pressures, the United States and its partners had a bargaining incentive to stress the command and control system. Regardless of how sophisticated or capable the information technology was, NATO could push it near the breaking point in order to challenge Milosevic's resolve. Clearly, Western leaders hesitated to raise the stakes by setting off a costly ground war, even one they would eventually win. Accelerating the bombing too quickly might split NATO or convince the Serbs that they nevertheless confronted all-out war and had nothing to lose by resisting through NATO invasion and occupation. On the other hand, stressing the alliance's command and control reminded Milosevic that despite the preferences and political constraints of NATO crisis managers, things could still slip too far: a false move could initiate a chain of events—reactions more than choices—leading to escalation on the ground or in the air that neither side wanted.[143]

Comparing Crisis Series: Berlin and Yugoslavia

In the chicken game of the 1950s, oncoming drivers could create fear in their opponent by making it obviously more difficult to steer their vehicle clear of the center line, in the extreme, throwing their own steering wheel out the window in an obvious bid to win the game. It does not much matter whether the steering was Model T vintage or Formula One, the tactic for convincing the other side to give way remains basically the same. Because leaders hesitate to surrender control permanently, in practice, the ploy is more akin to dangling the wheel out the window. State-of-the-art command and control may change details of the procedure, but in the end, dangling always means operating on the edge, raising the probability of catastrophe in order to win a competition in risk taking and end the crisis on favorable terms.

The dual challenges of overloading and over filtering—navigated under uncertainty and the pressures of surprise—reduce information technology performance during crisis. These suboptimal conditions combine with a perverse incentive to abuse

140 Clark (2001: 272–3, 443); Halberstam (2001: 469).

141 Ministry of Defense, France (1999); Rouleau (1999); Whitney (1999); Peters, et al. (2001: 40–1).

142 Ignatieff (2003); Prestowitz (2003); Chomsky (2004); Bacevich (2005).

143 Hosmer (2001: 93–8).

the system for bargaining leverage and raise chances of failure still further. With regard to the conventional purpose of fixing an adversary's resolve and suggesting an optimal strategy for managing a crisis, information technology appears to be an inadequate tool. Given an advanced information system for collection, analysis, and distribution, it does not follow that a state so endowed will have superior advantage for prevailing in crises.

If the technology cannot be employed directly by its owner to solve the policy problem, this begs the question of whether information systems might be used some other way to improve crisis outcomes. In fact, the role of Secretary General Solana in preserving NATO unity during the coercive bargaining over Kosovo suggests an alternative.

In the weeks leading up to the October 1998 ACTORD, Solana worked for unanimous approval, a necessary condition to engage NATO's military power and legitimacy against Milosevic. Besides extraordinary diplomatic skill, the Secretary General employed two principles to keep NATO together even without official UN sanction. He insisted that NATO's decision to use force have a legal basis, and he, rather than President Clinton or General Clark, took the public lead in executing NATO strategy.[144]

Both of these principles predisposed hawks and doves within NATO to compromise. Insistence on action to prevent massive human rights violations as a general obligation under the UN Charter reassured hesitant NATO countries that they were not surrendering their foreign policy to American power and Clinton administration priorities. If the Americans wanted to bomb Kosovo, rather than corralling the Allies using hard power, at least they were agreeing to craft a legal justification first. In the same vein, with Solana instead of an American representative articulating NATO policy and requesting delegation of authority from NATO heads of state, he provided the service of an honest broker. NATO decisions would not be mere aggregations of national priorities weighted according to the lopsided distribution of power. Solana, fastidiously consulting with all the members, opened the door for deliberation as an alternative to strong arming the Alliance. With Solana facilitating and announcing compromises, the United States could not be sure of obtaining every decision it wanted from NATO, but at the same time, the space allowed for allied rejection or amendments was limited, and the United States could be more confident that the Allies would stick by NATO's plan—after the Solana process—once the stakes increased and the going got tough.

If information process rather than product is shared, technologies operated in common could aid honest brokers in the Solana mode. Building and operating a NATO crisis information system together—not simply passing prefabricated packages through narrow, nationally-based, declassification gates—would promote deliberation by extricating discussions of adversary resolve and appropriate crisis response away from raw, geopolitical asymmetries. Information management procedures could be adapted so that the NATO crisis table was round. Like Solana's consulting, crisis information procedures could invite full participation in the

144 Hendrickson (2002: 245–6, 250–1).

determination of crisis risks and opportunities while at the same time preserving a pragmatic awareness of special resources riding on US support.

"The acid test of policy," Henry Kissinger once reflected, "is its ability to obtain domestic support. This has two aspects: the problem of legitimizing a policy within the governmental apparatus…and that of harmonizing it with the national experience." This dictum from a realist geopolitican has special relevance for international crisis management, when judging the balance of resolve matters as much as calculating the correct balance of power.[145] The next chapter explores a corollary to Kissinger's idea in the context of the Atlantic Alliance. The acid test of international crisis response is its ability to rally NATO even as the bargaining intensifies and adversaries attempt to break NATO resolve. This ability rests on two requirements, legitimizing a policy within the alliance's information management system and harmonizing it with diverse national perspectives of the member states. Despite the work of another astute secretary general, the test was not met during the Iraq crisis of 2002–2003. Information technology was available on a national basis and intelligence on Iraq to an extraordinary degree was declassified across allied boundaries and beyond. The question for the next chapter asks whether, in the case of Iraq, legitimizing and harmonizing through common information infrastructure would have done better than parallel crisis intelligence systems. In the event, national information management generated prodigious amounts of data and analysis but failed to deliver a favorable settlement.

145 Indeed these words were quoted by the famous scholar of international crisis management, Alexander George in one of his last works, *On Foreign Policy: Unfinished Business* (2006: 15).

Chapter 5

Common Assessment and Transatlantic Cooperation: Crisis Management before the War in Iraq

> The ability of the United States to lead its allies and the United Nations depends not only on its unquestioned military power but on its trustworthiness (Whitney [2005: xxvii] in The WMD Mirage).

Careful comparison of crises involving the Western allies over Berlin versus Yugoslavia in the previous chapter highlighted how fundamental political-psychological dilemmas of crisis management recur despite dramatic advances in collection and analysis of intelligence. Even with, or perhaps because of clear superiority in information assets, US leaders still face the urgent requirement to develop a personal rapport with coalition allies and the adversary in order to steer negotiations. Modern computer memory capacity and rapid micro-processing accommodate massive information flows, but these flows, rather than eliminating uncertainty, force leaders to make difficult decisions about how to filter the data and about who should respond to the cues they themselves do not have time to analyze. The persistence of filtering and delegation dilemmas presages imperfect information conditions and strategic surprise. As elaborate as the new systems are, crises still force them to operate under unanticipated circumstances and outside of standard procedures.

A great irony of information age crisis management is that while the enormous amount of data and analysis emerging from state-of-the-art national systems will not make escalation or concession decisions easier, leading nations and especially the United States jealously guard both the data and the networks. Whether or not it revealed the intentions of a crisis adversary, freely shared intelligence might say too much about sources and methods, not just for crisis but for war preparations. In most nations, the hardware and bureaucracy for information management are one and the same for crisis and war, even though as we have seen, the role of information changes across these different phases of conflict.

So it is that for reasons linked to the risks of future war, much cooperation among allies is forgone during crisis. Inefficient information sharing means that sovereign governments with fundamental values in common still struggle to form a common assessment of the threat.[1] The difficulty and unreliability of interpolating future behavior from an adversary's electromagnetic traces implies that the quality of the

1 Müller-Wille (2004); Dempsey (2004).

sharing process matters as much as the volume and fidelity of what is transferred. Friction within coalitions results not so much from the margin of data held by one country over the others but from mistrust engendered in debates where officials each cling tight to exclusive sources and methods.[2] These same sources and methods may support a hidden agenda, which prompts fear among coalition players who are caught between an inscrutable adversary and a powerful leader capable of hijacking the group's "multilateral" response.

At present the United States has mustered all instruments, including military force, to fight global terrorist groups. It will likely encounter militarized crises with state sponsors of terror in the years ahead at locations where it needs to win the conflict but can ill afford another drain on its armed forces.[3] As of now, there is only one previous crisis to show in the context of this global conflict how outcomes might have been different had intelligence sharing between the leading power and the international community been different.

The crisis during fall 2002 and winter 2003 over how to neutralize the weapons of mass destruction (WMD) and terrorist threat from Iraq ended with destruction of Saddam Hussein's regime, but the costs of the invasion and its aftermath handicapped military enforcement against other proliferators. Russia and China notwithstanding, disarming Saddam would have been easier if the United States had secured beforehand greater cooperation from France and Germany. By January 2003, there would have been a NATO bloc on the Security Council, consisting of the United States, the United Kingdom, France, Germany, Spain, and Bulgaria (as a NATO invitee from 2002) that would have proven tough to resist, as it had over Kosovo in 1999. In particular, the postwar costs would have been less burdensome for the United States if France and Germany had chosen to set positive examples for financial aid and training missions to Iraq rather than raising objections.[4]

Iraq, as explained in Chapter 3, provides a recent case in which suboptimal crisis outcomes for the United States coincided with the old "lock-and-key" mode of information sharing. This association does not by itself prove that exclusive information technologies and layered declassification procedures caused the

2 Emphasis on the sharing process has marked efforts to improve cooperation between intelligence agencies within the executive branch, and across the executive and legislative branches of the US government (Pincus 2005; Whitney 2005: 354–7, 652–3, and other passages reprinted from report of the *Commission on the Intelligence Capabilities of United States Regarding Weapons of Mass Destruction*, Washington, D.C., March 31, 2005). A recent study on inter-organizational trust in the *American Political Science Review* recorded stronger coefficients for perception related process variables over interest gaps among disparate stakeholders deliberating watershed policy in California and Washington (Leach and Sabatier 2005). "The paramount importance of stakeholders' perceptions of the fairness and legitimacy of the process (the variables *consensus norms* and *procedural fairness*) parallels the finding of Hibbing and Theiss-Morse (2001,2002) that people's attitudes toward government are driven primarily by their satisfaction with *how* government operates, not by its track record of producing agreeable policies" (p. 500).

3 See the assessment of British and American experts in McCausland and Stuart (2006), for example, pp. 127–31, 155–6.

4 Gordon and Trainor (2006: 457–60).

transatlantic meltdown. Yet, many analyses of the Iraq Crisis and the rupture in the Atlantic Alliance focus attention on the irreconcilable motives of an imperious United States or a conniving France. At the same time, very few questioned that the European states and America still face common vulnerabilities from the terror campaign unleashed by Islamic extremists. Almost regardless of the charges hurled at the French or American leaders, there remains agreement among governments as well as pundits that West Europeans and North Americans are, after all, the long-term guardians of liberal constitutionalism and market-based economics.[5] Peoples on both sides of the Atlantic have much to gain from an international order that reflects both of these innovations. Why then, it might be asked, could sophisticated states not get the intermediate steps right?

The answer so far has implied that one side or the other, by accident of leadership or the unintended consequences of indulgence in the easy life, turned out to be less sophisticated than expected.[6] Certainly, an alternative reply is possible: the national security establishments among core NATO countries could not agree on means to pursue their common interests because intergovernmental institutions were not optimized for producing a genuine social choice during crisis. Specifically, the information age brought new images and new signal intercepts to national intelligence without changing the way such information was shared among allies. Immersed in a complex crisis, reliant on the lock-and-key mode, and denied knowledge of how their partners were massaging raw data, sophisticated states with compatible objectives lost their way in disarming Iraq.

The Iraq Case

Because there are few clear cases to show the importance of different intelligence sharing regimes among coalition crisis actors, the research method must shift now from the structured-focused comparison of previous chapters to idiographic counterfactual analysis.[7] Just two international crises have occurred with the US high-bandwidth network in place that involved intensive information sharing:

5 BBC News (2005d); Hill (2005). See, also, several of the analyses in Andrews (2005), although many authors there remain pessimistic about transatlantic gaps on *how*, if not whether, to promote a liberal-democratic international order.

6 Depending on whom they wished to blame, analysts attributed mistakes on Iraq to Jacque Chirac, Gerhard Schroeder, or George Bush as these leaders attempted to cover one weakness or another in domestic politics. With respect to blunders brought on by the easy life, American critics spotlighted France's profitable relationship with Iraq and the financial gains to be made for French companies once US-backed sanctions against Iraq were lifted. For their part, European critics pointed out that the United States was prone to overreaction because it had not experienced terrorism or wartime destruction on its home ground, nor had it suffered the same immigration pressures from the greater Middle East. Gordon and Shapiro (2004) balanced criticism against all the primary players; Shawcross (2004) tilted against Chirac; Hiro (2004) tilted against Bush; Kagan (2003) criticized Europe's ease in enjoying a good life under the US security umbrella; and Serfaty (2004) noted the intoxicating effects of America's easy life prior to September 11.

7 Tetlock and Belkin (1996: 7–8).

Kosovo in 1999 and Iraq 2003.[8] Of the two, Iraq was less successful in terms of keeping the coalition together, so it is relevant to explore what would have happened had NATO allies in the crisis performed their deliberations with the advantage of a common information infrastructure designed to manage all three major functions in the intelligence process: collection, analysis, and dissemination. In the event, when it came to judging the magnitude and imminence of the threat from Saddam Hussein, the Americans and the Europeans relied on the antiquated, nationally-based lock-and-key model, which severely restricted joint activity in all three areas.

In order to see how the outcome for US leadership might have improved with an allied crisis management system, subsidiary research questions should follow a disciplined plan. For example, this study asks about plausible changes flowing from a NATO system, not a utopian situation center for all democracies or a single facility for all permanent members of the Security Council. NATO's fifty-seven year record of institutionalized cooperation on matters of collective defense and its achievement in the struggle for interoperability of allied military forces makes the counterfactual of common assessment easier to contemplate.[9]

Starting with a plausible hypothetical lays the groundwork for the next criterion of counterfactual analysis, the minimal rewrite rule. During the fifteen years since the end of the Cold War, NATO has extended common infrastructure projects to include the development of an Alliance Ground Surveillance (AGS) system that could have crisis management as well as tactical military significance.[10] The vast majority of circumstances surrounding the Iraq case do not have to be altered in order to accommodate a common collection and analysis system of meaningful capability installed among several of the main protagonists: especially the United States, the United Kingdom, Spain, France, and Germany. The causal linkages flowing from a different information system to improved crisis outcomes for the United States and its partners must also be cotenable with the mass of historical information on the case, including genuine conflicts of interest and perceptions regarding the future of Iraq. As Tetlock and Belkin (1996) advise, one of the most effective ways to demonstrate plausibility, minimal rewrite, and cotenability is to make observable projections based on the counterfactual. If, for example, the political benefits of common intelligence would have come from a richer process of deliberation, we should find evidence that key allies, despite the extraordinary declassification that did occur, still felt as if they were snubbed and left in the dark by the United States.[11]

8 For the breakdown of Israeli-Palestinian negotiations at Wye River Plantation in 2000, the United States was a mediator rather than a crisis actor. During the EP-3 Spy Plane crisis with China in 2001, few partners were intensely involved on the US side. Of course, in both of these cases any sharing by the United States was done according to lock-and-key rather than common assessment mode. Counterfactuals are the only way to vary the independent variable for testing our hypothesis (King, Keohane, Verba 1994).

9 Systematic criteria for counterfactual analysis are elaborated in Tetlock and Belkin (1996: Ch. 1) and Chapter 3 in this book.

10 NATO (2004).

11 Indeed, evidence of this nature does turn up. See, for example, Gordon and Shapiro (2004: 135–6), Woodward (2004: 312), and De Villepin (42–5, 53–4).

The emphasis of the counterfactual on information processing means that this study will track the crisis with respect to two parallel sequences. The first follows the classic set of decision nodes, the tactical concessions and escalation maneuvers that led ultimately to final breakdown and war in March 2003. The second sequence spotlights information transfers during the crisis among the state players attempting to address the threat posed by Saddam Hussein. With few exceptions, states transferred but without relaxing their guard on national sources and methods; these transactions are where the counterfactual asks us to initiate a historical alteration and trace likely consequences. In March 2003, the Iraq crisis ended in a failure of deliberation, that is, without any real synthesis of allied views.[12] As the strongest power, the United States pushed its perspective on the problem with the greatest force, and incompatible approaches simply fell by the wayside. This case study explores how the resolution of distinct allied positions and the social choice by the coalition might have been different had those players belonging to NATO operated a common technical intelligence service for crisis management.

Iraq and WMD: September 2002

Several opponents of the invasion have concluded that President Bush chose war with Iraq soon after the American military victory over the Taliban in Afghanistan.[13] In his January 2002 State of the Union address, Bush identified Iraq as a member of the Axis of Evil, a loose grouping of states distinguished by development programs for chemical, biological, and nuclear weapons and links to international terrorism. Iraq was not as far along as North Korea in the nuclear field, but its record of aggression against Iran in 1980, against Kuwait in 1990 and 1994, against UN mandated inspectors in 1998, against US and UK air forces patrolling internationally sanctioned no-fly zones, and even against the first President Bush after his retirement in 1993 put Iraq at the top of the list.[14]

Indeed, Bob Woodward later reported that the younger Bush asked Central Command's Tommy Franks to review invasion plans for Iraq while Afghanistan was still in full swing.[15] Deputy Secretary of Defense Paul Wolfowitz advocated military means to topple Saddam Hussein well before the fall of 2002, and by August both Bush and Vice-President Cheney, almost in defiance of Old-Guard balance of power Republicans, spoke publicly as if a US military strike against Iraq were all but inevitable.

Yet, something changed between the President's retreat to his Crawford, Texas ranch and his address to the United Nations on September 12. Woodward attributes the shift to a sober one-on-one intervention by Secretary of State Colin Powell; others

12 Payne (2005–2006).

13 Hersch (2003); Kessler (2003); Dreyfuss and Vest (2004); Kaufmann (2004); Pollack (2004); BBC News (2005b).

14 Gordon and Trainor (2006: 131).

15 Woodward (2004: 8).

give more weight to Prime Minister Tony Blair's visit on September 7.[16] Both men urged that the United States take its case against Saddam Hussein to the international community and the Security Council, not because of any legal requirement under the UN Charter, nor because either man doubted the severity of the threat posed by Saddam Hussein, but because both dreaded the consequences if Saddam were removed by an illegitimate war. Without legitimacy that the UN process could afford, the United States, despite its military might, could bog down in reconstruction after the combat phase, or it might face even more resistance from its partners in the next international crisis. Transnational problems on the horizon beyond Iraq, ranging from nuclear proliferation, to terrorist networks, to global economic recovery would be far more difficult to solve if remaining good will and trust toward US leadership were compromised.[17]

Avoiding illegitimacy is not the same as avoiding war, but once Bush promised to work with the Security Council and seek the appropriate resolutions, true crisis dynamics kicked in. Regardless of what occurred at the United Nations, US officials could expect widespread public opprobrium against the US war threat and a coterie of implacable opinion makers who would never concede that US diplomacy was anything but a sham. On the other hand, it would have been exceedingly risky to actually conduct *faux* diplomacy—without any chance of a peaceful resolution—because other countries could punish the United States worse than if it simply went to war on the basis of previously violated UN resolutions.

Moreover, the reactions of various parties to the crisis indicated that peace was a real possibility. Hardliners in the US administration led by Vice-President Cheney judged that the safest course was to forcibly remove Saddam Hussein from power. They genuinely worried that a UN resolution or even a sequence of resolutions would be crafted to let some Security Council members rationalize away the threat and perpetually postpone the day of reckoning for Hussein's Iraq. On the other side of the argument, Prime Minster Blair also saw the threat from Iraqi WMD, but his support for Bush's muscular policy met with skepticism in Britain. Facing the prospect of a Labour rebellion in Parliament, Blair could not commit British resources to the US-led operation without a domestic vote of confidence, and he was likely to lose that vote unless diplomacy was first given a genuine opportunity.[18]

Finally, President Bush himself appealed to several different audiences, including the US Congress, where the Democratic Party held a majority in the Senate, and

---

16 Woodward (2004: 149–53, 174–9); Ramesh (2003: 25); Bluth (2004: 879); Gordon and Trainor (2006: 71–2).

17 In a manuscript for the Ridgway Center's Working Group on Preventive Military Intervention, Rodger Payne (2005–6) argues that the Bush administration was aware of the dangers of a preventive war strategy and sought to impose deliberative requirements on the application of what they called preemptive war in the National Security Strategy (September 2002). For more on deliberative principles among sovereigns, see Payne and Samhat (2004).

18 Ramesh (2003: 26); Gordon and Shapiro (2004: 107); Woodward (2004: 102–3). On the eve of war, March 18, 2003, the vote in British Parliament finally did take place with a record high 139 MP's resisting Blair. Nevertheless, after the UN process, the House of Commons voted 2–1 behind war, overcoming continuing negative public opinion and the resignation of Blair's leader in Commons, Robin Cook (Ramesh 2003: 46).

allied governments in the Middle East which would have to live with a vengeful Saddam Hussein if US coercion failed to remove or disarm him. In each case, these groups responded as if they believed the United States would accept peaceful disarmament of Iraq rather than wage an illegitimate war. The real prospect of peace moved the conflict closer to the crisis model, placing familiar limits on how the United States could employ its instruments of military and information power and granting Saddam Hussein room to maneuver as he sought to split the coalition of states arrayed against him.

Besides triggering the "chicken game" dilemmas of international crisis, Bush's UN address on September 12 also started the clock on Iraq's weapons of mass destruction.[19] In the end, a legal standard would not determine whether Iraq was punished, but the quasi-legal process set in motion by Bush's promise to "work with the UN Security Council for the necessary resolutions" moved inexorably toward a conclusion of the conflict one way or the other.[20] Limited time meant extraordinary pressure—on the United States, Iraq, and major players on the Security Council—to abandon the status quo and enter the sequence of tactical maneuvers involved in crisis bargaining.

It is still possible that President Bush preferred several likely war scenarios over most plausible peace settlements, but this does not make the Iraq crisis a sham in the same way that Adolph Hitler portrayed his conflict with Poland.[21] Particularly after Powell and the allies overcame objections of the conservative hawks in late August 2002 and Bush opened the question to the United Nations, only a certain kind of war, sanctioned by an overwhelming majority in the international community, was preferable to peaceful disarmament. War was nevertheless likely because the administration committed itself, in the event no UN-brokered settlement were reached, to wage a unilateral war in no one's best interests. In other words, as in many cases studied in the past, a costly war was this crisis' *ultima ratio.* What Bush extracted from the bargaining on Iraq, despite the United States' clear military and information superiority, came perilously close to the suboptimal unilateral war outcome. The disappointing crisis performance illustrates why it is worthwhile inquiring about processes, such as information sharing among allies, that might have improved the result.

Crisis Maneuvers

Once the US challenge was made before the UN General Assembly, most observers could anticipate the basic stages of the crisis to follow. There would have to be some sort of resolution addressing Iraq's WMD capability and stipulating the steps Saddam Hussein would have to take in order to remove the punishment of sanctions as well as the threat of war. Hussein would have to be given a certain amount of time to declare his weapons status. Verification involving more intrusive inspections

19 Robert Pauly and Tom Lansford (2005: 59) called it the opening of the formal campaign to oust Saddam. See also, the weight given to September 12 in Fallows (2004).

20 Bush (2002).

21 Lebow (1981).

would have to be arranged. Inspectors would need time to complete their work. The Security Council would take time to evaluate inspectors' reports and determine whether Iraq's level of cooperation was sufficient for the inspectors to continue their disarmament mission. It was not clear precisely how long each of these stages would take, but most of the players, particularly the United States and France, knew them to be finite. Hussein may have felt that he could stretch the timeline by cooperating just enough to isolate the United States, but after Bush's commitments on September 12 and the subsequent US military build-up, he could not put off concessions forever.[22]

US military preparations in the Persian Gulf and the Mediterranean ramped up in December 2002 and January 2003, deploying some 200,000 US forces alongside 44,000 British by the end of February.[23] The troops could go into Iraq or back home, but Bush was unlikely to order them to freeze in place merely as a guarantor of agonizingly deliberate inspections. When the timeline could be stretched no further, Hussein may have hoped to discourage the Americans by forcing them to act alone, and until Blair received his vote of support from Parliament on March 18, the Iraqi dictator could still succeed, if not in saving his regime, at cornering the Americans into paying a steep price.

The first main hurdle—the adoption of a final opportunity from the Security Council demanding that Iraq surrender all chemical, biological, and nuclear weapons, dismantle long-range missiles, and discontinue related programs—vanished in dramatic fashion when all fifteen Council members, including Syria, backed resolution 1441. The resolution was powerfully worded, recalling a long list of ongoing violations by Iraq, placing the issue squarely in Chapter VII, and promising that if international peace and security were not restored due to partial accounting or less than immediate cooperation, Iraq would face enforcement in terms of "serious consequences."[24]

In fact, shortly after the resolution passed, Bush appeared with his secretary of state, thanking Powell and praising him for engineering the unanimous vote supporting such firm terms for Saddam Hussein.[25] Yet, the credibility of the American threat in terms of both gathering forces in the Gulf and the hardening political will of the international community was undermined by other aspects of the UN process.

Unlike the first Bush administration before the 1991 Gulf War, George W. Bush's advisers saw the 2003 crisis as a last chance not just for Saddam Hussein but for the United Nations. The younger President Bush decided to go to the US Congress sooner rather than later. The domestic vote in his favor would underscore his promise to the General Assembly that if the UN Security Council did not act against the long brewing WMD threat from Iraq, the United States still would. Despite several questions from Democratic senators about the circumstantial nature of evidence on Iraq's WMD and Hussein's al Qaeda connections, both houses of Congress

22 Gordon and Shapiro (2004: 8–9).

23 Woodward (2004: 328).

24 The text of resolution 1441 is available at www.un.int/usa/sres-iraq.htm.

25 Woodward (2004: 226).

provided Bush with substantial majorities: 296–133 in the House and 77–23 in the Democratically controlled Senate.[26]

Had the Democrats resisted Bush at this point in the crisis, mid-October 2002, the bargaining phase might well have gone to Saddam Hussein, and Bush would have been faced with a stark choice between political defeat and war with neither domestic nor international support. A similar argument subsequently persuaded Syria. As the only Arab state on the Security Council, Syria could back the consensus on 1441 as a means to shock Saddam Hussein into negotiating seriously, perhaps prompting the kind of concessions that would preserve peace.

Unfortunately, Hussein, simply by following open sources on the debate, could see that many votes in the US Congress and at the UN were actually declarations against war. If he had any doubts, the length and drama of the resolution negotiations, nearly eight weeks from Bush's UN address to the November 8 vote and France driving a hard bargain till the very end, almost seemed designed to dispel them.

To be sure, Hussein had to avoid embarrassing the reluctant members of the coalition by defiantly withholding *all* cooperation. Yet, with France insisting on a Security Council interpretation of whether Hussein's response at any given time constituted full cooperation, as long as France commanded diplomatic support of permanent members Russia and China along with NATO countries like Germany, resolution 1441 might as well have been an invitation for Hussein to create mischief inside the coalition.[27]

Iraq's 12,000 page report of December 8, 2002 arrived to the Security Council on time, but no one asserted that it fully accounted for all of the prohibited weapons systems encompassed by the string of resolutions referenced in 1441.[28] Four tons of VX gas, officially acknowledged but never controlled before UN Special Committee (UNSCOM) inspectors left under duress in 1998, essentially disappeared without a trace. Similarly unsupported claims about the unilateral destruction of other chemical and biological weapons disturbed not just US officials but Hans Blix, former director of the International Atomic Energy Agency (IAEA) and now head of the United Nations Monitoring, Verification and Inspection Commission (UNMOVIC).[29]

Blix saw UNMOVIC as the last hope for peace in the Gulf. From his point of view, Iraqi resistance in the late-1990s was a positive sign that inspections could be an effective means of disarming the dictator. With the provisions of 1441, UNMOVIC could penetrate and dismantle the Iraqi weapons complex far more efficiently.

For its part, France balanced the risk that UNMOVIC could not completely eliminate Saddam's WMD against the likely price of doing away with the Iraqi state, which included ethnic violence in that country, expanding anti-western

26 Woodward (2004: 193–99; 203–4).

27 Gordon and Shapiro (2004: 113).

28 Head of the UN inspection team, Hans Blix, responded to inaccuracies and omissions in the report, saying, "An opportunity was missed" (Purdum 2003: 65). This was strong language given that 1441 was passed as a final opportunity for Iraq to come back into compliance. French experts also deemed the Iraqi record incomplete (Gordon and Shapiro 2004: 116).

29 Secretary Powell referred to UNMOVIC's early reports in his February 5, 2003 address to the Security Council (Powell 2003).

extremism throughout the region, and greater incentives for WMD proliferation in places like Iran and North Korea.[30] Though France did not succeed in inserting an explicit requirement in 1441 for a subsequent resolution to legitimize the war, it did insist on language that included formal evaluation of Iraq's cooperation with UNMOVIC beyond any omissions in its December declaration. As American and later British troops streamed into the Gulf, the crisis now came down to whether or not UNMOVIC's progress reports implied full cooperation on the part of Iraq.

Through all the weeks of the crisis, the period that saw the greatest likelihood of the Security Council moving together, with no outcries against the war's legitimacy, passed between January 27 and February 9. Prior to this period, before Blix's first report to the Council on Iraq's biological and chemical weapons, France maneuvered with Germany and Russia to stretch the time available to UNMOVIC.[31] Eleven undeclared chemical warheads had been found in Iraq—a technical violation of 1441, which referenced all related equipment—but they were empty of toxic agents, so they could be accepted as preliminary evidence that the inspectors were making progress after all. On January 20, after a ministerial-level meeting of the Security Council on terrorism, French foreign minister Dominique de Villepin, who held a press conference as then-serving president of the Council, flatly rejected the idea that emerging difficulties with the inspections were sufficient to make 1441's war track inevitable.[32] Powell interpreted De Villepin's "there is no reason to choose the worst of all solutions" and "we shall stand by them (principles) to the end" as a warning that, barring a dramatic change in the status quo, France and likeminded states would attempt to block military enforcement of 1441. By contrast, the secretary along with other Bush administration officials had been staking his own diplomatic claim on the Sunday talk shows that time was running out, and unless there were dramatic concessions by Iraq to rescue the inspections and disarmament process, the United States, backed by the international community on the basis of 1441, would soon intervene.[33]

With the coalition against Saddam Hussein crumbling before the first UNMOVIC report under 1441, US Secretary of Defense Donald Rumsfeld, voicing frustration and determination to prevent Hussein from escaping yet again, fired back across the Atlantic his infamous repudiation of France and Germany as "Old Europe." However, in reminding Hussein that plenty of countries, enough countries, stood with the United States to make the war threat credible, Rumsfeld raised the stakes of the crisis even higher, now placing NATO unity on the table.

Such was the atmosphere when Blix and the IAEA's Mohamed ElBaradei made their much awaited appearance before the Security Council on January 27. His reputation for consummate professionalism notwithstanding, Blix's report sounded as if he preferred UNMOVIC rather than the United States to play the decisive role in defanging Saddam Hussein. The yawning gap between the United States and its allies was a problem because it made Hussein less likely to actually comply with

30 De Villepin (2004: 30–8).

31 Woodward (2004: 266–7).

32 De Villepin (2004: 35–6).

33 Gordon and Shapiro (2004: 122).

the provisions of 1441. In a phrase that was bound to raise the heat on the dictator to meet inspector demands, Blix warned that "Iraq appears not to have come to a genuine acceptance—not even today—of the disarmament, which was demanded of it and which it needs to carry out to win the confidence of the world and to live in peace."[34]

However, with troop levels rising quickly in the region surrounding Iraq, US aggressiveness threatened to undermine UNMOVIC as well. Despite several concerns involving large, unaccounted for quantities of chemical and biological agents and prohibited long-range missile programs, Blix asserted that "Iraq has decided in principle to provide cooperation on process" and reminded the Council that since the readmission of inspectors, UNMOVIC's capacity has been on the rise. Why rush the war, France, Germany, and Russia would subsequently argue, when Blix's new and improved "inspection apparatus" was now operating "at the disposal of the Security Council"?[35]

For the United States, the answer had something to do with maintaining more than 200,000 troops in a high state of readiness to launch an invasion of Iraq, perhaps in temperatures of 110 degrees or higher if the attack were to occur during summer. In the language of resolution 1441 agreed to by all fifteen Security Council members back in November, Iraq had failed to provide a currently accurate, full, and complete declaration of its WMD activities, and by Blix's impartial accounting, it had failed the standard of full, immediate, and unconditional cooperation laid down in action paragraph 9.[36]

Legal and international scholars still debate whether the promise of "serious consequences" in 1441 was sufficient to sanction war after Blix's January 27 report.[37] In their book-length explication of what went wrong on both sides of the transatlantic divide, Philip Gordon and Jeremy Shapiro reported that French officials understood the consequence of excluding any specific requirement for a second war resolution from 1441. Persuading the United States on legal grounds became much less feasible, and political-strategic arguments came more to the fore.[38] Especially after Blix voiced his continuing concerns on January 27, weight of the argument shifted toward the perceived magnitude of the threat from Iraqi WMD and the perceived risks of neutralizing them.

So profound was the change in terrain that the bickering allies actually exchanged positions on the question of a second resolution before the month of February was out. The United States, concerned about the risks of making war without the legitimizing presence of the British, eventually acquiesced to Prime Minister Blair's

34 The text of Blix's remarks is available among other places at www.un.org/Depts/unmovic/Bx27.htm.

35 Ibid.

36 Reference the text of resolution 1441 at www.unint/usa/sres-iraq.htm.

37 Bush administration officials argued that war was legal under resolution 1441. Dominique de Villepin and later UN Secretary General Koffi Annan maintained that the invasion of Iraq by a US-led coalition had been illegitimate. For a legal argument against the war, see Kramer and Michalowski (2005). For criticism of the legal brief against the United States, see Trachtenberg (2005: 213–24).

38 Gordon and Shapiro (2004: 120).

request for a second resolution. By that time, the French had abandoned the legal prohibition. On February 21, French Ambassador to the United States David Levitte met privately with Deputy National Security Adviser Stephen Hadley to press the case that if the United States decided to go, it would be best for the international community if it did not attempt to isolate France—or humiliate France—by insisting upon a second resolution.[39]

As legal strictures were harder to apply after the UNMOVIC reports, both the French and the US sides made urgent attempts in late-January and early-February to frame the strategic threat posed by Iraq. In response to Secretary Rumsfeld cleaving Europe in two, German Foreign Minister Joschka Fischer protested that Old Europe was not creating a problem. It was making a "constructive contribution," offering a corrective to US misapprehensions of the strategic situation.[40] However, on January 30, France and Germany's partners in the European Union reminded all parties that Jacque Chirac and Gerhard Schroeder could not claim to be exercising Common Foreign Policy even for traditional Europe. Countries like Spain, Great Britain, Italy, Denmark, and Portugal also brought much of New Europe with them. New members and aspirants to NATO and the European Union signed on to either the so-called Group of Eight letter of January 30 or the subsequent Vilnius Group (Seven) solidarity message with the United States that came out soon after Colin Powell's February 5 presentation to the Security Council.[41] Just before that speech, on February 3, Blair's government released yet another dossier to parliament, this time titled "Iraq: Its Infrastructure of Concealment, Deception, and Intimidation."[42]

With much of Europe gathering behind him, Powell took the global stage and for two hours held the world's attention as he presented the US brief against Iraq. Seated directly behind Powell in the Security Council chamber was US ambassador to the United States John Negroponte and a rather stern Director of Central Intelligence George Tenant. Back in October 1962, Adlai Stevenson's presentation on Soviet missile installations had drawn the attention of delegates to enlarged easels at the side of the chamber, so some stood up and others craned from their seats to have a better view. By contrast, Powell, flanked by Tenet, commanded from the center, the images and the sound recordings whirling around his presence.

For all the diplomatic gravity and high-tech wizardry, evidence presented on February 5 was circumstantial rather than determinative: there were no stockpiles, samples, or confessions of usable WMD. Nevertheless, even if what was said could support multiple interpretations, *who* said it left little doubt. Secretary Powell, the reluctant warrior, the perceived moderate who had counseled patience and multilateralism against Iraqi intransigence, now committed the United States to a stark and rapidly worsening strategic conception.

39 Gordon and Shapiro (2004: 148).

40 Purdum (2003: 67); BBC News (2003d).

41 Pauly and Lansford (2005: 94). Gordon and Shapiro (2004: 133) explain that Chirac's fury was in part due to his realization that written acceptance of the US presentation had been composed before Powell actually gave his address.

42 Hiro (2004: 131).

Immediately after Powell concluded, the international community held its fire, taking time to study the secretary's revelations and perhaps waiting to see which countries would remain unpersuaded after the American peroration. Woodward later reported that longtime Saudi ambassador to the United States Prince Bandar believed that Chirac might shift after Powell's performance, return to his line of early-January, and begin coordinating French contributions for a coalition war against Saddam.[43] On February 6, the BBC reported De Villepin's public offer of Mirage jet fighters in the event of war in an article titled, "France Tread's Carefully on Iraq," and on February 7, Chirac had a respectful phone conversation with Bush.[44] Chirac urged Bush to consider a Saudi proposal that would allow Saddam to go into exile in order to avoid war and pointed out that if war came despite attempts to avoid it, France and the United States should work together on Iraqi reconstruction. Bush, in turn, thanked Chirac for sharing French intelligence and allowed that their opposed positions on the war could both be moral.

Yet, the next opportunity after Powell's speech for better allied coordination on Iraq fell flat, and the rhetoric supporting French and American views never recovered. It seemed to spiral down into greater, more acrimonious discord until well after the war. At an annual ministers meeting on security policy held February 7–9 in Munich, Secretary of Defense Rumsfeld began in the afterglow of Powell's call for unity, softening his remarks on Old Europe and diminishing the present American disputes with France and Germany by placing them in context with larger achievements of postwar transatlantic cooperation. Then, of course, he proceeded to press the US vision of strategic challenges confronting the allies. In front of the press, in English, and in obvious exasperation, German Foreign Minister Fischer broke the momentum, "Excuse me! I am not convinced."[45] A short time later on February 10, Chirac invited Gerhard Schroeder and Vladimir Putin to Paris in order to reiterate, jointly, that, Powell's evidence not withstanding, none of his information justified war and that Iraq should be disarmed peacefully through continued inspections.[46] That same day, Iraq finally approved UN overflights of suspect facilities using American, French, and Russian spy planes.[47]

These events heralded an unremitting assault on the US position. On February 14, Hans Blix and Mohamed ElBaredai gave their second formal report to the Security Council. Though there were 8500 liters of anthrax still unaccounted for, Blix's main points validated Iraqi cooperation.[48] He directly questioned Powell's interpretation of the US imagery and noted that governments with large intelligence assets could facilitate the inspectors' task. He implied that with the cooperation of national intelligence agencies and the Iraqis themselves, the time required for peaceful disarmament of Iraq would not be long. In accordance with the basic position of France, Germany, and Russia, the inspectors should be granted more time—war was

43 Woodward (2004: 313).

44 Coomarasamy (2003); Woodward (2004: 313).

45 Gordon and Shapiro (2004: 135–6); Shawcross (2004: 126).

46 Woodward (2004: 315).

47 Pauly and Lansford (2005: 93).

48 Hiro (2004: 144).

not necessary. In his response for the other Security Council members, De Villepin said as much and received a surprising round of applause inside the chamber.[49]

During the weekend following Blix's second, more optimistic report, massive anti-war protests rocked world cities around the Atlantic community. London, Madrid, Rome, and New York saw hundreds of thousands of demonstrators essentially amplifying De Villepin's message: nothing, including all the US arguments presented on February 5, justified war.[50] Meanwhile, the transatlantic fissure highlighted earlier by Rumsfeld opened even wider as France, Germany, and Belgium blocked a US inspired move to have NATO send defensive equipment such as Patriot anti-missile batteries and biological-chemical decontamination units to Turkey.[51] The French saw this as an underhanded way to have NATO support a US-led war against Iraq. Not surprisingly, Turkey saw the issue differently, petitioning for the NATO protection under Article IV of the alliance treaty but not going so far as to permit US invasion forces a staging ground for a northern thrust against Baghdad.[52] It took until February 16, time enough to reroute the military preparations from the Atlantic Council through NATO's Defense Planning Committee, which does not include France, before the alliance could cooperate on a seemingly basic issue of common defense.[53]

By this time, there were small signs of relief from what had been a punishing couple of weeks for the US position. At an emergency summit, the European Union managed to declare a unified position on Iraq that bridged the French and American views. It echoed the language of resolution 1441, firmly stating that Iraq had one final chance to disarm, but it also noted that war was not inevitable and that inspectors should be given more time to complete their work.[54] Chirac had done his best to leverage EU agreement against Central and Eastern European states supporting the United States, haranguing them for juvenile misbehavior as he left the Brussels summit, but New Europe deftly fought back, endorsing the EU position while roundly criticizing Chirac. Charges of international bullying and arrogance during the Iraq weapons debate had been until then reserved for the Americans. Anti-Chirac reaction from countries like Poland, the Czech Republic, Bulgaria, and Romania bought badly needed cover for the hawks on Iraq. As the United States, Britain, and Spain introduced their "second UN resolution" on February 24, it appeared there might still be a chance to turn the tables and isolate France, which explains why Ambassador Levitte around this time privately encouraged the United States to fight, if it must, *without* publicly broaching a follow-on resolution.[55]

Blix's third report for the Security Council, completed on March 1, featured more impressive examples of unprecedented cooperation, including site visits and missile destruction. Some items found did not clearly violate resolution 1441, but Iraq was

49 Shawcross (2004: 138).
50 BBC News (2003a).
51 Marcus (2003); Pauly and Lansford (2005: 97).
52 BBC News (2003e).
53 Pond (2005: 45–6); BBC News (2003b); Gordon and Trainor (2006: 113).
54 BBC News (2003c).
55 Ibid.; Gordon and Shapiro (2004: 147–8); Burrough, et al. (2004).

unilaterally destroying them anyway.[56] Blix now termed the regime's cooperation "proactive," and gave an upbeat assessment of UNMOVIC's chances for success if only the inspectors were given more time.[57] France, Germany, and Russia stood firm on the Security Council against any resolution that would legitimize an Anglo-American invasion. Also, on March 1, the Turkish parliament rejected an enormous US aid package and narrowly failed to approve access for the US Army 4th Infantry Division, which sought a direct route to northern Iraq.[58]

With over 200,000 troops in the region and General Franks ready to begin combat operations, the US group was anxious to force a conclusion to the debate, as President Bush would later say, to force everyone to lay their cards on the table. On March 7, the same day that Blix formally presented his report to the Council, British Foreign Minister Jack Straw introduced an amended second resolution, giving Iraq ten days to fully comply with outstanding provisions, so-called disarmament benchmarks based on 1441.[59] There ensued a scramble for votes on the Security Council. The United States, Great Britain, Spain, and Bulgaria supported the resolution. Six rotating members on the council had not yet committed their representatives: Chile, Mexico, Angola, Cameroon, Ghana, and Pakistan. If the US-led faction could sway five of the six, France would find itself in the nightmare scenario that had motivated Ambassador Levitte's early effort to forestall the second resolution. Assuming Russia abstained in order to preserve Vladimir Putin's working relationship with President Bush, France would either have to admit diplomatic defeat or cast a lone and ultimately humiliating veto.[60]

To prevent this from happening, Foreign Minister De Villepin countered US lobbying by barnstorming the African capitals. On March 10, Chirac administered the *coup de grace*, implying that France would veto this second resolution "under any circumstances," thus making it impossible for the swinging six to deliver a UN mandate for the United States.[61] By March 14, it appeared that French diplomacy would in fact succeed against the arguments of the United States, Britain, Spain, and even Prime Minister Koizumi of Japan, who braved opinion polls showing 80 percent of the Japanese public against war without UN backing to openly support the US position.[62]

On Sunday, March 16, Bush, Blair, and Aznar were hosted at a Portuguese airbase in the Azores for a one-day coalition summit to coordinate the last diplomatic steps before disarming Iraq by force. The threshold to avoid war now ratcheted upward: after agonizing over the significance of Iraqi half-measures through three

---

56 The text of Hans Blix's summary report before the Security Council on March 7, 2003 is reprinted at www.mideastweb.org/log/archives/00000039.htm.

57 Hiro (2004: 158).

58 Gordon and Shapiro (2004: 149).

59 Ramesh (2003: 37); Gordon and Shapiro (2004: 152).

60 If combat operations proceeded on a 9–4 vote, brushing aside France's veto and drawing abstention from China and Russia, France would have appeared out of step with the world community and too weak-willed to meet its obligations as a permanent member of the Security Council (Ibid.: 147).

61 Ibid.: 152; Shawcross (2004: 147–8).

62 Scanlon (2003).

UNMOVIC reports, the United States, as leader of the coalition and as the country most threatened by Iraqi WMD, would be convinced of Iraq's full cooperation under resolution 1441 only if Saddam Hussein left Iraq. Meanwhile, an Iraqi newspaper run by Saddam's son, Odai, taunted the coalition while "well-intentioned powers in the world" led by France wrecked the British benchmarking strategy. On the evening of March 17, with the second resolution withdrawn from consideration, Bush declared that the only acceptable benchmark for avoiding "serious consequences" was Saddam's exit within 48 hours.[63]

At this moment, the die was cast, and the crisis phase of the dispute over Iraqi WMD abruptly ended. The only remaining consideration for the war to come was whether Blair could win parliamentary approval to engage some 44,000 British troops in the conflict without a second UN resolution. Tory members supported a hard-line policy against Saddam Hussein, and for his own Labour Party, Blair turned the war resolution into a confidence vote on his leadership, even employing the personal endorsement of long-time political ally Bill Clinton.[64]

With the clock ticking on Bush's ultimatum, Blair's strategy garnered 396 votes in favor. These votes overwhelmed the 217 against and set the final stage for international enforcement against the regime of Saddam Hussein.[65] In the end, war came not under Chapter 7 of the United Nations Charter but under a second-best solution cobbled together by a coalition of the willing.

The Lock-and-Key System for Coalition Crisis Management

On several occasions during the course of the Iraq crisis, Americans and British seemed to push the lock and key system for intelligence sharing to its limits.[66] In each case, they made a show of opening the door into a secret world, risking the loss of sources and methods in order to reveal the true dimensions of the danger from Iraq. Each time a world that was less equipped but no less sophisticated answered back with an alternative interpretation for the evidence that undermined the immediacy of the threat.

At each stage throughout the crisis—as reports, dossiers, speeches, and briefings mounted—the French, especially, clung to their original rhetoric. The United States government, even on the basis of superior national intelligence, could not choose war on behalf of the Security Council, which worked through its own intelligence arm in UNMOVIC.[67] Nothing the United States presented in September 2002 or

63 Associated Press (2003); Hiro (2004: 168).

64 Ramesh (2003: 46).

65 Ibid.

66 Shawcross (2004: 150).

67 On several occasions Blix implied that UNMOVIC's conclusions, not those of US intelligence, were definitive for the Security Council. US information, as with that of other member states, should complement UNMOVIC's work, but it could never trump the Council's argument as, say, U-2 spy plane photos had done in 1962. Blix's insistence failed to win the confidence of US officials as a neutral investigator, but his substantive view on the intelligence process later received oblique support from Richard Kerr, a former CIA

again in February 2003 justified unilateral regime change and occupation of a UN member. On moral and strategic principle, "whatever the circumstances" of any conceivable information release or American arm-twisting, France always thwarted any resolution that would impose an automatic trigger connecting raw data to war. Such a mechanism was unacceptable because it bypassed the Security Council's deliberation and judgment at the point where it was most needed for defense of a legitimate world order.

So consistent was the French mantra—and the US rejoinder that America certainly would if the UN did not act against Saddam Hussein—some commentators have charged that all the information exchanges between Iraq, the United Nations, the French, the British, and the United States were not so much crisis bargaining as political theater. The outcome, according to this view, was pre-ordained since Hussein decided early on not to abandon WMD programs, the United States committed itself after 1998 to regime change, and France, after American arrogance in Afghanistan, perceived more risk in granting the Bush administration a free hand in the Gulf than in continuing its economic flirtation with Saddam Hussein.[68]

Yet, this sterile view of the diplomacy heavily discounts the intense debates between and within various governments over how to resolve the French and American positions. Both France and the United States had an interest in preventing Hussein from tearing apart the Security Council. There simply was too much activity—too much consultation, too many briefs, too much fluidity on 1441 and the question of a second resolution, and too much anxiety on the part of Arab allies, including defecting Iraqis whose cooperation would be punished if the United States backed down—to all be *pro forma*.

In fact, the sterile view basically misses the hard fought battle to convince international partners whether regime change was necessary in Iraq. With widespread suspicion that Saddam Hussein was hiding something, the international argument came down to varying interpretations of circumstantial evidence. Since countries had differing access to that evidence, persuasion hinged upon how much potential allies trusted information and interpretations that were provided to them via the lock-and-key system.

Although some countries had human intelligence channels unavailable to the United States, US technical systems for imagery and signals intercept far outstripped those of companions on the Security Council. Consequently, the struggle for persuasion and successful management of the Iraq crisis turned on the credibility of specifically American threat portrayals based on information commonly understood to be a carefully selected sample of the total available.

---

executive brought back to review American pre-war analysis. In part, Kerr concluded that the CIA underestimated how much its own human and technical sources were limited by the loss of first-hand knowledge when the UN Special Commission on Iraq (UNSCOM) was forced to abandon its mission in 1998 (Burrough, et al. 2004). All major parties to the subsequent crisis, including the United States, conceded that UNMOVIC enjoyed significantly more resources and better access than its predecessor, UNSCOM.

68 Again, contrast the perspectives of William Shawcross (2004) and Dilip Hiro (2004).

The following paragraphs highlight three periods of information exchange, primarily from the United States to potential coalition partners during the crisis. The three phases, arranged in rough symmetry around Secretary Powell's prosecutorial brief to the world on February 5, 2003 are; (1) President Bush's call to action at the United Nations on September 12, 2002 and the US Congressional vote on October 10–11 to authorize force against Iraq; (2) Powell's speech to the Security Council and Hans Blix's February 14 interim report on inspections; and (3) the diplomatic endgame that brought virtual defeat for the US-backed second resolution on March 17, 2003.

In each period, states receiving information did not complain about imprecision of American intelligence as much as selectivity or bias in the analysis. Mountains of data were pushed toward one driving theme: Saddam Hussein was approaching a WMD threshold where he would no longer be deterred.[69] The problem was that other information, perhaps not piled quite as high, nevertheless pointed to a less threatening answer. This information, circulating in UN inspection reports and the global media, reached a wider audience and begged the question of why the American side so thoroughly discounted it. After all the effort, technology and deep pockets failed to persuade in part because the steps from raw data to intelligence finding remained secret. Even certain agencies within the US government, much less those of other allies, could not be confident about how much the well-known US policy goal of regime change shaped official American and British presentations of the facts on Iraq.[70]

Energizing the International Community

President Bush's speech to the United Nations marking the first anniversary of the September 11 attacks galvanized the Security Council and started the clock on the Iraq crisis. After that point, Saddam Hussein would have to make concessions in order to avoid war. Hussein's record of aggression, his defiance of previous UN resolutions, and the fear of what he might be concealing persuaded many countries represented in the audience to craft a firm, last chance resolution.[71]

As the fall wore on, however, the bargaining between Iraq, the United States, and potential coalition partners intensified, for the extent of Iraqi concessions and the size of the US coalition to confront Iraq remained very much in play. On September 24, Prime Minister Blair issued a fifty-page dossier on Iraqi WMD programs.[72] In

69 In President Bush's phrase, Hussein's regime posed a "grave and gathering danger." See Office of the Press Secretary, US Government (2002).

70 Bamford (2004: *passim*, 313–20, 329–30, 342–3).

71 A background paper for President Bush's speech was released on the same day and outlined the international threat posed by Iraq. The paper supported charges, including violation of UN resolutions, pursuit of weapons of mass destruction, and harboring of terrorists. It relied upon information from defectors, accounting gaps reported by UN inspectors, documentary evidence of attempts to purchase equipment on the international market, and technical intelligence on former military and dual-use facilities (ibid.).

72 Purdum (2003: 43); Ramesh (2003: 28).

preparation for the US congressional vote to authorize war, the Bush administration declassified portions of a new National Intelligence Estimate on Iraq.[73]

In each instance, the press, allies, and the US Congress reacted as if the Bush and Blair governments were holding back. Many of the most damning assertions against Iraq were based on straight-line projections from old information. Tons of chemical weapons stocks, for example, documented by Iraq in the aftermath of the Gulf War remained unaccounted for. In the forward to the British dossier, Prime Minister Blair endorsed the claim of a single Iraqi source that some of these stocks could be readied for launch in forty-five minutes.[74] In similar fashion, other evidence left the final verdict open to competing interpretations. Specialized aluminum tubes had been purchased, but they could be used for either conventional or nuclear weapons production. US satellite photos in fact showed new construction at a French-built nuclear plant, but international inspectors did not draw the same conclusions from the same images.[75]

Skeptics on the Security Council led by France and doubters in the US Senate, including senior Republican Chuck Hagel of Nebraska, acknowledged Hussein's defiance, but on the basis of released information could not concur with Bush and Blair on the imminence of the WMD threat from Iraq.[76] Bush and Blair eventually succeeded in the first important steps toward isolating Hussein: the US House and the US Senate passed war authorization resolutions by wide margins in October, and the Security Council passed its "last opportunity" resolution 15–0 in early November. Yet, the real basis of these victories was consensus that Iraq was not presently cooperating and that a united front behind the Anglo-American military threat was the best way to make such cooperation happen.

Hussein's counter move of partial compliance foisted the onus of proof back onto US and British intelligence. The next step—passing a UN Security Council ultimatum or attacking together on the basis of resolution 1441—would demand a higher standard, and now Hussein was playing his own lock-and-key game. If the Security Council would wait a little longer, he would open another door—allow access to the suspect Al Sahoud missile, permit U-2 overflights, et cetera—but, of course, as time went on, it became more difficult for coalition forces to maintain themselves in the field.

73 In the process of declassification for the wider congressional debate, the National Intelligence Estimate shrunk from ninety to twenty pages (Burrough, et al. 2004). See also Purdum (2003: 58).

74 Hiro (2004: 65).

75 Ibid.; Gordon and Trainor (2006: 133).

76 Senator Hagel felt the administration was relying on a stand-by line, "Yes. I know there is evidence there, but I don't want to tell you any more about it." The administration approach of selective release to Congress—not entirely dissimilar from the lock-and-key method used for allies—did not "give to the American public a heck of a lot of faith that, in fact, what anyone is saying is true" (Purdum 2003: 56).

Texas Hold 'Em at the UN

The second watershed for information exchange from the US side was Secretary Powell's speech to the Security Council on February 5, 2003. Powell turned another key in the US system and revealed a deluge of images, intercepts, and testimony. His presentation tapped one hundred different sources, including some that debuted in closely held presidential briefings over previous months.[77] All reports that made it into the UN briefing were independently confirmed to maximize his credibility. In a sense, Powell posted his final bet, hoping that new US Government information along with what the international community already knew would be enough to win the crisis. Reminiscent of his military preference for decisive force, Powell brought to the chamber a scowling CIA Director George Tenet—one of the few remaining veterans of the Clinton administration—to sit directly behind him. So intense was Powell's diplomatic fire on February 5, Woodward recounts that National Security Agency employees watching the televised exchange at their offices cheered when Powell unveiled their handiwork for the first time to a spellbound global audience.[78]

Yet, within a few days, Jacque Chirac, Gerhard Schroeder, and Vladimir Putin met to jointly declare the need for extended inspections.[79] In what became a constant refrain through the start of the war, opponents insisted that none of the revealed evidence justified US use of force against Iraq.[80] In spite of the general consensus, including UNMOVIC's view, that Iraq was not in compliance with Security Council resolutions and that Hussein almost certainly possessed prohibited weapons of mass destruction, there persisted a crucial difference of opinion on the imminence of the threat. After all, with each of Hans Blix's reports, Iraq's cooperation and the knowledge of inspectors improved. Why not keep making progress without war?

After February 5, almost all steps in information exchange took place against a backdrop of recriminations. In his February 14 report to the Security Council, Blix referred directly to Powell's presentation. Seeing in it a veiled charge that UN inspectors were not sufficiently thorough, Blix answered with a hint that the United States was still keeping too much under lock and key. "Governments have many sources of information that are not available to inspectors," he said. "The inspectors, for their part, must base their reports only on the evidence which they can themselves examine and present publicly."[81]

Blix's standard rankled the United States because it attacked US credibility and thereby reduced available information to prosecute Saddam Hussein. It also implied that analysis really counted only when UNMOVIC—not a specially created Policy Counterterrorism Evaluation Group inside the Pentagon—examined the

77 Woodward (2004: 311). Purdum (2003: 63) reports that some of the most dramatic radio intercepts played on February 5 were first heard by the President during a classified meeting on November 26, 2002. An obvious starting point for Powell's preparations was Vice-Presidential Chief of Staff Lewis Libby's classified all-source presentation on January 22 (Woodward 2004: 289; Burrough, et al. 2004).

78 Woodward (2004: 309).

79 Ibid.: 316.

80 Ibid.

81 Ibid.: 317.

circumstantial evidence. Some of the satellite images in Powell's presentation, Blix pointed out, had been taken weeks apart. The changes Powell indicated might have resulted from routine movement rather than emergency concealment.

Much depended upon assumptions about Iraqi intentions that one plugged into the data analysis.[82] As the debate over a second resolution dragged into March, opponents of the war, none more important than transatlantic allies France and Germany, distrusted the US approach. If the US troops would just remain patient in the field, UNMOVIC could squeeze more cooperation out of Iraq, and the Blix standard would prove good enough to defuse the common threat posed by Saddam Hussein.[83]

Insufficient Information versus Insufficient Trust

Unfortunately, US tolerance for UN procedure was nearly exhausted. Six months earlier, President Bush had embedded his invitation for the Security Council to disarm Iraq in the principle of enforcing its own previous resolutions. From the beginning, Bush made clear that if the United Nations did not act fast, the United States would neutralize the Iraq threat without the international body's sanction. With some 250,000 US and coalition troops awaiting orders to execute the war plan, patience in March became harder to maintain.

Moreover, the Bush administration, including early advocates of the diplomatic track such as Colin Powell, gradually came to question UNMOVIC. Resolution 1441 was worded as a last opportunity for Iraq to disarm. By March, several UNMOVIC reports had indicated specifics where Iraq was not cooperating fully and that greater cooperation would shorten the time to peaceful disarmament. Instead of the "serious consequences" agreed to in the resolution, ElBaradei, Blix, and several countries on the Council insisted on more time.

The United States did forward leads and lend equipment as requested by Blix and De Villepin, but as an outsider in the neutral inspections process, the United States could not be sure whether UNMOVIC's negative findings were accurate or simply due to lack of aggressiveness operating on Saddam Hussein's tightly controlled territory.[84] At various times during the crisis, American intercepts, remote images, and human intelligence certainly seemed suspicious, and as Powell wondered, why

---

82 Lt Gen Michael Hayden, then director of NSA, later elaborated on the limitations of technical intelligence in this context for James Bamford (2004: 354–7, 373–4).

83 These ideas still flourished in Foreign Minister De Villepin's address to the Security Council on March 19, 2003, after the United States had issued its forty-eight hour ultimatum against Iraq. "(F)or France, war can only be the exception, and collective responsibility the rule. Whatever our aversion to Saddam Hussein's cruel regime, that holds true for Iraq and for all crises that we will have to confront together…[Blix and ElBaradei's] report confirms what we all know here: Yes, the inspections are producing tangible results. Yes, they offer the prospect of effective disarmament through peaceful means and in shorter time-frames" (De Villepin 2004: 81–82).

84 Woodward (2004: 355).

would Hussein incur all of the costs, stretching back years before the present crisis, if the dictator had nothing to hide?[85]

If Hussein was indeed hiding WMD, all other parties to the crisis had to confront seriously the question of whether UNMOVIC could find it. Piece by piece, UNMOVIC and the IAEA dismantled the circumstantial evidence. In addition to Blix emphasizing the time gap and the lack of context for voice recordings, on the nuclear side, ElBaradei in his March 7 report to the UN challenged the suitability of Iraq's aluminum tube order for centrifuge construction, and he flatly rejected as forgeries documents provided through the United States to the IAEA on attempted uranium yellowcake purchases by Iraq. What the United States saw as woven into a large, integrated scheme of Iraqi deception, inspectors and war opponents saw as individual scraps that never added up to a "smoking gun."[86]

What is worse, as the United States turned over its high cards to little effect at the Security Council, it lost confidence, despite having military and technological advantage, that it in fact held a winning hand for the crisis diplomacy against Iraq. As the US-British-Spanish sponsored resolution to gird the international community for forceful disarmament faltered, US information exchange with potential allies degenerated perilously close to intimidation and coercion, especially against Swinging Six council members Chile and Mexico.[87] The ultimate indictment of the present lock-and-key approach to coalition crisis management came when the global media in early-March 2003 embarrassed the United States. They reported that sophisticated US collection methods had, in desperation, been turned against partner nations on the Security Council in order to better corral votes.[88]

Towards Common Information Infrastructure

Without the confidence of France and Germany, there was little chance that the United Nations would actually come together and analyze the fragmentary evidence under the same light. No one can say for sure what might have happened if France and Germany, by virtue of their NATO membership, had operated a common collection and analysis system with the United States. Combined intelligence likely would have expanded the pool of common information, but each state actor would still have tapped its national classified systems and employed its own human agents. The lock-and-key method would still have been used to make one side's case without revealing sources and methods.

---

85 Woodward (2004: 298). Gordon and Trainor (2006: 55, 62) answer that Saddam did seek to hide weakness from internal enemies.

86 "You take an intercepted telephone call as he played in the Security Council chamber, and you don't know who intercepted it and who are the persons, et cetera…I went into the Council and reported on that skepticism" (Hans Blix on the *Newshour with Jim Leher*, March 17, 2004); transcript available at www.pbs.org/newshour/66??/international/jan-june04/blix_3-17.html. See also Hersh (2003).

87 Burrough, et al. (2004); Bamford (2004: 364).

88 Bright, Vulliamy, and Beaumont (2003); Burrough, et al. (2004).

Yet, scraps of information tossed over the transom to war allies would have landed in a different context. On November 8, 2002, all fifteen members of the Security Council agreed that Saddam Hussein was in violation of previous resolutions to disarm and that continued violation would being serious consequences. Though President Bush's charges against Iraqi agents seeking to buy uranium from Africa would later be termed a mistake by the CIA, in the fall of 2002, they coincided with multiple British and, notably, French reports.[89] In late-January, there could still be rough consensus between French intelligence and the CIA on the suspicious nature of Iraq's aluminum tubes purchase.[90] The real falling out between transatlantic factions on the use of force did not take place with early disputes over Kyoto protocols for greenhouse gas emissions or the International Criminal Court. On the specific issue of the Iraqi WMD threat, breakdown began much later, after January 2003, when Blix's deadpan reports on Iraqi's partial compliance were juxtaposed against Powell's sweeping assertions on grave and imminent danger from much the same circumstantial evidence.

After that open conflict, but not before, whatever the United States poured into the Security Council or inspector mix fell under immediate suspicion. Each rebuttal by UNMOVIC or the IAEA in February and March dealt terrific blows to the mutual trust keeping the allies together on issues of high security. In the end, what separated long-time partners was not the quality of information but willingness to accept US interpretation of the threat.[91] Soon after Powell's presentation to the Security Council, French officials complained because the divisive Vilnius Ten letter of February 6, which supported Spain's Group of Eight letter from January 30 and added favorable references to the US revelations on February 5, had to have been composed prior to any painstaking review of the US case. Ironically, many of these Central and Eastern European states, several of them candidates for European Union membership, were behaving less like naïve children and more like De Gaulle himself in an earlier crisis. When John Kennedy sent former secretary of state Dean Acheson to Paris in October 1962, the normally demanding French leader did not seem overly concerned about the particulars of US intelligence on Soviet missiles in Cuba. "'I trust you,' De Gaulle told Acheson."[92]

In the early 1960s, trust among transatlantic partners who did not always see eye-to-eye was still available due to the sheer magnitude of the Soviet threat. In 2003, as French minister De Villepin expressed throughout the crisis, multilateral norms for an emerging order acceptant of US leadership, not simply one-shot gains in the overall balance of power, were at stake, so it was harder to allow any country, even the United States, to railroad the Security Council. A common technical intelligence

89 Whitney (2005: 42–3).

90 Gordon and Trainor (2006: 133).

91 Trachtenberg (2005: 231) remarked that "no real meeting of the minds" was possible due to the superficial way in which issues were negotiated. In other words, the transatlantic discussion on the Iraqi threat and alternative responses was shallow in the sense of a lack of deliberation. Yet, deliberation presupposes an original clash of interests, so if Trachtenberg is correct, it would be overly far-sighted to see national differences as the sole cause of an eventual breakdown in coalition crisis management.

92 Quoted in Gordon and Shapiro (2004: 28).

system would not have eliminated all the significant sources of private information among allies on that Council. However, there are a number of ways in which sharing more of the process could have worked to reinforce confidence, at least within the NATO subgroup, in the absence of a single, highly organized, and overwhelming threat.

As experienced in other NATO missions before and after September 11, the practice of operating together could create its own momentum. International crews laboring toward a common goal, in this case intelligence production for crisis management, would have opportunities at every step to build rapport and invest confidence in one another. Initial success of a combined operation, the conditions for which existed in this case as late as January 2003, generally breeds greater trust, more efficient cooperation, and greater likelihood for future success.

This progressive characteristic sharply contrasts with the lock-and-key system, which exists primarily to maintain the national information advantage and only secondarily to enlighten partners. As subsequent crisis decisions for escalation or concession induce higher costs, the lock-and-key approach becomes less, not more, likely to succeed. It sets up a reverse momentum compared to common infrastructure because the technologically advanced supplier has fewer doors that it is willing to open, and junior partners worry about what the supplier is not telling them: the limits to trust become obvious and less flexible at the crisis stages when intra-alliance trust is most needed.[93]

Of course, initial failure of combined operations can be devastating to trust. The suspicion, for example, that individual French officers were leaking NATO information to Serbs during Operation Allied Force hampered French-American cooperation during air operations over Afghanistan a few years later. In this regard, however, some faith is warranted in the capacity for democracies to sustain cooperation over the long haul. Temporary setbacks notwithstanding, the NATO allies are liable to succeed with common crisis information systems in ways that the full Security Council, which includes non-democratic states, could not. Many of the NATO democracies can draw upon a tradition of cooperation with one another.

Indeed, NATO officials invoked this legacy in order to heal the transatlantic split over defending Turkey from potential Iraqi attack during early February 2003 when NATO deployment might have been misinterpreted as a consensus decision to escalate the crisis. In addition to diplomatic history, each of the NATO allies brings to common crisis management a commitment to democratic deliberation for smoothing out conflicts among parochial interests.[94] One reason why the United

93 For a similar dynamic involving the US-UN partnership, see Hans Blix's less than enthusiastic reaction to US Assistant Secretary of State John Wolf when the official dumped US surveillance photos on Blix's UN desk. The abrupt, lock-and-key style transfer came after UNMOVIC's February 14 report in support of continued inspections (Burrough, et al. 2004). In this case, the United States could not easily discuss sources and methods. Blix suspected that these were UN photos, intercepted and decoded from a UN secure fax (Bamford 2004: 359)!

94 Not surprisingly, process integration is also an important consideration for intelligence reform within the United States. The idea is to improve threat assessment by fostering higher quality deliberation between various agencies within the executive as well as between the executive and Congress. See, for example, conclusions of the Commission on Intelligence

States and France might weather diplomatic incidents and stick by interoperability in intelligence operations as a priority within NATO transformation is that common infrastructure for collection, analysis, and distribution provides for early deliberation, democratic give and take, from the moment when value-laden assumptions are applied to make sense of circumstantial evidence.

Lock-and-key transfers, by contrast, resemble take-it-or-leave-it ultimatums, not the A-list invitations to quality conversation that some suppliers claim. By the time fully produced intelligence products were ready to be passed out the door from the Pentagon's Office of Special Plans to waiting allies, facts and values were tightly packaged and sealed with a political commitment.[95] The difference for transatlantic deliberation was poignantly captured after Powell's February 5 address by an awkward and exploitable gap separating French calls for more Council discussion from US expectations that there would be precipitous action.

Despite extraordinary lock-and-key transfers during the Iraq crisis, the United States failed to persuade the French and went to war without Security Council support. Even so, the United States did not fight entirely alone. Some partners such as Britain and Spain openly backed the United States. Others such as Saudi Arabia cooperated on a lower profile. How the Bush administration kept so many allies on board—without the kind of combined information management technology discussed here—provides another interesting wrinkle. Woodward reports that the Saudis cared as much or more about what Bush was going to do than whether the United States had correctly gauged the Iraqi threat. Rather than sharing in the process of threat assessment, Bush authorized the sharing of classified war plans to the Saudi ambassador in Washington so that Prince Bandar could then reassure Riyadh the United States would not at some point abandon Saudi Arabia to Saddam Hussein.[96] As a result, the United States, arguably, fared better with Saudi Arabia than it did with several of its NATO allies.

Yet, the coalition leader did so, in this case, by risking the integrity of combat operations and by narrowing its room for maneuver at a time when other partners were seeking US flexibility. Sharing instead the crisis management process through common information infrastructure, in addition to improving common threat assessment, might reduce the need to win trust by running combat risks of the kind employed for the Gulf States against Iraq. Benefits of better tools for crisis management do not necessarily stop if a war starts. A NATO information system tailored for crises could help the United States accumulate political capital—eventually sufficient for partners outside the alliance—that would facilitate aggressive US leadership in the event of war, which is, after all, the phase of conflict when autonomy, information superiority, and credibility with allies matter most.

Capabilities of the United States Regarding Weapons of Mass Destruction, reprinted in Whitney (2005: 598–615, 662–4).

95 Pillar (2006).

96 Woodward (2004: 263–7).

Chapter 6

Kantian Union in the Information Age

Shakespeare, the master at portraying human nature during England's ascendance in world politics, saw several paths between ignorance and war. Certainly there was the problem also captured in today's bargaining models: adversaries ignorant of the true extent of each other's power or resolve could fail to find a mutually acceptable agreement. In *The Merchant of Venice*, the playwright's allusion to music pointed toward a second connection.

> The man that hath no music in himself
> Nor is not moved with concord of sweet sounds,
> Is fit for treason, stratagems and spoils;
> The motions of his spirit are dull as night,
> And his affections dark as Erebus;
> Let no such man be trusted.

This book has mined Shakespeare's claim at the level of international relations. If a great power like the United States is ignorant of the sweet sounds and careful forms of legitimacy, such a state will not be trusted, even by its own allies on the eve of war. Trust, independent of material capability, counts in crisis bargaining, when the outcome depends not simply on the likelihood of victory in war but on the resolve of present and potential adversaries. A crisis actor's willingness to compromise, or alternatively fight to the death, is in the end a function of national disposition rather than hard power ratios, and disposition responds to the kind of soulful music identified in Shakespeare, in the form of diplomatic communication. Diplomacy, in turn, opens new vistas for the use of technology—particularly collection, analysis, and communication systems so prevalent in America's edge over other powers.[1]

When French foreign minister Hubert Védrine coined the term, *hyper-puissance*—or hyperpower—for America's international position at the end of the 1990s, he essentially accused the United States of being tone deaf, of being so much stronger than the rest of the world that it no longer discerned the niceties of style apart from substance, that it was succumbing to the temptation of substituting unilateralism for effective diplomacy.[2]

---

1 Nye and Owens (1996).

2 Kissinger (2001: 82, 286–8). "In the face of unilateralism, such as that deployed by the United States Senate, we advocate multilateralism that respects all the members of the international community, with the United Nations as its guardian" (Védrine 1999). Here, I elaborate what international respect means in terms of procedures for information management during crises, though the real guardian of a multipolar political order remains the United States.

There is a classic example of such a state, consumed by power, in Thucydides' Athens after its seeming victory in the great war with Sparta. Following the surrender of an army off the Peloponnesian coast at Pylos, Sparta soon sued for peace, and after that, no single state or foreseeable combination of states in the Hellenic system could stand against the Athenian navy.[3]

In terms of the balance of power, Athens could unilaterally demand obeisance from other cities, as it did from the small, neutral island of Melos in 416 B.C.[4] Melos responded with arguments grounded in hope, justice, and diplomatic tradition, but the irrefutable logic of power made Athens obdurate. In Shakespeare's terms, the motions of Athenian spirit were dull as night, its affections, even for fellow Greeks, dark as Erebus.

The classical scholar, Robert Connor, noted that in the original Greek, Thucydides inserted Persian-sounding phrases in the mouths of Athenian representatives for the Melian Dialog.[5] In short, without the forms required for legitimacy—without the usual music accompanying diplomacy among Greeks—the Athenians representing policy of a hyperpower did not sound like themselves, more as if they were alien invaders, coming from outside civilization. Cold calculation and naked self-interest stultified crisis communication. Because the power differential was so clear cut, dialog with the Melians had no significance for the Athenians; with their aloof, unmelodic approach, only actions counted.

Shakespeare, at the level of individual relations, and Thucydides, at the level of state interaction, warned us to pay attention to style, broadly conceived, as an extension of diplomatic substance. A powerful actor that becomes a hyperpower cannot be bothered with forms and will betray the laws of civilization for short-term advantage. "Treason, stratagems, and spoils," though, are not sustainable unless adversaries are permanently eliminated. Those that survive or develop later will not likely extend trust or negotiate in good faith only to be burned a second time.

Thucydides appreciated the long-term consequences of pure power politics that reduced international dialog to perfunctory performances with no effect on behavior. Firstly, Melos did not fall immediately. Athenian lines were broken, reinforcements were called, and months passed before even a few people inside the city were willing to betray Melian independence. Secondly, in their next venture, the would-be conquerors of Sicily found themselves handicapped by, among other things, their previous contempt for diplomatic music. Enemies were not easy to divide. Syracuse, especially, fought resolutely because Athenian occupation meant slavery or death, not the liberation so casually promised.

More importantly for our purposes, allies on the invading force were not easy to retain. Athens rallied partners primarily through fear of what would result from defying her power, not through principle, for she had already revealed herself, in Shakespeare's phrase, fit for treason, stratagems, and spoils. In her approach to Sicily, Athens was viewed as underestimating civic virtue and demanding too much of her foes. This perception of weakness in the Athenian coalition, among other

3 Strassler (1996: Book IV, 30; pp. 240–4).

4 Strassler (1996: Book V, 84; p. 350).

5 Connor (1984: 155–6).

factors, gave courage to Syracuse though they entered the contest with no guarantee of Spartan assistance and certainly as the inferior power.

The experiences of Athens at Melos and Sicily have much to recommend for American internationalism. Both states favored expansion in order to secure new areas for commerce. Though Athens controlled an empire, its military expeditions yet depended upon democratic consensus at home. Most importantly, Athens and the United States held the highest rank of powers in their respective systems while neither had enough absolute power to dominate all other states at once. Even with unrivaled militaries, both states employed coalitions for the use of force and crisis management. In the maintenance of those coalitions, diplomacy had the potential akin to music for the soul, and for the American case, technology—information technology in particular—had the potential to transform diplomacy.

Music and Diplomacy

In his history of the twenty-seven year Peloponnesian War, Thucydides noted plagues and civil wars as the utter breakdown of civilization, which turned the natural order of life inside afflicted cities upside down.[6] Where an outside observer expected to find trust and compassion, Thucydides instead reported betrayal and indifference. When he likened international war against Athens, the hyperpower, to civil war and pestilence, he revealed what could happen when political bonds unraveled in a double sense. When the rules governing how states should treat one another in the Hellenic system were imperiously discarded, the protective distinction between state and individual level conflict also broke down.

Writing from his precarious vantage point in tumultuous seventeenth-century England, Thomas Hobbes (c1651) made a sharper distinction between civil and interstate conflict, at least in a world without a hyperpower. As a translator of Thucydides, Hobbes may have had barbaric civil war scenes from the classical History in mind when he described man exiled back to his natural state.[7] By contrast, healthy, stable states made the condition of international anarchy less severe than a war of all against all. Under the protection of states, even non-democratic ones, individuals had more to lose: peace was more valuable, and aggressive war, since states never slept or tired with age, presented a costlier proposition.[8]

At the same time, Hedley Bull's (1977) 20th century perspective, implying an actual society of states was misleading.[9] States never formed full-fledged societies among themselves that could relegate musical diplomacy to a kind of effortless response, or second nature. Human identification and the intensity of interdependence

6 Strassler (1996: Book II, 52–3; pp. 120–1); Ibid. (Book III, 81–4; pp. 198–201); Connor (1984: 98–105).

7 Doyle (1997: 112).

8 Ibid. (pp. 116–7).

9 Sartori (2005), in her book on diplomacy as reputation building, makes a complimentary point. Preserving reputation once established, by honoring commitments even if they demand short-term sacrifices, can be a Nash equilibrium strategy with material benefits accruing in the long run.

attaching an individual to his family, neighborhood, city, province, and country even today far outshine sensitivity and vulnerability across state frontiers.[10] Advances in transportation and information technology notwithstanding, powerful states by comparison to other institutions are autonomous in supplying the necessities of social existence. In the contemporary world, as before, societies with shared legal codes and norms flourish inside states not among them.[11]

Music and Strong States

In the late 1970s, an era when stark lines of the Cold War appeared to be fragmenting, jumbling together sub-state, state, and supra-state actors, Kenneth Waltz (1979) took his theory of international politics in the opposite direction.[12] For him, emergent notions of complex interdependence discounted the one rock solid feature of the international landscape, state structures with capability and interest in preserving their power. Deep causes of war lay below the web of interactions that occupied daily attentions of international bureaucrats. War was not a daily event any more than the slower but more relevant shifts in the distribution of power among state behemoths.

While atmospherics indicated increasingly intertwined economies and merging legal systems, the massive concentrations of war making power in armies and state treasuries still set the foundation of international politics. The reason states did not attack each other had less to do with the incalculable effect on global investment than the more direct consequences to be suffered in a counterattack.

No society, in the true sense of the word, domesticated the superpowers. These monsters were held at bay by the same raw force that brought peace at Westphalia, Vienna, and Potsdam: knowledge and fear of each other's independence. Should a power position be threatened—and the lack of society among states actually made this destabilizing event less likely—any one of these creatures, armed to the teeth, could rear up in defense, tearing the fabric restraints of complex interdependence and elevating great power war, once again, to global headlines. The way to peace, therefore, lay with recognition of sovereign autonomy and self-sufficiency, and in the art of counterbalancing states' power to harm.

Even in this spare, Waltzian view of the world, however, there remains a purpose for diplomacy, providing useful signals for states that must husband their power to survive. This hardly equates to the more expansive role of diplomacy under liberal institutionalism, but the spare version—small diplomacy—also demands time and effort. Small diplomacy belongs in a realist view because, although power and resolve are measurable, they are uncertain in the midst of crisis. Dues paid to maintain diplomacy reduce this uncertainty. They signal to others a reassuring presumption that a state's interlocutors will continue their independent existence in the international arena after the end of a given conflict.

---

10 Keohane and Nye (1977).

11 Krasner (1999).

12 Waltz (1979: 104–7, 138–9, 158, 192–3).

To return to the example of tiny Melos, despite its material disadvantages and the horrific prospect of war with Athens, the state could not easily bargain away its existence. Athens' utter lack of rhythm, intonation, and style in announcing its demands revealed no interest in the most basic courtesies for another Hellenic city. Internally consistent or not, the "dialog" gave no opportunity for two-way communication, leaving Melos with no option between slavery and death.

In the history of international relations, states faced with Melos' dilemma do not all decide the same way. Reviewing the opening gambits of World War II, for example, Czechoslovakia and Poland responded differently to Hitler's aggression as did France and Great Britain, the latter fighting on despite the likelihood of annihilation in summer 1940.[13]

Granted, the variation in states' crisis behavior may be explained in part by differences in geography and national capability. Yet, at the same time, the stiffness of British resistance and the suddenness of France's collapse amazed observers at the time.[14] The difficulty in forecasting responses or in explaining why some states but not all prefer slavery over death suggests that some determinants of crisis decision making are invisible outside the state itself.

James Fearon's (1995) microeconomic model describing so-called rationalist explanations for war captured this irreducible uncertainty in the concept of resolve. Just as economists argue there is no accounting for taste, Fearon argued it was impossible to know with certainty what price a state on the defensive would attach to concessions. An Athens or a Germany on the rise would demand more if an opponent was unwilling to sacrifice its people in order to maximize its chances, however meager, of winning the war.

Diplomacy in these situations may serve a communication function beyond the substantive meaning of verbal or written language. No state or coalition commands one hundred percent of all military potential in a crisis. Demands served in the appropriate style indicate a belief that the recipient country is highly resolved: officials of the beleaguered government are presumed to be thinking of their state, not just their individual lives, and given that states in the past have come back to life, a glorious death now is preferable to the humiliation of unconditional surrender. A challenger pausing to uphold diplomacy credibly signals its willingness to demand less than one hundred percent; it can be trusted to respect rather than disparage the other side's determination and take no more than what the limits of its own power would dictate.

Under the realist framework, then, the connection between diplomacy among states and music among Shakespeare's individuals is profound. Both function as a meta-language, enveloping words, altering their timbre without changing their literal signification. Diplomacy and music register at a non-verbal level prior to reason. They govern the formation of priors, inscribing judgments in the heart or in the collective consciousness of the body politic. They address the limits of scientific realism by providing answers that, while necessary for the rational evaluation of strategies, cannot be perceived with the five senses: how, for example, will another

13 Churchill (1949).

14 May (2000).

state in the system value its territory or its independence against the lives of its soldiers or the fortunes of its people?

In his book length analysis of the American Mind, Allan Bloom recognized in an early chapter the importance of music as it plays within a single state.[15] Accepting the ontology of man as both political and animal, Bloom singled out rock-and-roll for transporting the soul away from political activity, from philosophizing about human nature and the public good. Popular rhythms exiled human souls from civic life and imprisoned them in a grind of bestial, self-centered satisfaction.[16]

At the same time, Bloom distinguished classical music for its orchestration, forms, and discipline—its ability to express variety within a natural order. Such music called souls to community not just to satiate appetites held in common but to participate in a structure, constituted through human reason and greater than the sum of individual concerns. Bloom's most important model among the Greeks, Plato, also reserved a special place for music with respect to the state.[17] The best music answered the needs of the Republic while the basest poetry broke it apart, luring citizens away from the pleasures of great works and civic identification to obsession with narrow-minded, short-sighted physical escapes.

Putting these ideas in international context, small diplomacy on the outside works like establishment music on the inside, with due regard for the taste of many states instead of one republic. Diplomacy's forms and melodies remind negotiators of long-term pleasures of peace as well as the unforeseen consequences of war—the potential for a quagmire to follow initial victory. Under diplomacy, other members of the international system are presumed highly resolved. If demands are rational, then they must be restrained to what the distribution of power in the system will bear. Without diplomacy, a superpower metastasizes into a hyperpower, a power trapped in a logic of continuous aggrandizement that leads, sooner or later, to defeat and decline.

A hyperpower comprehends calculations of force on force, but its priors going into crises are self-referential. No other nation will genuinely fight, it is assumed, because as lesser entities, they fear losing in the end. The hyperpower's perception of the world conforms to its own desires. For the voracious, world historical state, only today's meal matters. Relative power calculations pointing to present satisfaction overwhelm concerns about reverberations in the system or the potential for future complications. Without diplomacy, complications are difficult to foresee since any state that dreams of creating them must, presumably, succumb quickly and rationally to the same intimidation tactics.

Since the birth of the modern state system, though, every insatiable power center has fallen short of the capability to dominate every other member of the system at once. At least according to Waltz's theoretical structure, true unipolarity would put an end to the system as a historical object for study: the autonomy of its members and their *raison d'etre* would change. The Earth would have one world empire—Dante's vision of stability—or a world federation in which every territory and every

15 Bloom (1987: 68–81).

16 Ibid. (p. 75).

17 Bloom (c1968, 1991: 54 (376e), 200 (522a)).

population had its security guaranteed by a power *prima entre pares*—a scenario closer to Kant's perpetual peace. Despite the collapse of the Soviet Union, and a half-trillion dollar US defense budget, there is still no real world precedent for that sort of power.[18]

Against the United States in the 21st century, as against ancient Athens, complications are bound to arise, even if the world is more or less as described by realism. Without the accompaniment of diplomatic music, the first power will tend to overplay its military hand and neglect the resolve of rogue adversaries, some of which like Melos will refuse to cower in the face of long odds. When fighting begins—and Fearon (1995) carefully explained why consistent underestimation of resolve leads to fighting—war will unfold like a lottery.[19] Rational policy makers know what to do to maximize their expected value, but war carries a risk, rising with the total number of rounds played, that military operations will not turn out as expected. All to the good if the foe collapses quickly, but eventually, the enemy will get lucky and win on a long-shot or impose significantly greater costs than the victor anticipated.

When that moment comes, the lead power, the first among equals, will need help from its allies. Without diplomacy, in the Waltzian sense, those partners will find more reasons to abandon their leader. They might still acknowledge the champion's economic and military strength, and they will not forget common interests, but as the individual soul without music, or with the wrong kind of music, clutches immediate gratification in a kind of death grip, so the leading international power without diplomacy cannot be trusted, lest it drag allies to the same violent denouement.[20]

Diplomacy and Technology

So far, a connection has been made between music and diplomacy, but still open is the question of how a leading power like the United States can use its technological lead in a musical way. In fact, the most significant contemporary advantage is in information technology. Compared to margins in energy or work like those produced by the Manhattan Project, the information advantage is actually easier to convert into a diplomatic one. Such technology can be shared in a way that preserves the balance of power while thawing, or civilizing, the disposition of the leader. A militarily powerful country that also moves "with concord of sweet sounds" avoids the mistakes of Athens at Melos and Sicily. This champion becomes a trusted guardian of international mores rather than a dreaded predator, or hyperpower, operating outside any peace oriented federation of nations.

---

18 Waltz (1979: 111–2, 118, 136). The measurement and significance of unipolarity after the Cold War has been hotly debated. See, for example, Nye (1992); Huntington (1999); Wohlforth (1999); and Mowle and Sacko (2007).

19 Modern game theorists debate whether war is best modeled as a single-shot lottery or a complex sequence involving several roles of the dice, but within the community, there is broad agreement that war is a gamble (Reiter 2003).

20 Fukuyama (2006: 100–5).

To this point, the American debate over how to use the new technologies has played out in all the realms of strategy except the most expansive, and, ironically, the most familiar to students of politics: grand strategy.[21] At the levels of military strategy, operational art, and tactics, the dramatically improved capacity to collect, analyze, and disseminate information has, for many, occasioned a revolution in military affairs. Forces with an information advantage can potentially find, fix, and kill the enemy without exposing themselves to danger.[22]

Advanced information networks drive defense transformation toward lighter, faster, more precise, and more lethal units at whichever scale: army corps, divisions, brigades, or squads of Special Forces using lasers and the Global Positioning System to target air strikes. In short, easy access to information has greatly reduced the time, energy, and collateral damage necessary to produce kinetic effects on the battlefield. Not surprisingly, this development has encouraged a militaristic grand strategy. "Since 2001, neoconservatives have often advocated a non-status quo policy of transformational democratic change in hostile regimes…unilaterally and militarily if necessary."[23]

As might have been predicted, when US strategy discounted diplomacy as a waste of time, it embroiled itself in a sequence of fights with rogue states until "recent events in Iraq…so undermined the approach as to leave the grand strategic direction of the War on Terror largely adrift by January 2007."[24] Yet, that aimlessness might trace back to fundamental choices about how to exploit America's technological advantage. The musical aspects of technology, including its potential for reinforcing the rhythms and melodies of diplomacy have been overlooked.

This becomes clearer upon an examination of information sharing during international crisis. The conventional technique for exploitation gathers and analyzes data at the national level. US packages are then selectively declassified in order to transfer information while protecting sources and methods.

The briefings at their best provide open-and-shut cases, and on occasion, they seem to have persuaded other countries to change their diplomatic stance. US negotiators at Dayton, for example, employed sophisticated mapping technology to settle federal boundaries in Bosnia.[25] In other instances though, the packages have not dissipated resistance to US plans.

Some of the problems parallel those with the hyper-realism of the Athenians. Observable traces give a good notion of national capability, but they may not reveal relevant details of secret weapons programs or asymmetric tactics. With the most advance suite of antennas, cameras, satellites, and computers, the United States has still struggled to accurately describe the chemical weapons capabilities of Saddam Hussein's Iraq, as well as the nuclear programs of North Korea and Iran.[26] Though Operation Iraqi Freedom succeeded within three weeks in capturing Baghdad, intrepid

21 Biddle (2007: 461).

22 Owens (2000).

23 Biddle (2007: 461).

24 Biddle (2007: 462).

25 Johnson (1999).

26 Flawed intelligence on foreign WMD programs in 2002–2003 prompted calls for significant reform (Pincus and Baker 2005).

military correspondents and analysts Michael Gordon and Bernard Trainor (2006) recorded numerous surprises encountered by American forces at the tactical level against non-uniformed Fedayeen.[27] The greatest surprises awaited Americans after the putative end of major combat operations, as conventional Army soldiers and Marines discovered they were unable to prevent the rise of Sunni insurgents or Shia militias.[28]

Related to the problems of unanticipated weapons and novel strategies is the question of capturing the adversary's intent through intelligence operations. The appearance of new weapons facilities or the build-up of army divisions do not in themselves reveal how hard a state is going to fight once actual combat begins. Secret capabilities and hidden wells of resolve work against the precision and processing capacity of advanced information systems. Intelligence packages thrown over the wall of classification are unlikely to placate neutrals or allies because more often than not the data are open to multiple interpretations: they do not point conclusively to a single rational course of action.

The particulars of the 2003 Iraq Crisis illustrate another complication with information sharing through selective declassification. Recipients of the finished product cannot be sure that the sole supplier has not, under the guise of protecting sources and methods, doctored information to encourage a preferred policy. Both the French and the United Nations inspection team, as beneficiaries of US transfers, complained that American analysts were jumping to conclusions. Almost as soon as Secretary of State Colin Powell presented his aggressive interpretation of US satellite images and radio intercepts to the world on February 5, 2003, UN inspector Hans Blix countered with alternative theories for the presence of trucks outside certain factories and the fragments of Iraqi dialog ordering a clamp down on chemical weapons chatter in the field.

For those listening to the US case and deciding whether to stake their national honor by lining up with the superpower, the juxtaposition of shrill certitude against ambiguous evidence made their policy dilemma more frustrating. If the United States had information that could help the UN team on the ground in Iraq or the so-called Swinging Six countries on the Security Council draw correct conclusions, why was the United States refusing to divulge it? Ironically, the result of unprecedented declassification was even more intense speculation about what the United States suppressed and about whether it took advantage of its superior technology by distorting intelligence for political purposes.[29]

Certainly, the temptation is to use new collection and analysis systems to upgrade technical intelligence. Such an effort might help make sense of conflicting human intelligence reports or reduce uncertainty about adversary maneuvers. In addition, it could squelch the propensity for time consuming debate with coalition partners. From the perspective of a hyperpower, freedom within an alliance just impedes the will of the leading state when necessary information to determine the optimal course

27 Gordon and Trainor (2006: 214–25).

28 Ibid. (p. 495).

29 Questioning grew louder after no WMD stockpiles were found in Iraq. A Senate Intelligence Committee investigation eventually found major reasons for reform but no criminal or impeachable offenses by the President (Pincus and DeYoung 2007).

is already known. It requires nothing more than a straightforward confirmation of the facts—in the mold of the Athenian presentation at Melos—to end all argument and move to action. Rational expectations are that action should consist of surrender and subjugation since all the parties can predict the outcome of a war with the hyperpower beforehand, and the costs of actually fighting tax all sides. In this manner, hyper-realist logic eliminates the need for musical diplomacy or trust; the balance of power and interest is plain enough. Moreover, application of these hard calculations never ends until all the states in the world have lost their independence, or until a disaster—a Sicily or an Iraq, proves the original premises inadequate.

Even after a disaster, a hyperpower might stubbornly cling to the old logic. It could restrict its ambition, hesitate more to intimidate other rogue states with so many of its forces lost or tied down in a quagmire without ever appreciating the power of music, that is, diplomatic forms, to charm allies and impress foes. Accordingly, we find headlines proclaiming *déjà vu* on Iran, as the United States scrambles, so far in vain, to assemble slide shows that can cement a coalition against the latest upstart's bid for nuclear weapons.[30]

An alternative to finer data resolution and modernized declassification gates does, however, exist. The principle has been labeled in this book as Common Information Infrastructure, and the essential change is to share the processes rather than just the products of information management. Like opera, common information infrastructure alters the mode of communication without changing the literal significance of words. Presumably, ordinary transfers at the current level of information quality could still occur, but now they would take place in a different context where nationals from different allies sat shoulder to shoulder through the entire intelligence cycle, operating the same equipment. Analytical judgments in common infrastructure operations would be matters for deliberation in a senate like atmosphere with equal representation for each state regardless of its natural military capability or the size of its economy.[31]

Sharing in the labor rather than just the tainted fruit of technology makes fine international music that can alter others' dispositions. The substance of the material interests does not change, but in face of the inevitable uncertainties, states modulate their prior assumptions. Going through the effort to compose diplomatic music, or employ information technology in this way, only makes sense if the supplier has expectations of permanent partnerships that will pay off in future crises, only if the leader assumes interlocutors highly resolved in defense of their national interests, and only if the first state among equals is willing to limit its demands accordingly. Investing in common information infrastructure rather than selective declassification plainly shows that a great power values the concord of sweet sounds, that it comprehends not just superiority in relative power but finiteness in its own absolute power to reorder the world. Unlike Athens before Sicily in 416 B.C. or the United States before Iraq in 2003, such a power may be trusted by its natural allies and believed by its foes.

30 Linzer (2005a); Geyer (2006); Sanger and Broad (2006).

31 Prerequisites for deliberation are discussed in Habermas (c1981) and extended in an international context by Crawford (2002) and Payne and Samhat (2004).

Reasons for Optimism

The plan of this book was designed to show both the logical consistency and empirical evidence supporting a new approach to information sharing, starting with members of NATO. Early chapters explained why advanced technology generating more data at higher rates will leave statesmen confronting the same basic dilemmas of crisis management. No amount of computer bytes can anticipate an adversary's imagination when it comes to political-military strategy or an adversary's resolve when it comes to trading lives for state objectives.

A second stage of the logic examined whether sharing the collection, analysis, and dissemination functions as opposed to declassified information products could bring about better crisis bargaining outcomes for the leading power. If sharing functions promoted deliberation that produced a common position, essentially a common judgment on adversary resolve, the United States could end up winning more by placing stricter, European limits on its demands. The key to unlocking the benefits would be the effect on the opponent. Seeing all the sovereign states of NATO, perhaps along with several others, aligned on a single position, backing one coherent set of demands, a recalcitrant would find it more difficult to maintain his own state's resolve. Alliance sharing at the beginning turns the tables on a holdout. Instead of preserving his country's dignity against a monstrous empire, he is throwing away lives for a vain delusion that his country can somehow opt out of the system and escape the forms of civilization. The coalition leader as Trusted Guardian remains in tune with the song of nations while the rogue is cut out, like a hyperpower but without the material capability.

In order to check whether the theories in support of trusted guardianship could be supported in the historical record, empirical chapters of the book reported on two case comparisons. With respect to the first study on the effect of advancing information technology, two series of crises were selected. The Berlin series included situations when the allies had to resolve crises with the Soviet Union using relatively low levels of collection and communications technology. At the other end of the spectrum, many of these same allies engaged Slobodan Milosevic of Serbia over the future of Kosovo, this time with video conferencing, satellite imaging and far more sophisticated communications intercept technology.

Despite the dramatic upgrade in information systems, serious disagreements, leading to stark differences in apprehending the threat and formulating crisis demands, continued within the US decision making elite and among various allies. In every case, whether the adversary was Stalin, Khrushchev, or Milosevic, an important element of the opponent's strategy to improve bargaining position featured multiple ploys to split the coalition against him.

Intra-alliance conflicts across the crisis episodes hinged on divergent estimates of adversary resolve. Because the United States could not use its superior information or military systems to prove these claims one way or another, there was always the possibility that allied judgment was correct and that they, not US leaders, advocated the optimal strategy. In certain instances, despite the lopsided distribution of power and technology, allies were able to stand their ground—delaying certain currency steps during the Berlin Airlift, for example, or restricting targets during the Kosovo campaign—creating openings for the Soviet Union or Serbia, as the case was, to temporarily paralyze the coalition.

With the subsequent episode of Iraq in mind, it is interesting that certain coping strategies continued from the low technology through high technology bargaining. For example, General Lucius Clay had a unique personal touch. He seemed to possess special insight into Soviet resolve, pushing them on occasion during the Airlift of 1948 and the Wall crisis of 1961, without taking the world over the edge. Over many years, Clay made several important bargaining moves, and the rest of the US policy machinery as well as allied governments followed suit. The rise of instant communications and remote imaging over subsequent decades did nothing really to phase out this sort of protagonist. Richard Holbrooke, after years of diplomatic effort on war torn Bosnia, developed a unique relationship with Serbian negotiators and Slobodan Milosevic. In the military escalation of October 1998, Holbrooke used his personal skill to gauge Milosevic's position; he improvised, recasting the zone of agreement, and the rest of the US government as well as its allies were persuaded, with some subsequent modifications, to take up the settlement.

The prominence of the personal touch in both the early and late cases indicates the limits of information technology for directly solving the basic crisis dilemma, that is, deciding on the right mix of escalation and concession that will resolve the conflict on the most favorable grounds. At the same time, the tactic of sending a talented envoy has its own limitations. With ultimate responsibility for national security falling squarely on their shoulders, heads of government hesitate to potentially compromise their control by delegating their authority. In both the Berlin and Yugoslavia series, presidents eventually curtailed the maneuvering room for their fixer, and in the end, neither Clay nor Holbrooke were prominent in the ultimate resolutions for Berlin and Kosovo.

Supplementing the personal touch, presidents have tried deliberation—within their national security councils and across allied governments—as an alternative coping mechanism. Intriguingly, the most remarkable instance came during the high technology bargaining against Serbia. President Clinton reinforced the notion that Secretary General Javier Solana spoke with the authority of NATO's North Atlantic Council. Informally, this gave NATO's top official unprecedented power since he was not merely reporting the consensus of national representatives but actively participating, helping to shape the course of debate. No doubt, Solana was aware of the power distribution on the council and the large percentage of sorties in Operation Allied Force flown by the United States, but he also knew the importance of preserving allied cohesion. To resolve the differences between the most aggressive and the most cautious allies with respect to Serbia, he became a repository for neutral, mutually acceptable judgment. His voice informed General Clark what sort of bombing NATO would tolerate, and it persuaded the allies about what Clark needed to win. Even in a high tech age with much of the technology controlled by one party, the deliberation function was crucial for coalition crisis management.

In the future, it should be possible to institutionalize the personal effect achieved by Secretary Solana. Giving equal access to alliance members at every step of the crisis intelligence process creates a roundtable for open discussion. Common information infrastructure, akin to what Solana accomplished with personal credibility and diplomatic skill, sets the preconditions for deliberative judgment about important unknowns such as adversary resolve. From the US perspective, these judgments may not match precisely what its representatives initially had in mind, but alliance positions benefiting from process legitimacy will inspire stronger commitments from partners as the stakes and the stress rise during crisis.

Counterfactual analysis of the Iraq crisis indicated that stickiness for a NATO approach—in other words, one that could bind the United States, the United Kingdom, France, and Germany—would improve the United States' crisis performance. Based on the rhetoric of France's foreign minister at the time, Dominique DeVillepin; the closed door meetings between French Ambassador to the United States David Levitte and Deputy National Security Adviser Stephen Hadley; and France's actions in other parts of the world, France acknowledged the danger posed by Saddam Hussein's consistent violations of UN Security Council resolutions. Depending on how post-war policies played out, France's economic interest in Iraq's future differed from America's. Even so, France signaled multiple times in January 2003, that force was a viable option for neutralizing the security threat—as long as that decision was taken according to a reasonable international process, which had already been initiated at the Security Council.

Both France and Germany, as a non-permanent Security Council member, cooperated in the conventional way, sharing selective information with US intelligence services, but especially after Colin Powell's mega-presentation on February 5, they complained that either the United States was not being sufficiently transparent, or it simply did not have the evidence for justifying an invasion to eliminate the Iraqi regime. Moreover, Saddam Hussein read the split within the West and relied on it to gird his own country for resistance against the more stringent American demands.

The Iraq case points to another flaw with conventional declassification versus common information infrastructure. As the crisis deteriorated toward war, the United States as coalition leader became more desperate to keep its partners on board. Realizing this, the partners viewed US transfers with increasing skepticism, even as the US, sliding closer to combat operations, felt more pressure to protect sources and methods for the information vaults that yet remained off limits. Supply and demand for selective declassification worked at cross purposes. When demand triumphed, as in President Bush's authorization, late in the deployment period, to release US war plans for Saudi Arabia's review, the lack of trust among partners meant that the United States had no other options to demonstrate its credibility except to offer a peek at its sources and methods. In the long run, exclusive reliance on the complex system of locks and keys for sharing information may increase the chances that secrets vital to US military success must be revealed in order to purchase momentary cooperation.

Information Sharing and the Kantian Peace

Taken together, the logic of crisis management and the history of crisis bargaining across several cases support a policy that would shift US information sharing from selective declassification to common infrastructure. The question of whether such an initiative is practical in today's environment merits an answer on two levels. First, are there any empirical precedents or institutional antecedents for sharing the process in areas of activity vital to national security? Second, given what we understand about the motives of international cooperation, is there any reason to think that changing technology could profoundly alter behavior patterns in the international system?

With regard to the first question, examples of process integration relevant to crisis intelligence exist at various levels of national and international organization. Putting the steps together within the context of NATO would require policy innovation, but for a number of reasons, this does not seem like an impossibly giant leap forward. The United States, which as the leading state would come closest to the ideal role of Trusted Guardian and would pay for most of the equipment, is currently reforming its national intelligence system.[32] An independent, bipartisan commission after the 9/11 attacks criticized the fragmentation and lack of coordination at the level of intelligence operations and oversight. Perhaps the most salient recommendation eliminated the dual-hatted position of CIA director and coordinator of the intelligence community in favor of a dedicated national intelligence director who could impose standards of collection and analysis to permit free access across technical, human, and military intelligence organizations, and even break down traditional fire walls between foreign intelligence and law enforcement without compromising civil rights.[33]

In an article written during a push for intelligence reform but before 9/11, Stephen Chan (1979) warned about preserving pluralism even in a system with independent agencies.[34] Groupthink, for example might end up being more pernicious than in a formally centralized structure because the phenomenon could catch policy makers unawares. Competing agencies, after all, still benefited from pleasing the president. Simply making his policy preferences clear early in a crisis could steer the entire bureaucracy away from an alternative interpretation of the data.

Interestingly, Chan's objections might be overcome if pluralist architecture were employed across a union of states rather than within a single government. The United States has moved to internationalize its *National Intelligence Strategy*, creating a Combined Enterprise Information Exchange System (CENTRIXS) based on NATO's lock-and-key arrangements.[35] The European Union, also contemplating new requirements and interested in encouraging a common foreign policy, has considered developing common information infrastructure as an aid to developing a coherent EU bargaining position during crisis management.[36] In this case, the stumbling blocks have more to do with lingering conflicts of national interest than groupthink. The EU network would not include the United States, and certain European countries would prefer to limit their participation in EU deliberations rather than jeopardize special intelligence sharing relationships—even of the old lock and key variety—with the largest technical system in the world.

---

32 Turner (2005); Betts (2007).

33 National Commission on Terrorist Attacks upon the United States (2004: Section 13.3, p. 416).

34 Chan (1979: 177–8).

35 Reveron (2006: 458–9).

36 Villadsen (1999). See also Burwell et al. (2006: 16, 20–1).

NATO, of course, already includes the United States in combined crisis management and military operations. Here was an added reason to feature major NATO allies in all the cases for this research: if the logical propositions and empirical hypotheses supporting a shift toward common information infrastructure held true in cases like Berlin, Yugoslavia, and Iraq, this particular group of crisis managers was well positioned to actually carry the policy forward. While not yet at the order of magnitude necessary to fund satellite and computer networks for a full intelligence suite, NATO already runs a successful Security Investment Program (NSIP), coming in at nearly a billion dollars for fiscal year 2008.[37]

NATO common budget items are funded more or less according to members' ability to pay. The United States, for example, currently contributes 23.2 percent of the investment program budget for the twenty-six-nation alliance. Projects covered by the program include airfields and headquarters at European bases serving multinational contingents. Typically, infrastructure includes information technology like air defense radar or communications equipment.

Other combined programs besides NSIP indicate that a NATO proprietary system for collection and analysis of crisis intelligence data could be quite sophisticated without compromising US military secrets. Several major European allies are joining efforts to procure the next generation imaging satellite from the old Helios line, and many of these same countries are cooperating to construct the next generation satellite navigation system called Galileo.[38] Already, many of these partners sit shoulder-to-shoulder to analyze mostly commercial take—down to one meter resolution—at the EU Satellite Center in Torrejon, Spain.[39] With the Americans on board, NATO is developing an Alliance Ground Surveillance (AGS) radar, which improves on the American JSTARS concept for tactical military operations and crisis management, and NATO is reorienting its Special Committee from conventional military intelligence to combine sources that would better characterize the global terrorist threat.[40]

During the last five years, US defense acquisition has also evolved to include more participation from European countries. Though the share of Pentagon spending remains low, contractors from the United Kingdom, France, Germany, and beyond have captured important development contracts. In 2005, the *New York Times* reported that "the newest army spy plane will be a variation of the Brazilian Embraer," and "twelve of the biggest weapon systems used in Iraq—including Predator drones and Tomahawk missiles—could not be built without foreign suppliers," providing German aluminum tubes, Italian guidance systems and Swiss data terminals.[41] Large European contractors such as BAE Systems (United Kingdom) and European

---

37 NATO Security Investment Program: Budget Justifications for FY2008 President's Budget. Available at www.defenselink.mil/comptroller/defbudget/fy2008/budget_justification/pdfs/nsip/02_NSIP_FY%202008.pdf.

38 Hitchens (2006: 16, 20).

39 See the EU Satellite Center website at www.eusc.europa.eu/index.php?option=com_frontpage&Itemid=1.

40 GlobalSecurity.org (2005). Reveron (2006: 460–1).

41 Wayne (2005: 15).

Aeronautic Defense and Space (France-Germany) are implementing strategies to penetrate the American defense market, including multi-billion dollar acquisitions of US companies; international consortia with American flagship firms like Lockheed and Northrop; and foreign direct investment for production facilities in the United States. The Pentagon has considered the risk of becoming strategically dependent on foreign suppliers. At the same time though, top officials acknowledge that for some applications, the best research and technology may be overseas. Globalized acquisition promises "the best capability at the most cost-effective price and from the best suppliers we can find."[42]

At the same time, requirements of the war on terror, including a wider range of force protection missions for NATO, are ratcheting up incentives for intense cooperation on technology. The CIA now operates Counter Terrorist Intelligence Centers employing high end espionage devices and secure communications, side-by-side with foreign intelligence officers.[43] The cooperation not only takes place within front-line states in the war on terror such as Uzbekistan and Indonesia. In Paris, a multinational operations center called Alliance Base institutionalizes intense cooperation among agents from Britain, France, Germany, Canada, and Australia. While it is not clear that US partners in these centers such as the National Security Agency have moved beyond traditional methods, in other words, loosening the rules for sharing signals intelligence rather than producing and using technology together, dramatic lowering of the old classification barriers could be a preparatory step toward common information infrastructure.

As confirmed by the eventual falling out with Uzbek officials over democracy promotion in their country, selective declassification even at unprecedented levels buys only momentary trust: at the next fork in the road, the supplier state is asked to do more when it has less remaining to give. Common infrastructure, by contrast, sets up a virtuous cycle through permanent councils deliberating how to connect the dots, or interpret incoming data streams. The more the combined agency works, the more contributing members have incentive to stay. Common infrastructure is a natural development as US foreign intelligence strategy shifts from recruiting anti-government spies to partnering with other governments against terrorists.[44]

Focusing on relationships within the Atlantic Alliance, this book has implied that deep ties altering the emphasis from information sharing to "shared information" should begin with the most institutionalized alliance of democracies. One might ask, why start with this group of states rather than Western style democracies outside of Europe like Australia or Japan? Alternatively, the project could begin with a group such as the five permanent members of the UN Security Council with obvious responsibility for countering threats to international peace and security. The answers to these questions speak to the theoretical plausibility of common information infrastructure and trusted guardianship. Given that we can point to precedents in the record for high quality technology production outside the United States and for deeper intelligence ties against terrorist networks and nuclear proliferation, it

42 Ibid. Bruno (2005).

43 Priest (2005).

44 Ibid.

remains to explain how sharing the process of information management—creating a roundtable for allies to interpret data during crisis—accords with standard accounts of how world politics unfolds.

The roundtable proposed here is broadly consistent with the pluralistic security community in the North Atlantic area discussed by Karl Deutsch (1957: 6) and the ascendant security community described by Adler and Barnett (1998: 53–5). NATO, of course, was born to counter a common threat. The initial need for coordination to face the Soviet Union all but guaranteed repeated interactions on security issues such as military preparedness and deterrence, which extended time horizons and laid the groundwork for increasing trust among partners. Cultural ties, along with the common rejection of both fascism and communism meant a certain level of political, social, and ideological homogeneity, or at least compatibility among alliance members. At the same time, with the United States' superior economic and military position after World War II, the grouping had the benefit of a core state, what Immanuel Kant (c1795) called a powerful and enlightened focal point for free federation, to keep the alliance growing toward an ascendant community.[45]

At this second stage, the relationship between national identities and the group identity began to change. Cooperation in theory moved beyond the level of international institutions performing monitoring, verification, and brokering functions among members with competing interests. Preferences drew closer together. Security and economic benefits of continual cooperation became more of a common concern. Countries in this more advanced security community perceived the value of sharing intelligence as part of the process for developing a common threat picture; there was more interest in analyzing and debating the merits of each other's interpretations. Rather than a temporary alliance of convenience, the community took on the aura of a congress in which representatives harbored dual loyalties—to their geographic constituency and to the good of the whole.[46]

Interestingly, in the afterglow of NATO's victory against Slobodan Milosevic's murderous policy in Kosovo, Alex Bellamy (2002: 209) judged that the Atlantic Alliance was already demonstrating properties of a mature security community, including not just diplomatic understanding, self-restraint, and default to multilateralism, but the development of a common discourse that allowed a single definition of the outside threat. As a cautionary note, though, events after September 11 seemed to show a clash of discourses, the Bush administration arguing that unilateral strength was necessary to preserve international order against the nexus of terror and proliferation in weapons of mass destruction while several NATO allies countered that this approach undermined international norms in the long-run by violating the principles of a mature security community as promulgated by NATO and the United Nations.

Regardless of which constructivist account of evolving identities is correct, the implosion of the Soviet threat delivered a significant shock midway through the historical process. Even after the shift in relative power toward the United States,

45 Adler and Barnett (1998: 50–7) define different levels of security community, ranging from nascent to ascendant and mature communites.

46 Ibid. See also Russett (1998: 374, 377, 386).

it remained the case that NATO allies rejected the notion of war against the lead state—the main concern of Deutsch's political communities. However, NATO never reached the point where identical priorities and a common discourse were available for managing crises *out of area*. As demands on the Atlantic community for global crisis management approached those of a common security and defense policy, they far exceeded the level of identification required for the original mission of collective defense.

If it is planted in fertile soil, trusted guardianship stands a better chance of succeeding. Although not a mature community in the context of defending international order outside the alliance, NATO still exemplifies an ascendant community, which can provide a solid foundation.[47] Common Information Infrastructure is one of those institutional, or technological, options that can accelerate progress through the final steps toward a fully mature community. Specifications and technical parameters of a NATO crisis information system have less importance than creating a roundtable, nurturing a deliberative process with equal access, and fostering that common discourse for community judgments weighty enough to ameliorate discordant national priorities.[48]

Relative to the constructivist understanding of emergent, supranational identities, trusted guardianship is somewhat less consistent with institutional liberalism.[49] Building a crisis information system for the Atlantic Alliance with reporting obligations to national delegations on the North Atlantic Council does not automatically create meaningful legislative, executive, or judicial authority favored by institutionalists. It does not compare, for example to the growth of a World Trade Organization with enforcement powers out of the General Agreement on Tariffs and Trade, or the shift from consensus to qualified majority voting for binding regulations of the European Union.

Relative to institutions designed to promote open economies and encourage liberal democratic political arrangements, trusted guardianship imposes few new regulations. In some cases, it may actually reduce the amount of information from that which could be produced, at least in principle, by national systems pooling their resources using the old lock and key approach. Trusted guardianship promotes transparency, but it does not regulate it in the sense of conventional confidence building measures. The proposal draws strength from liberal ideas of an older vintage, before the complex institutions of the Bretton Woods system or the collective security of the League of Nations.

---

47 NATO provides a solid foundation, or a solid core, for expanding an international zone of stability and cooperation. In telling fashion Fukuyama (2006: 100–5) arguing from the ascendance of liberal-democratic ideas and Kagan (2004) arguing from the ascendance of American power both saw close allies in Western Europe as crucial but not automatic sources of legitimacy. Despite their relative material weakness, NATO allies still counted as critical participants for successful U.S. grand strategy.

48 Crawford (2002); Payne and Samhat (2004).

49 Deutsch's (1957: 25–8, 129–30, 164–7) policy recommendations emphasized responsiveness—especially getting a core state to listen to its partners' discourse—without coercion of "community-wide laws, courts, police forces, and armies."

Common Information Infrastructure makes more sense for the Atlantic Alliance than the UN Security Council because although the Security Council under codified international law has authority to intervene for the preservation of international peace and security, its members do not all have republican civil constitutions—in contemporary terms, they are not all liberal democracies. While a roundtable conceived by shared technology will not compel members to become more democratic, the success of crisis deliberations at this table does depend on the constitutions of its members. For the same reason that the American Constitution in Article IV guaranteed a republican constitution for all member states in the Union, trusted guardianship works best among national representatives who are accountable to the long-term interests of their people.

This claim aligns perfectly with Immanuel Kant's ideas on how to establish perpetual peace in the international system. Taking their cue from his culminating essay on "Perpetual Peace," modern institutionalists may underestimate the efficacy of Kant's free federation and endeavor to supplement it with "modern" variables. In an article on the neo-Kantian perspective, Bruce Russett (1998), a leading researcher on social scientific evidence for the democratic peace, argued that a late-20th century reading of Kant led directly to the notion of triangulating peace, bringing in representative democracy, economic interdependence, and international organizations.[50]

For Russett, these vertices were analytically separable and measurable variables. Consequently, in his work and several supporting investigations, democracy, economic interdependence, and the density of international organization networks were observed across thousands of interstate relationships, and their individual effects were calculated statistically, independent of so-called realist variables such as power distribution or territorial proximity. With minor revisions, notably the substitution of a dyadic score referring to a pair of states rather than individual state scores on democracy, all of Kant's ideas associated empirically with greater incidence of peace. These results led Russett away from trusted guardianship and toward cautious optimism that the United Nations—not the Atlantic Alliance—could, under conditions of spreading democracy and economic globalization, midwife a global security community.[51]

Several years after the 9/11 attacks and the Iraq Crisis, the United Nations still stands for peaceful conflict resolution, but the organization appears too weak to impose standards on recalcitrant states, whether they be upstarts like North Korea, Iran, and Iraq or impatient champions tending toward unilateralism as the United States did in 2002–2003. These disappointments, however, do not debunk all the plausible interpretations of Kant. Trusted guardianship, for example, matches Kant's advice on his second Definitive Article for perpetual peace better than the United Nations or many other international institutions.

Michael Doyle, who rekindled interest in Kant's essay with a series of articles during the 1980s, subsequently placed Kant at the system level of analysis.[52] This

50 Russett (1998: 370–1); Russett and Oneal (2001).

51 Russett (1998: 368, 370–1, 386–7).

52 Doyle (1983); Doyle (1997: 252; 252–84, *passim*).

represents an important difference from the modern social scientific understanding that translates Kant's three articles into three variables, each with independent causal force toward peace. At the state level of analysis, directly addressed by Kant's first Definitive Article, it is true that the causes of peace are monadic: the people pay the costs of war, so in a republic, they can prevail upon their representatives in government to avoid war.[53]

Yet, in the second Article, aimed at the system level, the one that Doyle emphasizes, a peace-loving disposition on the part of one state is not sufficient to extract that state from a condition of war with other nations. "For the sake of its own security," any nation, including one with a republican constitution, "can and should demand that the others enter into a contract."[54] Without "a league of a special sort" among nations, "peace can be neither inaugurated nor guaranteed."[55]

The contracting members of this league are free nations seeking a less brutal, less destructive way of maintaining their security than waging war—a republic "by its nature must be inclined to seek perpetual peace."[56] The free federation, though, extends the blessings of peace only to state members who have consented to bind themselves. In other words, between the league of liberal democracies and authoritarian governments outside the federation, relations in the state of nature, which is to say the state of war, still exist. From a close reading of the second Article, Doyle demonstrates that no modifications to the first Article are required to derive the dyadic, or more properly, the polygonal peace among democracies, even as they continue to war with non-democracies.[57]

Unlike the United Nations or the League of Nations, but like Kant's free federation, trusted guardianship has neither executive authority nor a pact to enforce peace among its members. States can leave at any time. In fact, "there will always be constant danger of their breaking loose." Why then is the liberal federation likely to endure, expanding incrementally, country by country, until the entire surface of the globe becomes a zone of peace? In his reply, Kant tests his ideas not by the postulates of liberalism but by the pessimistic assumptions of realism: "Perpetual peace is insured (guaranteed) by nothing less than that great artist *nature*, whose mechanical process makes her purposiveness visibly manifest, permitting harmony to emerge among men through their discord, even against their wills."[58]

Kant's opening salvo for a liberal order could have inspired Kenneth Waltz's neorealism, in which states pursuing their own interests in conflict with one another produce against their individual designs a stable balance of power.[59] In Kant's defense against the criticism that his Articles of peace were not sufficiently realistic, Waltz's balance indeed appears: "Unlike that peace that despotism brings about by vitiating all powers, this one is produced and secured by an equilibrium of the liveliest

53 Russett (1998: 388, fn 7).
54 Kant (c1795: 115).
55 Ibid. (pp. 116–7).
56 Ibid. (p. 117).
57 Doyle (1997: 260–5).
58 Kant (c1795: 120).
59 Waltz (1962).

competing powers."[60] The difference between Kant's liberalism and Waltz's neo-realism is not that one is idealistic while the other is scientific. Kant, too, discovers natural justification for his predictions.

Where Waltz applies the condition of war exclusively to nations, Kant observes it enveloping individuals as well. War, in a sense, becomes a more pervasive problem, but paradoxically one that is more amenable to resolution because there has already been progress in two out of the three types of interaction that could generate war: individual-on-individual, nation-on-nation, and nation-on-individual. Kant termed these the three domains of public right: civil, international, and cosmopolitan right. These interactions originated in a primal state of war, which in the language of modern game theory was an equilibrium condition based on the capabilities and competing interests of political actors as they came into existence. In *all three* arenas, Kant claimed that natural circumstances admitted an alternative equilibrium, a peaceful, Nash solution, in which no actor would rationally deviate given its knowledge of other players and their rational strategies.

Individuals interacting in the state of nature, for example, were compelled by costs of internal discord and the threat of conquest by an outside power to submit themselves to a civil constitution complete with executive, legislative, and judicial authority. Successful republics confirmed that it was possible for individuals, at least, to escape the insecurity of their original condition and enter another equilibrium. Similarly, successful trade delegations demonstrated that nations with a hospitality law for foreign individuals could in fact discover a mutually beneficial arrangement under which trade representatives enjoyed substantial protections in each other's countries. In terms of levels of interaction, that left, of course, nation-on-nation and a demonstration that countries could mutually consent to leave their original condition and enter a league of peace with one another.

Kant argued that nature conspired to bring this superior equilibrium into existence and to make the problem of its achievement solvable. He hesitated to call the free federation a theoretical certainty, because this alternative solution was difficult to see given the constant pressures and dangers of an anarchic system and what Nash would later recognize as a requirement for common knowledge, or mutual recognition. At the same time, success in the civic and cosmopolitan arenas made the theoretical existence of the peace equilibrium easier to preserve in the public imagination; a Waltzian balance of power—coming about just as the realists described—would provide a temporary respite from actual combat, so extant republican powers could reflect on how to make the peace permanent; finally there were the arguments of philosophers—disinterested so far as they were attached to scholarly rather than political life—if only those in power would take an enlightened view of their own good and consent to listen.

Modern game theory, in particular Fearon's rationalist model for war, which encapsulated in precise mathematical form Waltz's neo-realist assumptions about the world, surprisingly confirmed Kant's assertion about the existence of a peace equilibrium. One of the main difficulties in recognizing it may be blamed on the historical tendency to underestimate an adversary's resolve and therefore overestimate

60 Ibid. (p. 125).

the true optimal crisis demand in pursuit of the national interest, not unlike what occurred to ancient Athens in its sequence with Melos and Sicily.

Leaders of republics might acknowledge the resolve of fellow republics—essentially the right of others to coexist as separate, independent nations—on the idea that representatives forced by their civic constitution to seek the long-term interest of their people are likely to take an interest themselves in the peace equilibrium. In such a manner, the mutual recognition required to achieve permanent peace could emerge among representative authorities. By contrast, the bargaining relationships between republics and despotisms are fraught with difficulty. With no free federation between them, the hope of establishing one is quite remote. An authoritarian has no way of offering to recognize the international right since his credibility has been expended in disposing of civic right. A republic facing a Saddam Hussein is terribly vulnerable to preventive, or in the age of WMD what amounts to preemptive, war arguments: as soon as the rogue outside the federation of free nations has the means it will, all but inevitably, discount the republic's resolve and initiate a crisis that will leave that republic worse off unless it fights.

For these among other reasons, Kant anticipated that, although the peace equilibrium existed, it would require practical work to climb there from the war equilibrium of the original system. Those efforts might come to pass "if good fortune should so dispose matters that a powerful and enlightened people should form a republic…"

> It will provide a focal point for a federal association among other nations that will join it in order to guarantee a state of peace among nations that is in accord with the idea of the right of nations, and through several associations of this sort such federation can extend further and further.[61]

We find ourselves, today, in times when a powerful republic exists and several other powers with representative governments have freely joined it. Within this informal federation, war is not contemplated as a rational option for conflicts among members. Doubts linger, though, whether the lead republic is sufficiently enlightened to preserve its commitment to the international right within the zone of peace as it violates those precepts outside the federation, which indeed remains in a state of war.

In order to sustain its position in this mixed condition, with the world in both stations at once, the champion's own interest impels it to accept a new labor—to design for itself a new role of Trusted Guardian. If the United States is to serve as a Kantian focal point, a kind of beacon, during the turbulent shift from the state of war to a new equilibrium, then it will have to be a capable guardian, strong-willed and militarily equipped to deter or defeat outsiders who view the free federation as a threat to their national security. At the same time, it will have to be trusted by allies since no allied intelligence system can verify for certain—until it is too late—whether the United States has forsaken the international right, founded on mutual confidence that war is a barbarous and inefficient means to resolve conflict among republics and that republics will maintain an iron resolve to maintain their sovereign independence.

---

61 Ibid. (p. 117).

Military transformation and aggressive foreign policy outside the zone of peaceful democracies convey US seriousness with respect to the guardian aspect. The problem arises when militant internationalism becomes indistinguishable from the policies of a hyperpower seeking to maximize its security according to the old realist model by filling power vacuums wherever it encounters them. The disposition of a hyperpower, while rational in a state of war, tosses aside even the least burdensome musical accompaniment to the international power game. Other nations are viewed with contempt in that they are not expected to sacrifice in defense of their core principles, including their own independence. War costs for the home nation, on the other hand, are thought to weigh lightly given favorable odds for aggrandizing an empire.

Even in a mixed system with one region in the peace equilibrium and another at war, a leading state would have little reason to actually abandon a Kantian federation once established. Yet, under pressure—such as the stress of a devastating terrorist attack—governments like individuals can make mistakes. The champion, for example, could come to believe that its allies for some reason changed *their* disposition, that they raised questions against the leader's policy because they prioritized national investments or the interests of a corrupt domestic faction over security of the federation. Since mutual recognition is the only glue that makes the peace equilibrium self-enforcing, one pang of doubt can produce ripple effects that send every party scrambling back to what the game theorists call a babbling equilibrium, where strategies do not depend at all on what the players attempt to communicate.[62]

At this vulnerable moment in the whole Kantian scheme, information sharing can provide crucial support. Reinforcement lies not so much in the sophisticated content that might be distributed from sensors operating in one of the current lock and key networks. Worried allies discount this hard earned data as so much cheap talk. They cannot be sure if a hyperpower in the guise of a Trusted Guardian has doctored the intelligence packages for export. Style and process legitimacy, on the other hand, speak to independent governments the way music sways the disposition of individuals.

Without passing final judgment on the ultimate costs and benefits of waging war in Iraq, it was cavalier to do so without giving genuine voice to the allies. Open-and-shut evidentiary packages, stentorian prosecution briefs on the UN stage, and diplomacy that began, "you are either with us or against us," gave no real opportunity for federation partners to participate in the evaluations of Iraqi capability and resolve necessary to formulate the best crisis action plan. The US response became, by default rather than deliberation, the federation's response. That violated Kantian constitutionalism at the international level, where unlike the civic level, contracting parties stay on only through their continued informed consent. Not allowing them to voice their arguments in open deliberation was tantamount to

62 Kant believed that nations in perpetual peace were still in danger of slipping back to the less desirable but more robust war equilibrium. "And godless Furor shall sit/Inside on his frightful weapons, hands bound with a hundred/Brass knots behind him, and roar with bloody mouth" (Kant c1795, quoting Vergil, *Aeneid*, p. 140–1).

shearing these nations—the republics forming a security community in the North Atlantic area and perhaps beyond—of their separateness and independence, which *define* a free federation.

More crises for the present federation are on the way.[63] They will involve the same vexing issues of unaccountable authoritarian regimes, state sponsors of terrorism, and weapons of mass destruction. When the final decision is made to concede or escalate a crisis, it will not be known for sure how accurate the estimates for secret capability or adversary resolve were, but it will likely be quite clear whether a deliberative or despotic process produced those assessments leading to a final strategy.[64]

Common Information Infrastructure, sharing the intelligence process rather than just the content, even if it meant a second Marshall Plan to build a separate, proprietary system away from the Guardian's military secrets, would send an unmistakable signal that the most powerful republic was also enlightened. US policy needs to move with concord of sweet sounds if it wants to lead a Kantian community. Those sounds are the song of free nations calling for the American republic to act internationally, but not as a hyperpower, a world policeman, or even a unipole, for those types are easily seduced by the rationales of stratagems, spoils, and war. An America that appreciates the eventual strategic importance of keeping its democratic partners together, even when that means moderating crisis demands against outsiders, reconciles the tension between its ideals and its interests. Such an America is fit for trusted guardianship not over but within an expanding federation of democracies that might yet buoy international relations and secure a just peace.

63 The issue of Iran's developing nuclear capability might still drag the allies into a crisis (Wright 2007).

64 Linzer (2005a); Linzer (2005b).

Bibliography

Adler Emanuel and Michael Barnett (1998), "A Framework for the Study of Security Communities." In Emanuel Adler and Michael Barnett, (eds) *Security Communities*. Cambridge, UK: Cambridge University Press.

Agence France-Press (2004), "US Press Urges Kerry to Make Clear His Position on Defense." *Agence France-Press* (English) (July 29).

Albright, Madeleine Albright (2003), "Bridges, Bombs, or Bluster?" *Foreign Affairs* Vol. 82, No. 5 (September/October): 2–19.

Allison, Graham (1971), *Essence of Decision: Explaining the Cuban Missile Crisis*. USA: HarperCollins Publishers.

Allison, Graham and Philip Zelikow (1999), *Essence of Decision: Explaining the Cuban Missile Crisis*. 2nd edn NY: Addison Wesley Longman.

Andrews, David (2005), "The United States and Its Atlantic Partners." In David Andrews, (ed.) *The Atlantic Alliance Under Stress: US-European Relations after Iraq*. Cambridge, UK: Cambridge University Press, pp. 56–78.

Andrews, David, (ed.) (2005), *The Atlantic Alliance Under Stress: US – European Relations after Iraq*. Cambridge, UK: Cambridge University Press.

Appathurai, James (2007), The NATO Response Force. Press Briefing by NATO Spokesman, James Appathurai (September 21). Available at http://www.nato.int/docu/speech/2007/s070921a.html.

Armitage, Catherine (2004), "China Signals Timely Shift Against Proliferation," *The Weekend Australian* (February 21): 13.

Art, Robert (2003), *A Grand Strategy for America*. Ithaca, NY: Cornell University Press.

Art, Robert and Patrick Cronin, (eds) (2003), *The United States and Coercive Diplomacy*. Washington, D.C.: United States Institute of Peace Press.

Associated Press (2003), "Bush to Meet Blair, Aznar in Azores." (March 14). *Global Policy Forum*. Available at www.globalpolicy.org/security/issues/iraq/attack/2003/0314bushto.htm.

Bacevich, Andrew (2005), *The New American Militarism: How Americans Are Seduced by War*. Oxford, UK: Oxford University Press.

Baker, Peter and Jonathan Weisman (2007), "Patraeus Backs Initial Pullout." *Washington Post* (September 11): A01.

Bamford, James (2004), *A Pretext for War: 9/11, Iraq, and the Abuse of America's Intelligence Agencies*. NY: Doubleday.

Bamford, James (2006), "Big Brother Is Listening." *Atlantic Monthly* (April): 65–70.

BBC (2003a), "Millions Join Global Anti-War Protests." *BBC News* online (February 17). Available at http://news.bbc.co.uk/2/hi/europe/2765215.stm.

BBC (2003b), "NATO Scrutinizes Compromise Plan." *BBC News* online (February 16). Available at http://news.bbc.co.uk/1/hi/world/europe/2767537.stm.

BBC (2003c), "'New Europe' Backs EU on Iraq." *BBC News* online (February 19). Available at http://news.bbc.co.uk/2/hi/europe/2775579.stm.

BBC (2003d), "Outrage at Old Europe Remarks." *BBC News* online (January 23). Available at http://news.bbc.co.uk/2/hi/europe/2687403.stm.

BBC (2003e), "Turkey Ups the Stakes on US Troops." *BBC News* online (February 19). Available at http://news.bbc.co.uk/2/hi/europe/2773877.stm.

BBC (2004a), "Kerry, Bush Clash over Iraq War." (October 1). Available at http://news.bbc.co.uk.

BBC (2004b), "Spain's Government Ousted in Poll." (March 15). Available at http://news.bbc.co.uk.

BBC (2005a), "Blair Secures Historic Third Term." (May 6). Available at http://news.bbc.co.uk.

BBC (2005b), "Congressmen Probe Iraq War Memo." *BBC News* online (June 17). Available at http://news.bbc.co.uk/2/hi/americas/4101420.stm.

BBC (2005c), "Rice Sees New Chapter in Europe." (February 8). Available at http://news.bbc.co.uk.

BBC (2005d), "Rice Speech Wins Measured Reviews." *BBC News* online (February 9). Available at http://news.bbc.co.uk/2/hi/europe/4249753.stm.

BBC (2006), "NATO Takes Over Afghan Security." BBC (October 5): http://news.bbc.co.uk/2/hi/south_asia/5408332.stm.

Bellamy, Alex (2002), *Kosovo and International Society.* NY: Palgrave Macmillan.

Betts, Richard (1978), "Analysis, War, and Decision: Why Intelligence Failures are Inevitable." *World Politics* Vol. 31, No. 1 (October): 61–89.

Betts, Richard (2000), "Is Strategy an Illusion?" *International Security* Vol. 25, No. 2 (Fall): 5–50.

Betts, Richard (2002a), "Fixing Intelligence." *Foreign Affairs* Vol. 81, No. 1 (January/February): 43–59.

Betts, Richard (2002b), "The Soft Underbelly of American Primacy: Technical Advantages of Terror." *Political Science Quarterly* Vol. 117, No. 1 (April): 19–36.

Betts, Richard (2007), *Enemies of Intelligence: Knowledge and Power in American National Security.* NY: Columbia University Press.

Biddle, Stephen (1997), "The Gulf War Debate Redux." *International Security* Vol. 22, No. 2 (Fall): 163–74.

Biddle, Stephen (2002), "The New Way of War? Debating the Kosovo Model." *Foreign Affairs* Vol. 81, No. 3 (May/June): 138–44.

Biddle, Stephen (2004), *Military Power: Explaining Military Victory and Defeat in Modern Battle.* Princeton, NJ: Princeton University Press.

Biddle, Stephen (2007), "Strategy in War." *P.S.: Political Science and Politics* Vol. 40, No. 3 (July): 461–6.

Blechman, Barry and Stephen Kaplan (1978), *Force without War: US Armed Forces as a Political Instrument.* Washington, D.C.: Brookings Institution.

Blight, James and David Welch (1998), *Intelligence and the Cuban Missile Crisis.* London, UK: Frank Cass.

Blix, Hans (2004), Interview on the *Newshour with Jim Leher*, PBS (March 17). Transcript available at www.pbs.org/newshour/66??/international/jan-june04/blix_3-17.html.

Bloom, Allan (1987), *The Closing of the American Mind.* NY: Simon and Schuster.

Bloom, Allan (c1968, 1991), *The Republic of Plato*, 2nd Edition. Translation, Introduction, Notes, and Interpretive Essay. NY: Basic Books.

Bluth, Christoph (2004), "The British Road to War: Blair, Bush and the Decision to Invade Iraq." *International Affairs* Vol. 80, No. 5: 871–92.

Boin, Arjen (2004), "Lessons for Crisis Research." *International Studies Review* Vol. 6, No. 1 (March): 165–74.

Borden, Teresa (2004), "U.S. Tack on Trade Treaties Assailed." *Atlanta Journal-Constitution* (June 23): 6F.

Bouchard, Joseph (1991), *Command in Crisis: Four Case Studies.* NY: Columbia University Press.

Bowie, Robert and Richard Immerman (1998), *Waging Peace: How Eisenhower Shaped an Enduring Cold War Strategy.* NY: Oxford University Press.

Boyer, Glenn, (ed.) (1976), *I Married Wyatt Earp: The Recollections of Josephine Sarah Marcus Earp.* Tuscon, AZ: University of Arizona Press.

Boyer, Peter (2003), "The New War Machine." *New Yorker* (June 30): 55–69.

Bracken, Paul (1983), *The Command and Control of Nuclear Forces.* New Haven, CT: Yale University Press.

Brecher, Michael and Jonathan Wilkenfeld (2000), *A Study of Crisis.* Ann Arbor, MI: University of Michigan Press.

Bright, Martin, Ed Vulliamy, and Peter Beaumont (2003), "Revealed: US Dirty Tricks to Win Vote on Iraq War." *The Observer* (London) (March 2). Available at http://observer.guardian.co.uk/iraq/story/0,12239,905936,00.html.

Brodie, Bernard (1959), *Strategy in the Missile Age.* Princeton, NJ: Princeton University Press.

Brosky, John (2002), "It Takes Two to Interoperate." *Journal of Electronic Defense* (August): 43–46.

Brugioni, Dino (1993), *Eyeball to Eyeball: The Inside Story of the Cuban Missile Crisis*, Updated Edition. NY: Random House.

Bruno, Michael (2005), "Krieg: 'Creative' Acquisition Needed to Help Competition." *Aerospace Daily and Defense Report.* Excerpted from the Pentagon *Early Bird* http://ebird.afis.mil (September 8).

Bueno de Mesquita, Bruce (2000), *Principles of International Politics: People's Power, Preferences, and Perceptions.* Washington, D.C., CQ Press.

Bueno de Mesquita, Bruce and David Lalman (1992), *War and Reason: Domestic and International Imperatives.* New Haven, CT: Yale University Press.

Bull, Hedley (1977), *The Anarchical Society: A Study of Order in World Politics.* NY: Columbia University Press.

Burdick, Frank (1984), "The Christmas Bombing of North Vietnam: The Limitations of Force." *Journal of Political and Military Sociology* Vol. 12, No. 2 (Fall): 213–28.

Burrough, Bryan, Evgenia Peretz, David Rose, and David Wise (2004), "The Path to War." *Vanity Fair* (May): 228–45.

Burrows, William (1986), *Deep Black: Space Espionage and National Security.* NY: Random House.

Burwell, Frances, David Gompert, Leslie Lebl, Jan Lodal, and Walter Slocombe (2006), *Transatlantic Transformation: Building a NATO-EU Security Architecture.* Washington, D.C.: Program on Transatlantic Relations, Atlantic Council of the United States.

Bush, George (2002a), *The National Security Strategy of the United States of America.* Washington, D.C.: The White House (September). Available at www.whitehouse.gov/nsc/nss.html.

Bush, George (2002b), President's Remarks at the United Nations General Assembly, New York, September 12. Available at www.whitehouse.gov/news/releases/2002/09/20020912-1.html.

Bush, George (2006), *The National Security Strategy of the United States of America.* Washington, D.C.: The White House (March). Available at http://www.whitehouse.gov/nsc/nss/2006/.

Butterworth-Hayes, Philip (2004), "New Members Boost EU Aerospace Industry." *Aerospace America* (May): 4.

Byman, Daniel and Kenneth Pollack (2003), "Democracy in Iraq." *Washington Quarterly* Vol. 26, No. 3 (Summer): 119–36.

Byman, Daniel and Matthew Waxman (2000), "Kosovo and the Great Air Power Debate." *International Security* Vol. 24, No. 4 (Spring): 5–38.

Byman, Daniel and Mathew Waxman (2001), *The Dynamics of Coercion: American Foreign Policy and the Limits of Military Might.* NY: Cambridge University Press.

Carnesale, Albert, Paul Doty, Stanley Hoffmann, Joseph Nye, Scott Sagan, and Derek Bok (1983), *Living with Nuclear Weapons.* Cambridge, MA: Harvard University Press.

Carpenter, Ted Galen, (ed.) (2000), *NATO's Empty Victory.* Washington, D.C.: CATO Institute.

Carr, Edward Hallet (1964, c1946), *The Twenty Years' Crisis, 1919–1939.* NY: Harper and Row Publishers.

Chamberlin, Jeffrey (2004), *Comparisons of U.S. and Foreign Military Spending: Data from Selected Public Sources*, CRS Report for Congress (January 28). Available at www.policyalmanac.org/world/archive/defense_spending_comparisons.pdf.

Chan, Steve (1979), "Intelligence of Stupidity: Understanding Failures in Strategic Warning." *American Political Science Review* Vol. 73, No. 1 (March): 171–80.

Chan, Steve (1997), "In Search of the Democratic Peace: Problems and Promise." *Mershon International Studies Review* Vol. 41, No. 1 (May): 59–91.

Choi, Ajin (2003), "The Power of Democratic Cooperation." *International Security* Vol. 28, No. 1 (Summer): 142–53.

Chomsky, Noam (2004), *Hegemony or Survival: America's Quest for Global Dominance.* NY: Henry Holt and Co.

Churchill, Winston (1949), *The Second World War* (Vol. 2): *Their Finest Hour.* NY: Houghton Mifflin Company.

Clark, Wesley (2001), *Waging Modern War: Bosnia, Kosovo, and the Future of Combat.* NY: Public Affairs.

Clodfelter, Mark (1989), *The Limits of Air Power: The American Bombing of North Vietnam.* NY: Free Press.

CNN (2001), "Hit Smarter, not Harder? Gulf War Strikes Marked a Sea Change in Air Tactics." *CNN.com In-Depth—The Unfinished War: A Decade Since Desert Storm.* Available at http://www.cnn.com/SPECIALS/2001/gulf.war/legacy/airstrikes/index.html.

Coletta, Damon and Peter Feaver (2006), "Civilian Monitoring of US Military Operations in the Information Age." *Armed Forces and Society* Vol. 33, No. 1 (October): 106–26.

Commission on the Intelligence Capabilities of the United States Regarding Weapons Of Mass Destruction – Report, Washington, D.C. March 31, 2005. Available at www.wmd.gov.

Connor, W. Robert (1984), *Thucydides.* Princeton, NJ: Princeton University Press.

Coomarasamy, Jamie (2003), "France Treads Carefully on Iraq." *BBC News* online (February 6). Available at http://news.bbc.co.uk/2/hi/middle_east/2732939.stm.

Council on Foreign Relations (2003), "Iraq: What is the Fedayeen Saddam?" CFR Backgrounder (March 31): http://www.cfr.org/publication/7698/.

Crawford, Neta (2002), *Argument and Change in World Politics: Ethics, Decolonization, and Humanitarian Intervention.* Cambridge, UK: Cambridge University Press.

Daadler, Ivo and James Lindsay (2003), *America Unbound: The Bush Revolution in Foreign Policy.* Washington, D.C.: Brookings Institution Press.

Daalder, Ivo and Michael O'Hanlon (2001), *Winning Ugly: NATO's War to Save Kosovo.* Washington, D.C.: Brookings Institution.

Darilek, Richard, Walter Perry, Jerome Bracken, John Gordon, and Brian Nichiporuk (2001), *Measures of Effectiveness for the Information Age Army*, MR-1155A. Santa Monica, CA: RAND.

Davis, Joshua (2003), "If We Run Out of Batteries, This War Is Screwed." *Wired* Magazine (June). Available at www.wired.com/wired/archive/.

Davison, W. Phillips (1958), *The Berlin Blockade; A Study of Cold War Politics.* Princeton, NJ: Princeton University Press.

De Villepin, Dominique (2004), *Toward a New World.* Hoboken, NJ: Melville House Publishing.

De Wijk, Rob (2004), "European Military Reform for a Global Partnership." *The Washington Quarterly* Vol. 27, No. 1 (Winter): 197–211.

Dempsey, Judy (2004), "For EU and NATO, Snags over Intelligence." *International Herald Tribune* (November 11): 1.

Department of Defense, United States (1995), *Military Operations Other than War*, Joint Pub 3–07 (June 16). Available at www.dtic.mil/doctrine/jel/new_pubs/jp3_07.pdf.

Department of Defense, United States (2006), *Information Operations* (2006), Joint Pub 3–13 (Draft—February 13). Available at www.dtic.mil/doctrine/jel/new_pubs/jp3_13.pdf.

Desch, Michael (2003), "Democracy and Victory." *International Security* Vol. 28, No. 1 (Summer): 180–94.

Deutsch, Karl, Sidney Burrell, Robert Kann, Maurice Lee, Jr., Martin Lichterman, Raymond Lindgren, Francis Loewenheim, Richard Van Wagenen (1957), *Political Community in the North Atlantic Area: International Organization in the Light of Historical Experience.* Princeton, NJ: Princeton University Press.

Diehl, Paul and Gary Goertz (2000), *War and Peace in International Rivalry.* Ann Arbor, MI: University of Michigan Press.

Doyle, Michael (1983), "Kant, Liberal Legacies, and Foreign Affairs," Parts I and II. *Philosophy and Public Affairs*, Vol. 12, Nos. 3 and 4 (Summer and Fall): 205–54, 323–53.

Doyle, Michael (1986), "Liberalism and World Politics." *American Political Science Review* Vol. 80, No. 4 (December): 1151–69.

Doyle, Michael (1997), *Ways of War and Peace.* NY: W.W. Norton and Co.

Dreyfuss, Robert and Jason Vest (2004), "The Lie Factory." *Mother Jones* (January-February 2004). Available at www.motherjones.com/news/feature/2004/01/12_405.html.

Economist (2003), "Hell-bent: Dealing with the Danger of a Nuclear North Korea." (May 3): 11–2.

Eilstrup-Sangiovanni, Mette and Daniel Verdier (2005), "European Integration as a Solution to War," *European Journal of International Relations* Vol. 11, No. 1 (March): 99–135.

Elster, Jon (1998), *Deliberative Democracy.* Cambridge, UK: Cambridge University Press.

Etzioni, Amitai (2004), *From Empire to Community: A New Approach to International Relations.* NY: Palgrave.

Fabey, Michael (2005), "US Air Force Space Radar to Provide MOVINT." *C4ISR: The Journal of Net-Centric Warfare*. Defense News Media Group (July 7) www.isrjournal.com/story.php?F=921294.

Fallows, James (2004), "Blind into Baghdad." *Atlantic Monthly* (January/February): 52–74.

Fearon, James (1991), "Counterfactuals and Hypothesis Testing in Political Science." *World Politics* Vol. 43, No. 2 (January): 169–95.

Fearon, James (1994), "Domestic Political Audiences and the Escalation of International Disputes." *American Political Science Review* Vol. 88, No. 3 (September): 577–92.

Fearon, James (1995), "Rationalist Explanations for War." *International Organization* Vol. 49, No. 3 (Summer): 379–414.

Feaver, Peter (1992), *Guarding the Guardians: Civilian Control of Nuclear Weapons in the United States.* Ithaca, NY: Cornell University Press.

Feaver, Peter (1998), "Blowback: Information Warfare and the Dynamics of Coercion." *Security Studies* Vol. 7, No. 4 (Summer): 88–120.

Feaver, Peter (2003), *Armed Servants: Agency, Oversight, and Civil-Military Relations.* Cambridge, MA: Harvard University Press.

Feith, Douglas (2004), "Transformation and Security Cooperation." Remarks by Under Secretary of Defense for Policy, National Press Club Washington, D.C., September 8. Available at http://www.defenselink.mil/Speeches/Speech.aspx?SpeechID=145.

Feith, Douglas, US Undersecretary of Defense for Policy (2004), "Transformation and Security Cooperation." Speech before ComDef 2004, National Press Club, Washington, D.C. (September 28).

Franks, Tommy with Malcolm McConnell (2004), *American Soldier.* NY: HarperCollins.

Freedberg, Jr., Sydney (2004), "A Military Stretched Thin." *National Journal* (June 26): 2008–14.

Freedman, Lawrence (2000), *Kennedy's Wars: Berlin, Cuba, Laos, and Vietnam.* NY: Oxford University Press.

Fukuyama, Francis (2006), *America at the Crossroads: Democracy, Power, and the Neoconservative Legacy.* New Haven, CT: Yale University Press.

Fulghum, David (2003), "Embracing the Foe." *Aviation Week and Space Technology* (June 30): 54.

Gaddis, John Lewis (1983), "The Emerging Post-Revisionist Synthesis on the Origins of the Cold War." *Diplomatic History* Vol. 7, No. 3 (July): 171–90.

Gaddis, John Lewis (1986), "The Long Peace: Elements of Stability in the Postwar International System." *International Security* Vol. 10, No. 4 (Spring): 99–142.

Gaddis, John Lewis (2002), "A Grand Strategy of Transformation." *Foreign Policy* (November/December): 50–7.

Gaddis, John Lewis (2004), *Surprise, Security, and the American Experience.* Cambridge, MA: Harvard University Press.

Gaddis, John Lewis (2005), "Grand Strategy in the Second Term." *Foreign Affairs* Vol. 84, No. 1 (January/February): 2–15.

Garfinkel, Michelle and Stergios Skaperdas (2000), "Conflict without Misperceptions or Incomplete Information: How the Future Matters." *Journal of Conflict Resolution* Vol. 44, No. 6 (December): 793–807.

Garthoff, Raymond (1991), "Berlin 1961: The Record Corrected." *Foreign Policy* Vol. 84 (Autumn): 142–56.

Gartner, Scott and Gary Segura (1998), "War, Casualties, and Public Opinion." *Journal of Conflict Resolution* Vol. 42, No. 3 (June): 278–300.

Gartzke, Erik (1999), "War Is in the Error Term." *International Organization* Vol. 53, No. 3 (Summer): 567–87.

Gaubatz, Kurt (1996), "Democracy and Commitment" *International Organization* Vol. 50, No. 1 (Winter): 109–39.

Gaubatz, Kurt (1999), *Elections and War: The Electoral Incentive in the Democratic Politics of War and Peace.* Stanford, CA: Stanford University Press.

Gearson, John and Keri Schake, (eds) (2002), *The Berlin Wall Crisis: Perspectives on Cold War Alliances.* NY: Palgrave.

Gelpi, Christopher (1997), "The Role of Norms in Crisis Bargaining." *American Political Science Review* Vol. 92, No. 2 (June): 339–60.

Gelpi, Christopher and Michael Griesdorf (2001), "Winners or Losers. Democracies in International Crisis, 1918–94." *American Political Science Review* Vol. 95, No. 3 (September): 633–48.

George, Alexander (1991), "The Cuban Missile Crisis." In Alexander George, (ed.) *Avoiding War: Problems of Crisis Management.* Boulder, CO: Westview Press, pp. 222–68.

George, Alexander, (ed.) (1991), *Avoiding War: Problems of Crisis Management.* Boulder, CO: Westview Press.

George, Alexander (2006), *On Foreign Policy: Unfinished Business.* Boulder, CO: Paradigm Publishers.

George, Alexander and Andrew Bennett (2005), *Case Studies and Theory Development in the Social Sciences.* Cambridge, MA: MIT Press.

George, Alexander and Jane Holl (1997), *The Warning-Response Problem and Missed Opportunities in Preventive Diplomacy.* Washington, D.C.: Carnegie Commission on Preventing Deadly Conflict.

George, Alexander and Richard Smoke (1974), *Deterrence in American Foreign Policy: Theory and Practice.* NY: Columbia University Press.

George, Alexander, David Hall, and William Simons (1971), *The Limits of Coercive Diplomacy: Laos, Cuba, Vietnam.* Boston, MA: Little, Brown).

George, Alexander, William Simons, and David Hall (1994), *The Limits of Coercive Diplomacy*, 2nd Edition. Boulder, CO: Westview Press.

Gertz, Bill (2005), "Thefts of US Technology Boost China's Weaponry." *Washington Times* (June 27): 1.

Geyer, Georgie Anne (2006), "Iraq Déjà Vu all over Iran." *Washington Times* (May 15): 16.

Giffen, Sidney (1965), *The Crisis Game.* Garden City, NY: Doubleday and Co.

Gilmore, J. Michael (2006), "The Army's Future Combat Systems Program." Statement before the Subcommittee on Tactical Air and Land Forces, Committee on Armed Services, US House of Representatives, April 4, Washington, D.C.: Congressional Budget Office.

Global Security (2005), "Future Combat Systems" (June). Available at www.globalsecurity.org/military/systems/ground/fcs.htm.

GlobalSecurity.org (2005), "Alliance Ground Surveillance." GlobalSecurity.org. Available at www.globalsecurity.org/intell/systems/ags.htm.

Gordon, Michael and Bernard Trainor (2006), *Cobra II: The Inside Story of the Invasion and Occupation of Iraq.* NY: Pantheon Books.

Gordon, Philip and Jeremy Shapiro (2004), *Allies at War: America, Europe, and the Crisis over Iraq.* NY: McGraw-Hill.

Graff, James (2000), "The Shadow of a Spy." *TIME Magazine* (March 20): 24.

Gray, Colin (2004), *The Sheriff: America's Defense of the New World Order.* Lexington, KY: University of Kentucky Press.

Gudgel, Andy (2004), "Chinese Crisis Management." Strategic Studies Institute Conference Brief, US Army War College, Carlisle Barracks, PA, October 1–3.

Guggenheim, Ken (2004), "Kerry Offers Support for Pre-emptive Strikes against Terrorists." *Associated Press Worldstream* (July 16).

Guisinger, Alexandra and Alastair Smith (2002), "Honest Threats: The Interaction of Reputation and Political Institutions in International Crises." *Journal of Conflict Resolution* Vol. 46, No. 2 (April): 175–200.

Gutmann, Amy and Dennis Thompson (2004), *Why Deliberative Democracy.* Princeton, NJ: Princeton University Press.

Habermas, Jürgen (c1981, 1984–1987), *The Theory of Communicative Action.* Translated by Thomas McCarthy. Boston: Beacon Press.

Halberstam, David (1992), *The Best and the Brightest—Twentieth Anniversary Edition.* NY: Ballantine Books.

Halberstam, David (2001), *War in a Time of Peace: Bush, Clinton, and the Generals.* NY: Scribner.

Haley, P. Edward (2004), "A Defensive Grand Strategy for the United States." *Armed Forces and Society* Vol. 30, No. 3 (Spring): 461–81.

Handel, Michael (1984), "Intelligence and the Problem of Strategic Surprise." *Journal of Strategic Studies* Vol. 7, No. 3 (September): 229–81.

Hansen, Ryan (SSgt, USAF), (2006), "JDAM Continues to be Warfighter's Weapon of Choice." *Air Force Link* (March 17). Available at www.af.mil/news/story.asp?id=123017613.

Harwood, John and Jacob Schlesinger (2004), "Kerry Sets Test for Iraq Withdrawal." *Wall Street Journal* (July 16): A5.

Hendrickson, David (2002), "Toward Universal Empire: The Dangerous Quest for Absolute Security." *World Policy Journal* Vol. 19, No. 3 (Fall): 1–10.

Hendrickson, Ryan (2002), "NATO's Secretary General Javier Solana and the Kosovo Crisis." *Journal of International Relations and Development* Vol. 5, No. 3 (September): 240–57.

Herek, Gregory, Irving Janis, and Paul Huth (1987), "Decision Making during International Crises: Is Quality of Process Related to Outcome?" *Journal of Conflict Resolution* Vol. 31, No. 2 (June): 203–26.

Hermann, Charles (1972), "Threat, Time, and Surprise: A Simulation of International Crisis." Charles Hermann, editor. *International Crises: Insights from Behavioral Research.* NY: The Free Press, pp. 187–211.

Hersh, Seymour (2003), "Who Lied to Whom." *New Yorker* (March 31). Available at www.newyorker.com/fact/content/?030331fa_fact1.

Hersh, Seymour (2004), "Selective Intelligence." *New Yorker* (May 12): Available at www.newyorker.com/fact/content/?030512fa_fact.

Hewitt, J. Joseph and Jonathan Wilkenfeld (1996), "Democracies in International Crisis." *International Interactions* Vol. 22, No. 2: 123–42.

Hibbing, John and Elizabeth Theiss-Morse (2001), "Process Preferences and American Politics: What the People Want Government to Be." *American Political Science Review* Vol. 95, No. 1 (March): 145–53.

Hibbing, John and Elizabeth Theiss-Morse (2002), *Stealth Democracy: Americans Beliefs about How Government Should Work.* Cambridge, MA: Cambridge University Press.

Hill, Don (2005), "US: New Secretary of State Focuses on 'Common Goals' in Paris Speech." *Radio Free Europe – Radio Liberty.* Available at www.rferl.org/featuresarticle/2005/02/4bb2da74-7c00-4c04-9278-653217465413.html.

Hilsman, Roger (1987), *The Politics of Policy Making in Defense and Foreign Affairs.* Englewood Cliffs, New Jersey: Prentice Hall.

Hiro, Dilip (2004), *Secrets and Lies: Operation "Iraqi Freedom" and After.* NY: Nation Books.

Hirsh, Michael, et al. (2003), "Kim Is the Key Danger." *Newsweek* (January 13): 30.

Hitchens, Theresa (2006), "Military Satellites." Center for Defense Information. Available at www.cdi.org/PDFS/Microsat%202006.pdf.

Hobbes, Thomas (c1651, 1968), *Leviathan.* Edited and Introduction by C.B. Macpherson. NY: Penguin Group.
Hoge, Warren (2004), "Security Council Backs Resolution on Iraq Turnover." *New York Times* (June 8): A1.
Holland, Max (2005), "The 'Photo Gap' that Delayed Discovery of the Missiles." *Studies in Intelligence* Vol. 49, No. 4. Available at https://www.cia.gov/library/center-for-the-study-of-intelligence/csi-publications/csi-studies/studies/vol49no4/Photo_Gap_2.htm.
Holsti, Kalevi J. (2006), "The Decline of Interstate War: Pondering Systemic Explanations." In Raimo Varynem, (ed.) *The Waning of Major War: Theories and Debates.* NY: Routledge, pp. 135–59.
Holsti, Ole (1972), *Crisis, Escalation, War.* Montreal: McGill-Queens University Press.
Hosmer, Stephen (2001), *Why Milosevic Decided to Settle When He Did.* Santa Monica, CA: RAND.
Howard, Peter (2004), "Why Not Invade North Korea? Threats, Language Games, and US Foreign Policy." *International Studies Quarterly* Vol. 48, No. 4 (December): 805–28.
Howley, Frank (1950), *Berlin Command.* NY: Putnam's.
Howorth, Jolyon (2003), "France, Britain and the Euro Atlantic Crisis." S*urvival* Vol. 45, No. 4: 173–92.
Hubbard, Christopher (2005), *Australian and US Military Cooperation: Fighting Common Enemies.* Burlington, VT: Ashgate.
Huntington, Samuel (1999), "The Lonely Superpower." *Foreign Affairs* Vol. 78, No. 2 (March/April): 35–49.
Hutchings, Robert (2004), "X + 9-11." *Foreign Policy* (July/August): 70–2.
Hyland, William (1987), *Mortal Rivals: Superpower Relations from Nixon to Reagan* NY: Random House.
Ignatieff, Michael (2003), "Why Are We in Iraq? (And Liberia? And Afghanistan?)" *New York Times Magazine* (September 7). Available at http://query.nytimes.com/gst/fullpage.html?res=9805EED61538F934A3575AC0A9569C8B63&n=Top/News/World/Countries%20and%Territories/Liberia.
Ikenberry, John (2001), *After Victory: Institutions, Strategic Restraint, and the Rebuilding of Order after Major Wars.* Princeton, NJ: Princeton University Press.
Janis, Irving (1982), *Groupthink: Psychological Studies of Policy Decisions and Fiascoes*, 2nd Edition. Boston, MA: Houghton Mifflin.
Janis, Irving (1989), *Crucial Decisions: Leadership in Policymaking and Crisis Management.* NY: Free Press.
Jentleson, Bruce and Rebecca Britton (1998), "Still Pretty Prudent: Post-Cold War American Public Opinion on the Use of Military Force." *Journal of Conflict Resolution* Vol. 42, No. 4 (August): 395–417.
Jervis, Robert (1976), *Perception and Misperception in International Politics.* Princeton, NJ: Princeton University Press.
Jervis, Robert (1978), "Cooperation under the Security Dilemma," *World Politics* Vol. 30, No. 2 (January): 167–214.

Jervis, Robert (1989), *The Meaning of the Nuclear Revolution: Statecraft and the Prospect of Armageddon.* Ithaca, NY: Cornell University Press.

Johnson, Richard (1999), "Negotiating the Dayton Peace Accords through Digital Maps." United States Institute of Peace. Available at www.usip.org/virtualdiplomacy/publications/reports/rjohnsonISA99.html.

Johnston, Alastair Iain (2003), "Is China a Status Quo Power?" *International Security* Vol. 27, No. 4 (Spring): 5–56.

Kagan, Robert (2002), "Power and Weakness." *Policy Review* No. 113 (June/July). Available at http://www.newamericancentury.org/kagan-20020520.htm.

Kagan, Robert (2003), *Of Paradise and Power: America and Europe in the New World Order.* NY: A. Knopf.

Kagan, Robert (2004), "America's Crisis of Legitimacy." *Foreign Affairs* Vol. 83, No. 2 (March/April): 65–87.

Kant, Immanuel (c1784–1795, 1983), *Perpetual Peace and Other Essays.* Translation and Introduction by Ted Humphrey. USA: Hackett Publishing.

Kaplan, Robert (2002), "A Post-Saddam Scenario." *Atlantic Monthly* (November 2002): 88–90.

Kaufman, Joyce (2002), *NATO and the Former Yugoslavia: Crisis, Conflict, and the Atlantic Alliance.* Lanham, MD: Rowman and Littlefield.

Kaufmann, Chaim (2004), "Threat Inflation and the Failure of the Marketplace of Ideas: The Selling of the Iraq War." *International Security* Vol. 29, No. 4 (Summer): 5–48.

Kennedy, Paul (1987), *The Rise and Fall of the Great Powers: Economic Change and Military Conflict from 1500 to 2000.* NY: Random House.

Keohane, Robert and Joseph Nye (1977), *Power and Interdependence: World Politics in Transition.* Boston, MA: Little, Brown.

Kessler, Glenn (2003a), "N. Korea's Nuclear Ambitions Are Urgent Issue. Powell Says." *Washington Post* (June 19): 23.

Kessler, Glenn (2003b), "US Decision on Iraq Has Puzzling Past." *Washington Post* (January 12): A01.

King, Gary, Robert Keohane, and Sidney Verba (1994), *Designing Social Inquiry: Scientific Inference in Qualitative Research.* Princeton, NJ: Princeton University Press.

Kirshner, Jonathan (2000), "Rationalist Explanations for War?" *Security Studies* Vol. 10, No. 1 (Autumn): 143–50.

Kissinger, Henry (2001), *Does America Need a Foreign Policy?* NY: Touchstone.

Kitfield, James (2002), "Pox Americana?" *National Journal* (April 6): 982–6.

Kramer, Ronald and Ray Michalowski (2005), "War, Aggression and State Crime." *British Journal of Criminology* Vol. 45, No. 4: 446–69.

Krasner, Stephen (1973, c1972), "Are Bureaucracies Important? (Or Allison Wonderland)." *Foreign Policy* No. 7: 159–79. Reprinted in Richard Head and Ervin Rokke, (eds) (1973), *American Defense Policy*, 3rd Edition. Baltimore, MD: Johns Hopkins University Press.

Krasner, Stephen (1999), *Sovereignty: Organized Hypocrisy.* Princeton, NJ: Princeton University Press.

Kupchan, Charles (1994), *The Vulnerability of Empire.* Ithaca, NY: Cornell University Press.

Kydd, Andrew (1997), "Game Theory and the Spiral Model." *World Politics* Vol. 49, No. 3 (April): 371–400.

Lake, David (1992), "Powerful Pacifists." *American Political Science Review* Vol. 86, No. 1 (March): 24–37.

Lake, Stuart (1931), *The Life and Times of Wyatt Earp.* Boston, MA: Houghton Mifflin Co.

Lamb, Christopher (2005), "Information Operations as a Core Competency." *Joint Forces Quarterly* Vol. 36 (Winter): 88–96.

Lambeth, Benjamin (2001), *NATO's Air War for Kosovo.* Santa Monica, CA: RAND.

Lansford, Tom (2006), "Coalition Diplomacy and Iraq." In John Davis, (ed.) *Presidential Policies and the Road to the Second Iraq War.* Hampshire, UK: Ashgate, pp. 142–65.

Leach, William and Paul Sabatier (2005), "To Trust an Adversary: Integrating Rational And Psychological Models in Collaborative Policymaking." *American Political Science Review* Vol. 99, No. 4 (December): 491–503.

Lebow, Richard Ned (1981), *Between Peace and War: The Nature of International Crisis.* Baltimore, MD: Johns Hopkins University Press.

Lebow, Richard Ned (2000), "What's So Different about a Counterfactual?" *World Politics* Vol. 52, No. 4 (July): 550–85.

Leeds, Brett Ashley (1999), "Democratic Institutions, Credible Commitments, and International Cooperation." *American Journal of Political Science* Vol. 43, No. 4 (October): 979–1002.

Leeds, Brett Ashley (2003), "Do Alliances Deter Aggression? The Influence of Military Alliances on the Initiation of Militarized Interstate Disputes." *American Journal of Political Science* Vol. 47, No. 3 (July): 427–39.

Leng, Russell (2000), *Bargaining and Learning in Recurring Crises.* Ann Arbor, MI: University of Michigan Press.

Leppingwell, John (1987), "The Laws of Combat? Lanchester Reexamined." *International Security* Vol. 12, No. 1 (Summer): 89–134.

Leurdijk, Dick (1999), "Kosovo: A Case of 'Coercive Diplomacy.'" *Helsinki Monitor* Vol. 2: 8–17. Available at www.nhc.nl/hm/1999/vol2/leurdijk.pdf.

Levite, Ariel (1987), *Intelligence and Strategic Surprises.* NY: Columbia University Press.

Liddell Hart, Basil (1954), *Strategy.* NY: Praeger.

Lieber, Robert (2004), "Rethinking America's Grand Strategy." *The Chronicle of Higher Education*, Section B, The Chronicle Review (June 4): B6–B9.

Lieber, Robert (2005), *The American Era: Power and Strategy for the 21st Century.* Cambridge, UK: Cambridge University Press.

Linzer, Dafna (2004), "Worldwide Terror War Hindered by Secrecy." *San Diego Union-Tribune* (March 28): www.signonsandiego.com/uniontrib20040328/news ln28intel.html.

Linzer, Dafna (2005a), "US Deploys Slide Show to Press Case against Iran." *Washington Post* (September 14): 7.

Linzer, Dafna (2005b), "US Misled Allies about Nuclear Export: North Korea Sent Material to Pakistan, Not to Libya." *Washington Post* (March 20): A01.

Lloyd, John (2002), "An Old Continent, Tired and Important." *New Statesmen*, 18 (February): 21–2.

Lord, Carnes (2003), *The Modern Prince: What Leaders Need to Know Now.* New Haven, CT: Yale University Press.

Lowry, Rich (2004), "Two Johns, Many Positions on Iraq." *Seattle Post-Intelligencer* (Editorial) (July 16): B6.

Ludden, Jennifer and Sylvia Poggioli (2005), "Deadly Incident in Iraq Strains US-Italian Relations." *National Public Radio* (March 5): www.npr.org/templates/story/story.php?storyId=452452.

Lynn-Jones Sean (1987), "Lulling and Stimulating Effects of Arms Control." Albert Carnesale and Richard Haass, (eds) *Superpower Arms Control.* Cambridge, MA: Ballinger, pp. 223–74.

Macmillan, John (2003), "Beyond the Separate Democratic Peace." *Journal of Peace Research* Vol. 40, No. 2 (March): 233–43.

Mansfield, Edward and Jack Snyder (1995), "Democratization and the Danger of War." *International Security* Vol. 20, No. 1 (Summer): 5–38.

Marcus, Jonathan (2003), "NATO 'Bad Blood' Rocks Alliance." *BBC News* online (February 12). Available at http://news.bbc.co.uk/2/hi/europe/2744491.stm.

Matsumura, John, Randall Steeb, Thomas Herbert, Scot Eisenhard, and John Gordon (1999), *The Army After Next: Exploring New Concepts and Technologies for the Light Battle Force* DB-258-A. Santa Monica, CA: RAND.

May, Ernest (2000), *Strange Victory: Hitler's Conquest of France.* NY: Hill and Wang.

May, Ernest and Philip Zelikow (1997), *The Kennedy Tapes: Inside the White House during the Cuban Missile Crisis.* Cambridge, MA: Harvard University Press.

Mazzetti, Mark (2004), "Troops Could Stay Beyond Limit." *Los Angeles Times* (July 21): A5.

McCausland, Jeffrey and Douglas Stuart, (eds) (2006), *US –UK Relations at the Start of the 21st Century.* Carlisle Barracks, PA: Army War College – Strategic Studies Institute.

McGillivray, Fiona and Alastair Smith (2000), "Trust and Cooperation through Agent Specific Punishments." *International Organization* Vol. 54, No. 4 (Autumn): 809–24.

Mead, Walter Russell (2004), *Power, Terror, Peace, and War: American Grand Strategy in a World at Risk.* NY: Alfred A. Knopf.

Mearsheimer, John (1991), "Back to the Future: Instability in Europe after the Cold War." *International Security* Vol. 15, No. 1 (Summer): 5–56.

Mearsheimer, John (2005), "Hans Morgenthau and the Iraq War: Realism versus Neo-conservatism." Posted May 19; available at http://mearsheimer.uchicago.edu/pdfs/A0037.pdf.

Mearsheimer, John and Stephen Walt (2003), "An Unnecessary War." *Foreign Policy* No. 134 (January/February): 50–9.

Mearsheimer, John and Stephen Walt (2007), *The Israel Lobby and U.S. Foreign Policy.* NY: Farrar, Straus, and Giroux.

Miller, Benjamin (2001), "Systemic and Regional Effects in Post-Cold War Transitions." *Security Studies* Vol. 11, No. 1 (Autumn): 1–52.

Miller, Steven, Sean Lynn-Jones and Stephen Van Evera, (eds) (1991), *Military Strategy and the Origins of the First World War.* Princeton, NJ: Princeton University Press.

Ministry of Defense, France (1999), *Premiers Enseignements de la Crise du Kosovo—Evaluations Techniques et Operationnelles* (September).

Mitchell, Paul (2006), *Network Centric Warfare: Coalition Operations in an Age of U.S. Military Primacy* Adelphi Paper No. 385. London, UK: International Institute for Strategic Studies.

Morgenthau, Hans (c1950), "The New Balance of Power between the United States and the Soviet Union." Reprinted in Morgenthau, Hans and Kenneth Thompson, (eds) (1952), *Principles and Problems of International Politics.* NY: Alfred A. Knopf, pp. 303–16.

Morgenthau, Hans (c1966), "What Should We Do Now?" (August). Reprinted in Morgenthau, Hans (1970), *Truth and Power: Essays of a Decade, 1960–1970.* NY: Praeger Publishers, pp. 413–25.

Morgenthau, Hans (c1968), "The Doctrine of War without End" (November). Reprinted in Morgenthau, Hans (1970), *Truth and Power: Essays of a Decade, 1960–70.* NY: Praeger Publishers, pp. 413–25.

Mowle, Thomas and David Sacko (2007), *The Unipolar World: An Unbalanced Future.* NY: Palgrave Macmillan.

Mueller, John (1989), *Retreat from Doomsday: The Obsolescence of Major War.* NY: Basic Books.

Müller-Wille, Björn (2004), "For Your Eyes Only? Shaping an Intelligence Community Within the EU." Paris, France: EU Institute for Security Studies – Occasional Paper 50 (January).

Nardulli, Bruce, Walter Perry, Bruce Pirnie, John Gordon IV, and John McGinn (2002), *Disjointed War: Military Operations in Kosovo, 1999.* Santa Monica, CA: RAND.

Nathan, James (1995), "On Coercive Statecraft: 'The New Strategy' and the American Foreign Affairs Experience." *International Relations* Vol. 12, No. 6: 3.

National Commission on Terrorist Attacks upon the United States (2004), *The 9/11 Commission Report: Final Report of the National Commission on Terrorist Attacks upon the United States.* NY: Norton.

NATO (2004), "Briefing: Improving Capabilities to Meet New Threats—7. Alliance Ground Surveillance." NATO On-line Library. Available at www.nato.int/docu/briefing/capabilities/html-en/capabilities07.html.

NATO Ministerial (1999), "Statement on Kosovo Issued at the Ministerial Meeting of the North Atlantic Council, Brussels, 8 December 1998." *NATO Review* Vol. 47, No. 1 (Spring): 21.

Nomikos, John (2005), "The European Union's Proposed Intelligence Service World Security Network," *World Security Network* (June 27). Available at www.worldsecuritynetwork.com/printArticle3.cfm?article_id=11580.

Nye, Joseph (1992), "What New World Order?" *Foreign Affairs* Vol. 71, No. 2 (Spring): 83–96.

Nye, Joseph (1999), "Redefining NATO's Mission in the Information Age." *NATO Review* Vol. 47, No. 4 (Winter): 12–5.

Nye, Joseph (2003a), *The Paradox of American Power.* NY: Oxford University Press.
Nye, Joseph (2003b), "US Power and Strategy After Iraq." *Foreign Affairs* Vol. 82, No. 4 (July/August): 60–73.
Nye, Joseph (2004), *Soft Power: The Means to Success in World Politics.* NY: PublicAffairs.
Nye, Joseph (2005), *Understanding International Conflicts*, 5th edition. NY: Pearson-Longman.
Nye, Joseph and Admiral William Owens (1996), "America's Information Edge." *Foreign Affairs* 75, no. 2 (March/April): 20–36.
Office of the Press Secretary, US Government (2002), "A Decade of Deception and Defiance." September 12, 2002. Available at www.whitehouse.gov/news/releases/2002/09/20020912.html.
Owens, William (2000), *Lifting the Fog of War.* NY: Farrar, Straus, and Giroux.
Parker, Charles and Eric Stern (2005), "Bolt from the Blue or Avoidable Failures? Revisiting September 11 and the Origins of Strategic Surprise." *Foreign Policy Analysis* Vol. 1, No. 3 (November): 301–31.
Partell, Peter and Glenn Palmer (1999), "Audience Costs and Interstate Crises: An Empirical Assessment of Fearon's Model of Dispute Outcomes." *International Studies Quarterly* Vol. 43, No. 2 (June): 389–406.
Pasztor, Andy and Jonathan Karp (2004), "Defense Firms Face Global Obstacles." *Wall Street Journal* (July 22): A4.
Pauly, Robert and Tom Lansford (2005), *Strategic Pre-emption: US Foreign Policy and the Second Iraq War.* Hants, England: Ashgate Publishing Limited.
Payne, Rodger (2005–2006), "Deliberating Preventive War: The Strange Case of Iraq's Disappearing Nuclear Threat." Manuscript prepared for the Ridgway Center's Working Group on Preventive Military Intervention, University of Pittsburgh. Available at www.ridgway.pitt.edu/docs/working papers/Payne.pdf.
Payne, Rodger and Nayef Samhat (2004), *Democratizing Global Politics: Discourse Norms, International Regimes, and Political Community.* Albany, NY: State University of New York Press.
Perry, Walter (2003), Interview of former US secretary of defense by FRONTLINE(TR), February 26. Available at www.pbs.org/wgbh/pages/frontline/shows/kim/interviews/.
Peters, John, Stuart Johnson, Nora Bensahel, Timothy Liston, and Traci Williams (2001), *European Contributions to Allied Force: Implications for Transatlantic Cooperation.* Santa Monica, CA: RAND.
Pillar, Paul (2006), "Intelligence Policy and the War in Iraq." *Foreign Affairs* Vol. 85, No. 2 (March/April): 15–27.
Pincus, Walter (2005), "Roberts: Iraq Will Affect Future War Votes—Experience with Faulty Data Has Made Senators More Wary, Panel Chairman Says." *Washington Post* (November 14): 4.
Pincus, Walter and Karen DeYoung (2007), "Analysts' Warnings of Iraq Chaos Detailed."
Pincus, Walter and Peter Baker (2005), "Data on Iraqi Arms Flawed, Panel Says: Intelligence Commission Outlines 74 Fixes for Bureaucracy." *Washington Post* (April 1): A01.

Pollack, Kenneth (2004), "Spies, Lies, and Weapons: What Went Wrong." *Atlantic Monthly* (January/February): 78–92.

Pond, Elizabeth (2005), "The Dynamics of the Feud over Iraq," in David Andrews, (ed.) *The Atlantic Alliance under Stress: US-European Relations after Iraq.* Cambridge, UK: Cambridge University Press, pp. 30–55.

Porch, Douglas and James Wirtz (2002), "Surprise and Intelligence Failure." *Strategic Insights* Vol. 1, No. 7 (September). Available at www.ccc.nps.navy.mil/si.

Posen, Barry (2000), "The War for Kosovo; Serbia's Political Military Strategy." *International Security* Vol. 24, No. 4 (Spring): 39–84.

Posen, Barry (2006), "European Union Security and Defense Policy: Response to Unipolarity." *Security Studies* Vol. 15, No. 2 (July): 149–86.

Powell, Colin (1992–1993), "U.S. Forces: Challenges Ahead." *Foreign Affairs* Vol. 71, No. 5 (Winter): 36–41.

Powell, Colin (2003), Remarks, Secretary of State Colin Powell to the United Nations Security Council, February 5, NY. Available at www.un.int/usa/03clp0205.htm.

Powell, Colin (2004), "A Strategy of Partnerships." *Foreign Affairs* Vol. 83, No. 1 (January/Febrary): 22–34.

Powell, Robert (2002), "Bargaining Theory and International Conflict." *Annual Review of Political Science* Vol. 5: 1–30.

Powell, Robert (2004), "Bargaining and Learning While Fighting." *American Journal of Political Science* Vol. 48, No. 2 (April): 344–61.

Press, Daryl (1997), "Lessons from Ground Combat in the Gulf." *International Security* Vol. 22, No. 22 (Fall): 137–46.

Press, Daryl (2005), *Calculating Credibility: How Leaders Assess Military Threats.* Ithaca, NY: Cornell University Press.

Prestowitz, Clyde (2003), *Rogue Nation: American Unilateralism and the Failure of Good Intentions.* NY: Basic Books.

Priest, Dana (1999a), "Bombing by Committee: France Balked at NATO Targets." *Washington Post* (September 20): A01.

Priest, Dana (1999b), "Soldiering on in a War of Constraints: NATO's Top General Works around Politics." *Washington Post* (May 30): A01.

Priest, Dana (2005), "Foreign Network at Front of CIA's Terror Fight." *Washington Post* (November 18): 1.

Purdum, Todd (2003), *A Time of Our Choosing.* NY: Times Books, Henry Holt and Co.

Ramesh, Randeep, (ed.) (2003), *The War We Could Not Stop.* NY: Thunder's Mouth Press.

Ramsay, Kristopher (2004), "Politics at the Water's Edge: Crisis Bargaining and Electoral Competition." *Journal of Conflict Resolution* Vol. 48, No. 4 (August): 459–86.

Rapoport, Anatol (1966), "Strategic and Non-Strategic Approaches to Problems of Security and Peace." Kathleen Archibald, editor. *Strategic Interaction and Conflict.* Berkeley, CA: Institute of International Studies, University of California, Berkeley, pp. 88–101.

Reed, William (2003), "Information, Power, and War." *American Political Science Review* Vol. 97, No. 4 (November): 633–41.

Reiter, Dan (2003), "Exploring the Bargaining Model of War." *Perspectives on Politics* Vol. 1, No. 1 (March): 27–43.

Reiter, Dan and Allan Stam (1998), "Democracy, War Initiation and Victory." *American Political Science Review* vol. 92, no. 2 (June): 377–89.

Reiter, Dan and Allan Stam (2002), *Democracies at War*. Princeton, NJ: Princeton University Press.

Reiter, Dan and Allan Stam (2003), "Understanding Victory: Why Political Institutions Matter." *International Security* vol. 28, no. 1 (Summer): 168–79.

Reuters (2000), "NATO Denies Leak of Bomb Plans to Belgrade." *New York Times* (March 10): A7.

Reveron, Derek (2006), "Old Allies, New Friends: Intelligence-Sharing in the War on Terror." *Orbis* Vol. 50, No. 3 (Summer): 453–68.

Rice, Condoleezza (2000), "Promoting the National Interest," *Foreign Affairs* Vol. 79, No. 1 (January/February): 45–62.

Roberts, Jonathan (1988), *Decision-Making during International Crisis*. NY: St. Martin's Press.

Robinson, James (1972), "Crisis: An Appraisal of Concepts and Theories." Charles Hermann, (ed.) *International Crises: Insights from Behavioral Research*. New York: The Free Press, pp. 18–35.

Roeder, Tom (2006), "Bases in Springs Helped Find, Kill Al-Zarqawi." *Gazette* (Colorado Springs) (June 10): www.findarticles.com/p/articles/mi_qn4191/is_20060610/ai_n16475451.

Rogers, Philip (1991), "Crisis Bargaining Codes and Crisis Management." In Alexander George, (ed.) *Avoiding War: Problems of Crisis Management*. Boulder, CO: Westview Press, pp. 413–42.

Rosenau, James (1990), *Turbulence in World Politics: A Theory of Change and Continuity*. Princeton, NJ: Princeton University Press.

Rosenthal, Uriel, Michael Charles, and Paul 't Hart (1989), "The World of Crises and Crisis Management." Uriel Rosenthal, Michael Charles, and Pual 't Hart, (eds) *Coping with Crises: The Management of Disasters, Riots, and Terrorism*. Springfield, IL: Charles C. Thomas.

Rouleau, Eric (1999), "French Diplomacy Adrift in Kosovo." *Le Monde Diplomatique*. (December). Available at http://mondediplo.com/1999/12/04rouleau.

Russett, Bruce (1998), "A Neo-Kantian Perspective: Democracy, Interdependence, and International Organizations in Building Security Communities". In Emanuel Adler and Michael Barnett, (eds) *Security Communities*. Cambridge, UK: Cambridge University Press.

Russett, Bruce and John Oneal (2001), *Triangulating Peace: Democracy, Interdependence, and International Organizations*. NY: Norton.

Rutten, Maartje (2001), *From St. Malo to Nice, European Defence: Core Documents*, Chaillot Papers No. 47. Paris: Institute for Security Studies – Western European Union (May): 82–91.

Sanger, David (2004), "Bush's Pre-emptive Strategy Meets Some Untidy Reality." *New York Times* (July 12): A10.

Sanger, David (2005), "Prewar British Memo Says War Decision Wasn't Made." *New York Times* (June 13): 11.

Sanger, David and William Broad (2006), "Nuclear Déjà Vu: Now It's Iran that Does or Doesn't Intend to Make Nuclear Weapons." *New York Times* (September 6): 6.

Scanlon, Charles (2003), "Japan Backs US stance on Iraq." *BBC News online* (March 14). Available at http://news.bbc.co.uk/2/hi/asia-pacific/284915.stm.

Schelling, Thomas (1960), *The Strategy of Conflict*. Cambridge, MA: Harvard University Press.

Schelling, Thomas (1966a), *Arms and Influence*. New Haven, CT: Yale University Press.

Schelling, Thomas (1966b), "Uncertainty, Brinksmanship, and the Game of 'Chicken'". Kathleen Archibald, editor. *Strategic Interaction and Conflict*, Berkeley, CA: Institute of International Studies, University of California, Berkeley, pp. 74–87.

Schick, Jack (1971), *The Berlin Crisis, 1958–1962*. Philadelphia, PA: University of Pennsylvania Press.

Schmitt, Eric (2003), "Plans for Policing a Postwar Iraq." *New York Times* (April 9): B1.

Schultz, Kenneth (1998), "Domestic Opposition and Signaling in International Crises," *American Political Science Review* Vol. 92, No. 4 (December): 829–44.

Schultz, Kenneth (1999), "Do Democratic Institutions Constrain or Inform? Contrasting Two Institutional Perspectives on Democracy and War." *International Organization* Vol. 53, No. 2 (Spring): 233–66.

Schultz, Kenneth (2001), *Democracy and Coercive Diplomacy*. Cambridge, UK: Cambridge University Press.

Schuster, Jürgen and Herbert Maier (2006), "The Rift: Explaining Europe's Divergent Iraq Policies in the Run-Up of the American-Led War on Iraq." *Foreign Policy Analysis* Vol. 2, No. 3 (July): 223–44.

Sciolino, Elaine (2004), "Drifting NATO Finds New Purpose with Afghanistan and Iraq." *New York Times* (February 23): A6.

Scully, Megan (2005), "Chopper Contract Alarms Buy American Supporters." *TheHill.com* (February 3). Available at http://thehill.com/the-executive/chopper-contract-alarms-buy-america-supporters-2005-02-03.html.

Secretary General of the United Nations (2005), *In Larger Freedom: Towards Development, Security and Human Rights for All* (September). NY: United Nations Report.

Senate Panel Releases Assessments from 2003. *Washington Post* (May 26): A01.

Senese, Paul (1997), "Costs and Demands: International Sources of Dispute Challenges and Reciprocation." *Journal of Conflict Resolution* Vol. 41, No. 3 (June): 407–27.

Serfaty, Simon (2004), "Thinking about and beyond NATO," in Hall Gardner, (ed.) *NATO and the European Union: New World, New Europe, New Threats*. Hants, England: Ashgate, pp. 107–114.

Shawcross, William (2004), *Allies: The US, Britain, Europe, and the War in Iraq*. NY: Public Affairs.

Shenon, Philip (1999), "War Crimes Suspects Seen as Living Openly in Bosnia." *New York Times* (December 13): A14.

Shlaim, Avi (1983), *The United States and the Berlin Blockade, 1948–9: A Study in Crisis Decision-Making*. Berkeley, CA: University of California Press.

Slantchev, Branislav (2003), "The Power to Hurt: Costly Conflict with Completely Informed States." *American Political Science Review* Vol. 97, No. 1 (February): 123–33.

Slantchev, Branislav (2003), "The Principle of Convergence in Wartime Negotiations." *American Political Science Review* Vol. 97, No. 4 (November): 621–32.

Slantchev, Branislav (2004), "The Watchful Eye: Information Transmission and Political Failure." Unpublished manuscript (September). Available at http://dss.ucsd.edu/~bslantch/wp/pdf/bs012w00C.pdf.

Slevin, Peter (2004), "Retired Envoys, Commanders Assail Bush Team: Administration Unable to Handle 'Global Leadership,' 27-Member Group Asserts," *Washington Post* (June 17): 22.

Smith, Alastair (1998a), "Fighting Battles, Winning Wars." *Journal of Conflict Resolution* Vol. 42, No. 3 (June): 301–20.

Smith, Alastair (1998b), "International Crises and Domestic Politics." *American Political Science Review* Vol. 92, No. 3 (September): 623–38.

Smith, Alastair and Allan Stam (2002), "Bargaining and the Nature of War." Presented at the Annual Meeting of the American Political Science Association, Boston, MA, September 2002.

Smith, Jean (1963), *The Defense of Berlin.* Baltimore, MD: Johns Hopkins University Press.

Snow, Donald and Eugene Brown (2000), *International Relations: The Changing Contours of Power."* NY: Longman Addison Wesley.

Snyder, Glenn and Paul Diesing (1977), *Conflict Among Nations: Bargaining, Decision Making, and System Structure in International Crises.* Princeton, NJ: Princeton University Press.

Snyder, Jack (1991), *Myths of Empire: Domestic Politics and International Ambition.* Ithaca, NY: Cornell University Press.

Snyder, Jack (2004), "One World, Rival Theories." *Foreign Policy* (November/December): 52–62.

Sontag, Deborah (2004), "Early Tests for U.S. in Its Global Fight on AIDS." *New York Times* (July 14): A1.

Spiegel, Peter (2004), "Hoon Warns US of Retaliation against Arms Deal Protectionism." *London Financial Times* (July 30).

Stigler, Andrew (2002/2003), "A Clear Victory for Air Power: NATO's Empty Threat to Invade Kosovo." *International Security* Vol. 27, No. 3 (Winter): 124–57.

Stivers, William (1997), "The Incomplete Blockade: Soviet Zone Supply of West Berlin, 1948–9." *Diplomatic History* Vol. 21, No. 4 (Fall): 569–602.

Strassler, Robert (1996), *The Landmark Thucydides: A Comprehensive Guide to the Peloponnesian War.* Introduction by Victor Davis Hanson. NY: Touchstone.

Sullivan, Shannon, Lt Col, USAF (2002), "Globalized Security: An Allied Industrial Base for the 21st Century." *Acquisition Review Quarterly* (Spring). Available at www.dau.mil/pubs/arq/2002arq/SulliSP2.pdf.

Tetlock, Philip and Aaron Belkin, (eds) (1996), *Counterfactual Thought Experiments in World Politics.* Princeton, NJ: Princeton University Press.

Tetlock, Philip and Richard Ned Lebow (2001), "Poking Counterfactual Holes in Covering Laws: Cognitive Styles and Historical Reasoning." *American Political Science Review* Vol. 95, No. 4 (December): 829–43.

Tetlock, Philip, Jo Husbands, Robert Jervis, Paul Stern, and Charles Tilly, (eds) (1989), *Behavior, Society, and Nuclear War*, Vol. 1. NY: Oxford University Press.

Thompson, Llewellyn (1961), Classified Telegram to the Secretary of State Regarding Berlin Telegram to Department 572 and Bonn Telegram 1971 (May 27). Available from the National Security Archive, George Washington University.

Tiboni, Frank (2004), "Army's Future Combat Systems at the Heart of Transformation." *Federal Computer Week* on-line (February 9). Available at www.fcw.com/fcw/articles/2004/0209/pol-army-02-09-04.esp#related.

Trachtenberg, Marc (1990/1991), "The Meaning of Mobilization in 1914." *International Security* Vol. 15, No. 3 (Winter): 120–50.

Trachtenberg, Marc (2005), "The Iraq Crisis and the Future of the Western Alliance," in David Andrews, (ed.) *The Atlantic Alliance under Stress: US-European Relations after Iraq*. Cambridge, UK: Cambridge University Press, pp. 201–31.

Trauschweizer, Ingo Wolfgang (2006), "Tanks at Checkpoint Charlie: Lucius Clay and the Berlin Crisis; 1961–62." *Cold War History* Vol. 6, No. 2 (May): 205–28.

Truman, Harry S. (1956), *Memoirs* Vol. 2: *Years of Trial and Hope, 1946–1953*. London, UK: Hodder and Stoughton.

Turner, Michael (2005), *Why Secret Intelligence Fails*. Dulles, VA: Potomac Books.

US Senate Armed Services Committee (2003), Hearing on FY 2004 Defense Authorization. FDCH Transcript (February 25): http://search.epnet.com/login.aspx?direct=true&db=mth&an=32V0345319954.

Van Evera, Stephen (1990/1991), "Primed for Peace: Europe after the Cold War." *International Security* Vol. 15, No. 3 (Winter): 7–57.

Van Evera, Stephen (1997), *Guide to Methods for Students of Political Science*. Ithaca, NY: Cornell University Press.

Védrine, Hubert (1999), "Into the Twenty-First." Speech at the opening of the IFRI Annual Conference, Paris, November 3. Available at www.un.int/france/documents_anglais/991103_mae_presse_desarmement.htm.

Villadsen, Ole (1999), "Prospects for a European Common Intelligence Policy." Center for the Study of Intelligence, Central Intelligence Agency. Available at www.cia.gov/csi/kent_csi/docs/v44i3a07p.htm.

Wagner, Harrison (2000), "Bargaining and War." *American Journal of Political Science* Vol. 44, No. 3 (July): 469–84.

Walker, Martin (2002), "The Defense Gap." *Europe* (May): 8–9.

Walt, Stephen (2005), *Taming American Power: The Global Response to U.S. Primacy*. NY: W.W. Norton.

Waltz, Kenneth (1962), "Kant, Liberalism, and War." *American Political Science Review* Vol. 56, No. 2 (June): 331–40.

Waltz, Kenneth (1979), *Theory of International Politics*. Reading, MA: Addison-Wesley.

Wayne, Leslie (2005), "Pentagon Defends Its Growing Reliance on Foreign Contractors." *International Herald Tribune* (September 23): 15.

Weller, Marc (1999), "The Rambouillet Conference on Kosovo." *International Affairs* Vol. 75, No. 2 (April): 211–51.

White House Office of Homeland Security (2002), *National Security Strategy of the United States of America*, September. Available at www.whitehouse.gov/nsc/nss.pdf.

White, John and John Deutch (2004), *Building Capability from the Technical Revolution that Has Happened.* Carlisle Barracks, PA: Strategic Studies Institute, U.S. Army War College (June).

Whitney, Craig (1999), "U.S. Military Acted Outside NATO Framework During Kosovo Conflict, France Says." *New York Times*, (November 11): A6.

Whitney, Craig, editor (2005), *The WMD Mirage: Iraq's Decade of Deception and America's False Premise for War.* NY: Public Affairs.

Wirtz, Jim (2004), "The Balance of Power Paradox," in T.V. Paul, James Wirtz and Michel Fortmann, editors, *Balance of Power: Theory and Practice in the 21st Century* (Stanford, CA: Stanford University Press).

Wohlforth, William (1999), "The Stability of a Unipolar World". *International Security* Vol. 24, No. 1 (Summer): 5–41.

Wohlstetter, Roberta (1965), "Cuba and Pearl Harbor." *Foreign Affairs* Vol. 43, No. 4 (July): 691–707.

Woods, Kevin, James Lacey, and Williamson Murray (2006), "Saddam's Delusions: The View from the Inside." *Foreign Affairs* Vol. 85, No. 3 (May-June): 2–26.

Woodward, Bob (2004), *Plan of Attack.* NY: Simon and Schuster.

Wright, Robin (2007), "As US Steps up Pressure on Iran, Aftereffects Worry Allies." *Washington Post* (August 16): 9.

Yin, Robert (2003), *Case Study Research: Design and Methods.* Thousand Oaks, CA: Sage Publications.

Yost, David (1998), *NATO Transformed: The Alliance's New Roles in International Security.* Washington, D.C.: United States Institute of Peace Press.

Young, Oran (1968), *The Politics of Force: Bargaining During International Crises.* Princeton, NJ: Princeton University Press.

Zelikow, Philip and Ernest May (2002), *The Kennedy Tapes: Inside the White House during the Cuban Missile Crisis.* NY: W.W. Norton and Co.

Index